Costume Society of America series

Phyllis A. Specht, *Series Editor*

Also in the Costume Society of America series

American Menswear: From the Civil War to the Twenty-First Century, Daniel Delis Hill

American Silk, 1830–1930: Entrepreneurs and Artifacts, Jacqueline Field, Marjorie Senechal, and Madelyn Shaw

As Seen in Vogue: A Century of American Fashion in Advertising, Daniel Delis Hill

Clothing and Textile Collections in the United States, Sally Queen and Vicki L. Berger

Dressing Modern Maternity: The Frankfurt Sisters of Dallas and the Page Boy Label, Kay Goldman

Fashion Prints in the Age of Louis XIV: Interpreting the Art of Elegance, edited by Kathryn Norberg and Sandra Rosenbaum

Forbidden Fashions: Invisible Luxuries in Early Venetian Convents, Isabella Campagnol

M. de Garsault's 1767 Art of the Shoemaker: An Annotated Translation, translated by D. A. Saguto

Managing Costume Collections: An Essential Primer, Louise Coffey-Webb

A Perfect Fit: The Garment Industry and American Jewry, 1860–1960, edited by Gabriel M. Goldstein and Elizabeth E. Greenberg

A Separate Sphere: Dressmakers in Cincinnati's Golden Age, 1877–1922, Cynthia Amnéus

The Sunbonnet: An American Icon in Texas, Rebecca Jumper Matheson

Young Originals: Emily Wilkins and the Teen Sophisticate, Rebecca Jumper Matheson

Knock It Off

A History of Design Piracy in the US Women's Ready-to-Wear Apparel Industry

Sara B. Marcketti and Jean L. Parsons

Texas Tech University Press

Copyright © 2016 by Sara B. Marcketti and Jean L. Parsons

All rights reserved. No portion of this book may be reproduced in any form or by any means, including electronic storage and retrieval systems, except by explicit prior written permission of the publisher. Brief passages excerpted for review and critical purposes are excepted.

This book is typeset in Minion Pro. The paper used in this book meets the minimum requirements of ANSI/NISO Z39.48-1992 (R1997). ∞

Designed by Kasey McBeath
Cover photograph/illustration by LIFE, March 20, 1913, 61.

Library of Congress Cataloging-in-Publication Data
Names: Marcketti, Sara B., author. | Parsons, Jean Louise, 1952- author.

Title: Knock it off! : a history of design piracy in the US women's ready-to-wear apparel industry / Sara B. Marcketti and Jean L. Parsons.

Description: Lubbock, Texas : Texas Tech University Press, [2016] | Series: Costume Society of America series | Includes bibliographical references and index.

Identifiers: LCCN 2016011788 (print) | LCCN 2016015984 (ebook) | ISBN 9780896729667 (pbk. : alk. paper) | ISBN 9780896729674 (e-book)

Subjects: LCSH: Ready-to-wear-clothing industry—United States—History. | Fashion design—United States—History. | Fashion design—Law and legislation—United States—History. | Design protection—United States—History. | Fashion designers—United States—History. | Fashion—United States—History.

Classification: LCC TT496.U6 M37 2016 (print) | LCC TT496.U6 (ebook) | DDC 746.9/20973—dc23

LC record available at https://lccn.loc.gov/2016011788

16 17 18 19 20 21 22 23 24 / 9 8 7 6 5 4 3 2 1

Texas Tech University Press
Box 41037 | Lubbock, Texas 79409-1037 USA
800.832.4042 | ttup@ttu.edu | www.ttupress.org

Contents

Illustrations	*vii*
Introduction	*xi*

Chapter 1
Historical Overview of Evolving Design Protection Efforts — 3

Chapter 2
Design Piracy from a Legal Perspective — 16
    Available Legal Protection — 18
        Copyright
        Patents: Utility and Design
        Trademarks
    Bills Submitted to Congress for Design Protection — 28
    Industry Efforts — 33

Chapter 3
Origins of Design Piracy in the US Women's Ready-to-Wear
    Apparel Industry — 36
    Women's Ready-to-Wear: Rise of the Trade — 37
    Style Change and Competition — 41
    A New Industry Organization — 43
    The New Fashion Consumer — 46
    Cultivating a Style Industry — 50

Chapter 4
Development and Promotion of a US Design Presence — 55
    Fashion Design for the US Ready-to-Wear Market — 55
        Industry Organization
        French Fashion Industry Dominance
        The False French Label
    Creating Demand for an American Style — 70

American Designers and Stylists	75
Educating American Designers	
Promoting American Designers	
Protecting American Design	

Chapter 5
Design Piracy and Self-Regulation: The Fashion Originators' Guild of America	98
Impact of the Great Depression	98
The Fashion Originators' Guild of America	101

Chapter 6
Design Protection Arguments	112
Enforcement	113
Cost-Benefit Perspectives	114
Consumers' Entitlement to Fashion	117
The Industry Perspective	123
The Industry: Manufacturers	
The Industry: Retailers	
The Industry: Labor	

Chapter 7
The Fashion Originators' Guild of America: Controversy and Defeat	130
New Regulations and Controversial Policies	130
Legal Battles	135
Did the FOGA Monopolize the Industry?	142

Chapter 8
Original, Adaptation, Copy, Reproduction?	145

Appendix: FOGA Officers and Members, 1936	*153*
Notes	*157*
Sources	*193*
Index	*203*

Illustrations

Copies of Wallis Warfield Simpson's wedding dress, 1937	xiii
Original Yves Saint Laurent "Mondrian" dress and copy, 1965	xiv
Council of Fashion Designers of America promotional materials	xv
A 1935 advertisement offering variations at reasonable prices	8
"Paris Comes to Wanamaker's," advertisement, 1936	9
Oppenheim, Collins & Co. promises they do not sell forgeries, 1923	11
"Original models" heavily influenced by King Tutankhamen's tomb, 1923	12
Martin's store offered "originations" rather than originals, 1919	13
Women's Wear Daily regularly featured the workings of the FOGA, 1935	15
Advertisement stating "every precaution is taken . . . ," 1901	17
Rosen Bros. Company 1933 advertisement	20
Example of a utility patent issued for a combination corset and brassiere, 1933	21
Example of a design patent for a dress by Dorothy Long, 1930	22
Legal notice warning retailers and manufacturers of a patent, 1924	23
Design patent in dispute, 1935	24
Example of a 1941 design patent for a dress by Nettie Rosenstein	26
Invitation to a "Knock it off" purse party from 2007	27
An 1899 advertisement for Star brand shirtwaists	28

Illustrations • viii

"Every Dress Manufacturer Is Faced with a New Style Control Menace," 1935	32
Advertisement for Osias Nathanson, William Price, and Jack Adelman, 1934	34
A page of shirtwaists designed by Mrs. Le Roy-Huntington, 1909	38
An 1896 advertisement for Star brand shirts	42
Women in 1915 wearing the many shirtwaist style variations	43
One-piece dresses available by mail-order from Charles A. Stevens & Brothers, Fall/Winter 1908/1909	47
Gimbels emphasized the variety of styles, fabrics, and prices available, 1917	50
Designer working on a tailored suit, with model at right, 1916	56
Designs introduced at an "American Fall and Winter Fashion Show," 1913	59
Saks and Co. advertises reproductions and adaptation of Paris styles, 1916	62
R. H. Macy & Co. advertisement for an exhibition of fall fashions, 1913–1914	64
Callot Soeurs advertisement with Syndicat endorsement and list of members, 1913	66
Weingarten & Pearl advertisement for an exhibition of Paris designs, 1914	67
Garment designed by Madame Jenny especially for the *Woman's Home Companion*, 1915	69
American-themed styles for US cities, 1913	72
A Stein and Blaine suit that received accolades at the Fashion Fete, 1914	73
Dress designs inspired by the American Museum of Natural History collection, 1918	80
Advertisement for a *New York Times* design contest, 1912	86
Creator of "Art in Dress" Harry Collins, 1918	88
Dress design by E. M. A. Steinmetz for Stein and Blaine, 1918	89
A dress and its copy, offered as Exhibit E in an appeal case, 1923	91
Dress patent assigned to Franklin Simon Co., Inc., by designer Taubé Davis, 1927	93

Illustrations

Betty Wales advertisement, 1917	94
Maurice Rentner, chairman of the FOGA, c. 1935	99
Fashion Originators' Guild of America inaugural announcement, 1932	102
Advertisement promoting exhibition of guild members, 1933	103
Amelia Earhart designs registered with the FOGA and the National Recovery Administration, 1934	104
The FOGA had its own section in this issue of *WWD*, 1933	105
FOGA-registered dress worn by Ann Meany Appleton, 1938	106
Herbert Sondheim sketch registered with the FOGA, 1934	108
Announcement of the Registry Division of the FOGA with a sample label, 1933	109
Advertisement "shouting value" for the price-conscious consumer, 1932	113
Advertisement for a replica Vionnet collarless coat, 1931	115
Illustration showing the high-cost "original" down to lower-cost copies, 1933	118
Announcement of the formation of the Dress Creators' League of America, Inc., 1932	122
FOGA extends protection into the $4.75 field, 1935	131
Popular Priced Dress Manufacturers Group, Inc., announcement, 1936	133
Label from c. 1940 FOGA dress that indicates "U.S. Patent Applied For"	138
Samuel Zahn dress patent from 1944	139
Design patent by Syd Novak for Flora Dress Company, 1940	141
A worker in China preparing a copy of Kate Middleton's wedding dress, 2011	147
Diane Von Furstenberg bag, part of the "You Can't Fake Fashion" campaign, 2013	151

Introduction

How do fashion designers create show-stopping pieces that dazzle and amaze audiences around the world? Some say designers draw creative inspiration from nature, from architecture, or from the *zeitgeist*, the spirit of the times. Others might conclude that all designs are either derivative of past fashion or are variations on current styles. For more than a century, the process of copying has been an integral business and creative practice of the ready-to-wear apparel industry. Unlike other creative fields, or even the French protective system, US intellectual property laws do not fully protect apparel designs. Thus, companies are free to creatively borrow (or steal) from other designers and manufacturers.[1]

Different from counterfeiting, when objects are fraudulently branded with a designer's name or logo, design piracy is the unauthorized copying of another manufacturer's or designer's styles. It is a perpetual occurrence in the ready-to-wear apparel industry, popularized today by mass media. *Marie Claire*, for example, regularly publishes their feature "Splurge versus Steal." These comparisons of high-priced designer garments with the lower-priced, nearly identical "knock-offs" encourage consumer acceptance of piracy.[2]

While some view the entire fashion industry as a "well balanced system which succeeds by integrating a complicated blend of original ideas, individual creativity, and copying," others contend piracy detrimentally affects business practices.[3] Tobé Coller Davis, fashion consultant and founder of the Tobé-Coburn School and the Tobé Report, assumed that pirated designs were fundamental to the industry. She stated, "If there were no copying, we would have no industry."[4] Conversely, those in favor of design protection often cite statistics that demonstrate the enormous difference in quantity of sales between the original and a pirated copy, and while actual dollar amounts are seldom cited, the inference is that when cheaper copies begin to appear, sales for higher-priced designs decline.

As a case in point, designer Narciso Rodriguez estimated that he sold about forty versions of the exclusive wedding dress he designed for Carolyn Bessette's wedding to John F. Kennedy, Jr., while other firms produced and sold from seven million to eight million copies.[5] The pirated copies were sold by companies such as A.B.S. by Allen Schwartz, which operates openly as a copy house, in cheaper fabrics and at price points in the hundreds rather than the thousands of dollars. Whether Rodriguez would have sold more of his original copies if the dress had not been pirated is difficult to guess, let alone determine. There is surely a finite market for expensive originals. Furthermore, the story is more complicated, as some copied dresses were sold as interpretations rather than exact copies, in a variety of colors, and as evening dresses, short and long, rather than as duplicates of the Rodriguez-designed wedding dress.[6] Rodriguez argued, "All that publicity and the knockoffs didn't pay my bills or get me to where I am today."[7] However, some might contend that as he was a relative newcomer on the fashion scene, the publicity significantly aided Rodriguez's career. Indeed, Bernard Roshco, in his 1963 narrative on the US fashion industry, suggested that when there is a substantial price difference between an original and a copy, the cheaper version does not in fact "kill off" the more expensive version, but rather can help further its popularity.[8]

The dresses of the rich and famous are a common object of copying. For example, on May 20, 1937, a sketch of the $250 original Mainbocher dress Wallis Simpson wore for her wedding to Edward, Duke of Windsor, appeared in *Women's Wear Daily*. By June a close copy of the dress was available at Bonwit Teller for $39.95. Bonwit Teller also sold a short, daytime version for $25, creating a sketch for the dress in exactly the same pose as Simpson's wedding photos. A few weeks later, Lord & Taylor sold a version for $16.95, and a week later shoppers could purchase a short version for $8.90 at Klein's (Figure I.1).[9] Whether there was a loss of income to Mainbocher, or even to the stores that sold the higher-priced copies first is unknown. Even in blurred black-and-white, however, the illustration published in *LIFE* magazine of this example makes clear that the pirated copies were sold in cheaper fabrics with less detailed attention to fit. Presumably customers understood that they were purchasing copies of the highly publicized design. What is less clear is whether the women who purchased the cheaper imitations (or even those women who purchased the higher-priced originals) really cared.

While these examples are of highly publicized dresses worn by well-known women, they highlight the ambiguity of the arguments both for and against design protection for apparel, as well as the complexities of what constitutes an original, an adaptation, and a copy. These arguments have been deliberated within the US fashion industry for more than a century. These examples also highlight the critical role of fashion for consumers and underscore arguments about consumers' "rights" to access fashion at all price points. Debate and disagreement about the language used to describe fashion designs and about advantages and disadvantages of the copying process began at the very rise of the apparel indus-

• xiii •   Introduction

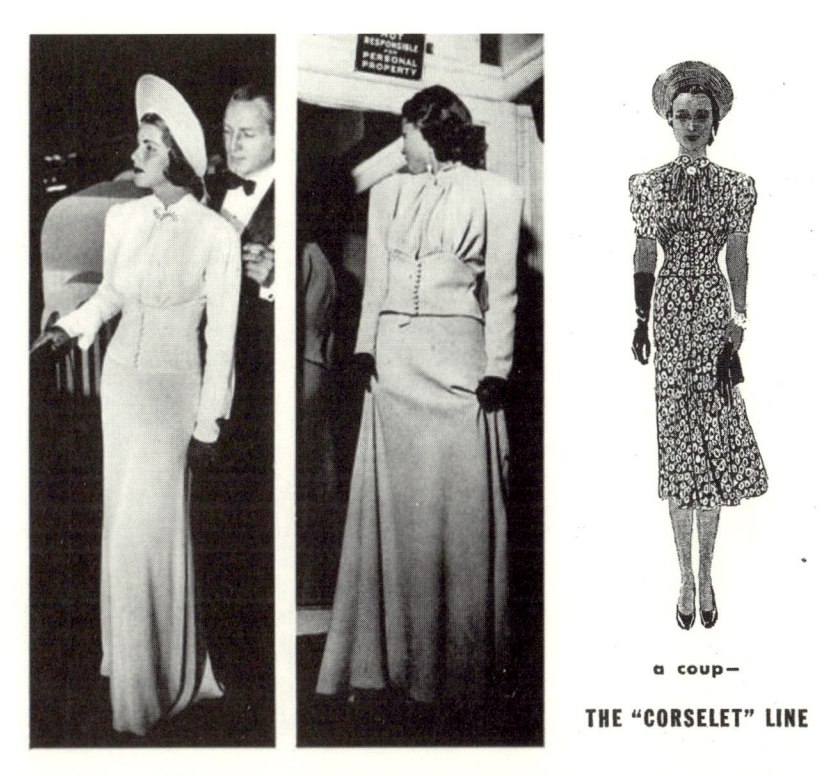

a coup—

THE "CORSELET" LINE

Figure I.1 Copies of Wallis Warfield Simpson's wedding dress by Bonwit Teller (l) and Klein's (c), with an advertisement for a day dress variation by Bonwit Teller (r). *LIFE*, August 9, 1937; *The New York Times*, June 13, 1937.

try. Indeed, issues of what constitutes an original fashion design and who benefits and who loses in the process often take precedence over ethical and moral issues related to piracy. The latter are more often underscored when the practice involves illegal counterfeiting of labels or brand trademarks rather than pirated copies of dress designs.

The apparel industry thrives on the practice of creating a presumably original design that is then interpreted into copies. And although design piracy is most often used to turn high-end designs into less expensive goods, haute couture designers have also been known to copy one another as well as other artists (Figure I.2).[10] Even within the educational system, copying is an important aspect of learning, as knockoff techniques are taught in apparel construction courses and as a component of patternmaking textbooks.[11]

Historically, some industry organizations and individual designers accepted

Introduction • xiv •

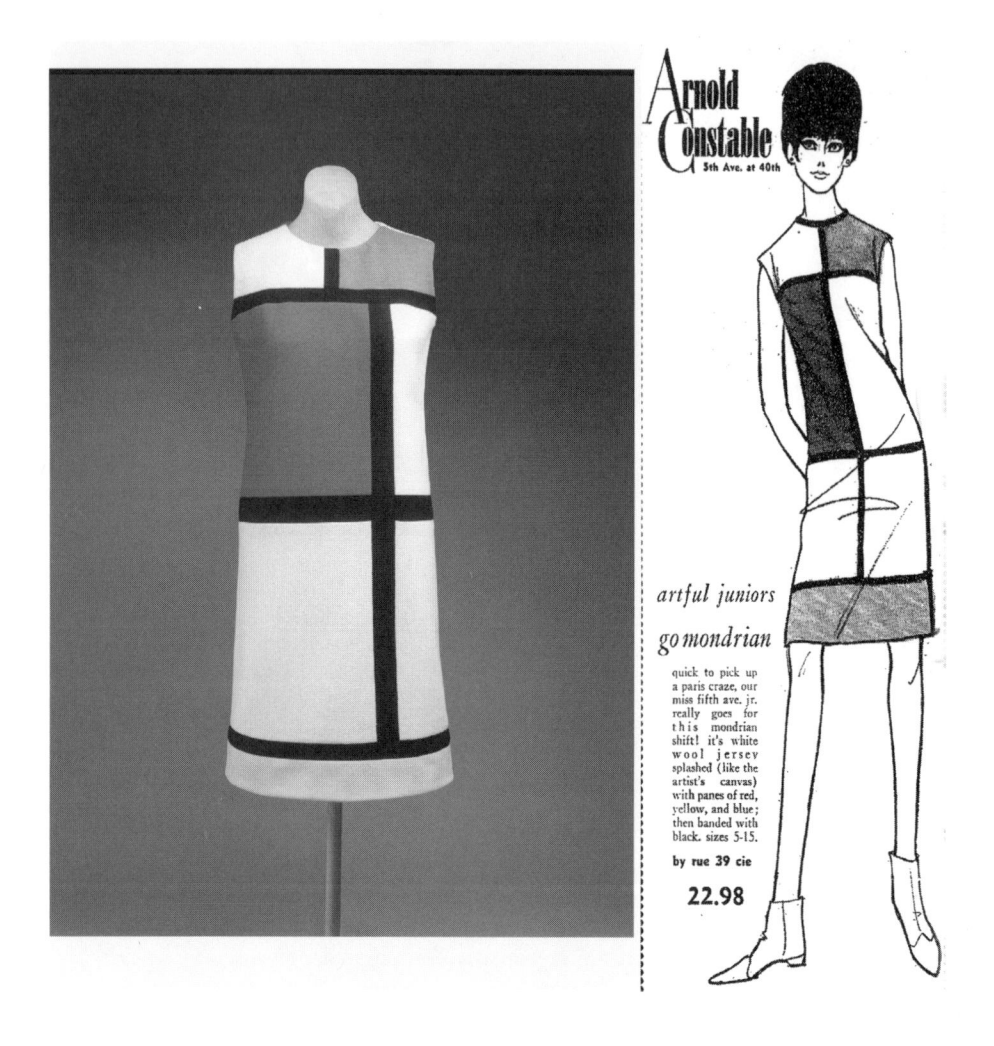

Figure I.2 Original Yves Saint Laurent "Mondrian" dress from fall/winter 1965–1966 (l) and copy from 1965 (r). The advertisement for the copied dress uses language that references the painting, but still notes that it is a "paris craze." Courtesy of The Metropolitan Museum of Art. Image source: Art Resource, NY; Arnold Constable advertisement, *The New York Times*, September 7, 1965.

Figure I.3 Council of Fashion Designers of America (CFDA) promotional materials supporting protection from piracy. Courtesy of CFDA.

and supported the practice as important to the transmission of fashion, while others actively tried to prevent copying, stating reasons ranging from loss of profits to the potential for unfair labor practices. In recent years the Council of Fashion Designers of America has sought legal remedies to curb piracy (Figure I.3). This was a renewed attempt at copyright legislation brought on, in part, by the increased competition from fast-fashion brands and retailers such as H&M, Zara, and Forever 21, companies that rely on knockoffs of higher-priced fashions.

First introduced to the US Congress in 2006 as the Design Piracy Prohibition Act, with variations introduced in 2009, 2011, and 2012, these bills proposed to give fashion design short-term protection. Unlike painting, music, and other creative arts, apparel has generally not been eligible for copyright protection because it is considered a utilitarian product. Additionally, the required step of separating unique design features from the purely functional aspects of clothing has been deemed too difficult. To remedy this problem, recent bills have proposed to protect only those designs that come closer to art than functionality and set a higher burden of proof than previous bills.[12] For instance, the bills required substantiation that the initial design was original; the alleged knockoff was "substantially identical"; and "the defendant [was] privy to the original design before it was publicly released."[13] Each of these bills has been controversial within Congress and the industry. One of the sticking points continues to be difficulties in determining originality, as well as the more basic question of how to define the term *original*. The American Apparel & Footwear Association, for instance, disagreed with the 2006 bill because of its overly broad definitions, which the trade association claimed would have "opened a Pandora's box of litigation," detrimental to the industry.[14] There were also suggestions that the bills would provide unfair advantage to more established designers who typically have larger financial and legal resources at their disposal to litigate against copyists.[15]

The 2006 proposed legislation is far from the first apparel industry effort to seek legal protection. Design piracy surfaced even before the rapid growth of ready-to-wear at the end of the nineteenth century, as did bills to prevent the practice. Failing consistently to secure legislated protection, industry groups of the 1930s, most notably the Fashion Originators' Guild of America (FOGA), attempted self-regulation with some success, until its ultimate failure in the court system in 1941.

The current arguments about whether fashion can or should receive governmental protection from piracy have largely been aired in the legal press, with passing references to the history of the US apparel industry.[16] However, all the attempts to regulate, legislate, and/or control design piracy of apparel are grounded in the history of ready-to-wear. The purpose of this book is to analyze design piracy within the historical context of the American ready-to-wear apparel industry. This includes examination of perceptions of what was defined as an original design versus the many design variations that began with an "original," then became a direct copy—usually but not always in a less expensive fabric—or an adaptation, that is, a similar but not exact version of the original. The study that follows puts into perspective the conflicting interests that have plagued the industry and that make true protection seemingly impossible.

Our purpose is not to offer solutions but rather to examine the inherent economic and social challenges faced by what is essentially a style industry, one that clothes women from the highest to the lowest price points. It is an industry that has always relied on the concept and importance of rapidly changing fashion, with an acceptance that there is such a conceit as an original design, and that copies of that original were and are essential to suggest democratic fashion for all.

We begin discussion in the 1890s, with the rise of the women's ready-to-wear apparel industry, and continue through the early 1940s, when the FOGA's brief but successful industry-run program of self-regulation against piracy ended. While the design piracy debate wears on within the fashion and popular press and within the legal system today, this book provides the critical historical context of the role of copying in the US women's ready-to-wear apparel industry. It also suggests that although many of the arguments are financial in nature, some depend on access to fashion by all women. The ethical questions concerning the copy are more ambiguous and often not included in these arguments for and against protection, due at least in part to the fact that many early manufacturers and retailers considered copying of Parisian designs both customary and acceptable. We highlight the Depression-era industry's attempts at controlling design piracy, emphasizing the legal, ethical, economic, and social considerations. We analyze legal documentation, including the incorporation papers of the FOGA and the docket of FOGA cases argued in the United States District Court in southern New York and the twelve briefs of the United States Supreme Court case, *FOGA v. Federal Trade Commission (FTC)*. We also evaluate governmental reports from the period, including the working papers of the National Recovery Administration's Division of Review on Design Piracy of 1935 as well as its Hearings on the Codes of Fair Competition for the Dress Manufacturing Industry. In addition, it was essential to take into account legal and apparel industry arguments for and against copying as published in the *Journal of the Patent Office Society*, the *Harvard Law Review*, and the *Journal of Retailing*. Primary research conducted in museums, archives, and special collections in New York City included the Fashion Institute of Technology's Costume Collection and Special Collections and College Archives, the Metropolitan Museum of Art's Costume Institute, the Metropolitan Museum of Art's Library, and the New York Public Libraries Science, Business, and Industry Library.[17]

The book is written both chronologically and topically. Chapter 1, Historical Overview of Evolving Design Protection Efforts, provides a general historical context for issues of design originality, copying, and the consumer in the apparel industry. Chapter 2, Design Piracy from a Legal Perspective, provides a background and explanation of the legal and governmental issues surrounding protection. Chapter 3, Origins of Design Piracy in the US Women's Ready-to-Wear Apparel Industry, describes the early years of the ready-to-wear industry and the reasons that design piracy came to be a dominant method of competition for manufacturers. Chapter 4, Development and Promotion of a United States Design Presence, demonstrates the steps the American industry and its supporters took to create a unique presence, not just in the United States but also abroad. This chapter also demonstrates the inherent complexities of the fashion design process within a system of creation, distribution, and advertising that esteems originality yet supports copying. Chapter 5, Design Piracy and Self-Regulation: The Fashion Originators' Guild of America, describes the beginnings of the FOGA and traces its persistent efforts to eradicate piracy. Chapter 6, Design Protection Arguments, explains the arguments for and against legalized design protection. While these arguments are discussed within the context of the controversy over the FOGA, they can be seen as broadly applicable to both earlier and later arguments related to design piracy and copyright. Chapter 7, The Fashion Originators' Guild of America: Controversy and Defeat, examines this nongovernmental group's policies and how they led ultimately to its demise. The final chapter, Chapter 8, Original, Adaptation, Copy, Reproduction?, summarizes the book and illustrates the numerous ways the apparel industry continues to grapple with design piracy. Throughout the book we argue that the way the industry grew, and its integrated use of often ambiguous design language that included "original," "adaptation," "reproduction," and "authorized copy," along with the preponderance of pirated copies, shaped business practices in a way that continues today.

Knock It Off

Chapter 1

Historical Overview of Evolving Design Protection Efforts

Prior to the 1860s, whether for geographical or economic reasons, clothing consumption meant personal production for most American women. "Babies," or dolls, dressed in European styles and fashion drawings published in magazines such as *Graham's* (1826–1857), *Godey's Lady's Book* (1830–1898), and *Peterson's* (1842–1898) informed clothing makers of the latest styles. Homemade clothing, created from patterns or based on existing styles, often did not fit well or look fashionable, partly because of the great complexity of the styles and the lack of training and skill of the maker. Wealthier clients could order clothing directly from Europe or commission tailors and dressmakers to faithfully copy the fashions. Clients often insisted on gowns that followed the fashionable silhouette and idea, yet were adapted to the particular form and personal characteristics of the individual woman. Even women in moderate income brackets would occasionally pay a local seamstress or dressmaker to do the complicated fitting involved in producing more elaborate dresses. In large cities there were also custom dress businesses that catered to the servant classes. Thus, women relied on a variety of resources to clothe themselves, choosing the options that best fit their budget and approach to fashion.

In the late nineteenth and early twentieth centuries, a complex interaction of social, cultural, and technological changes set the stage for rapid growth of the ready-to-wear apparel industry in the United States. An increase in the number of wage-earning women, especially in white-collar jobs, expanded college attendance, and participation in sports activities helped to create demand for ready-to-wear. By the beginning of the twentieth century, ready-to-wear clothing offered in a variety of styles, quantities, and prices was available in almost all markets.[1] Several factors led to this development. For instance, more single women entered the workplace as secretaries, factory workers, and saleswomen. Long working hours coupled with wider opportunities to fill leisure time, such as riding in automobiles, attending movies, or playing sports, meant less time to sew. In addition, the struggle to create a well-fitted, acceptable garment made home sewing even less appealing when it was possible to purchase a ready-to-wear garment. Active women increasingly chose to purchase their clothing in retail stores rather than to invest either the time to make it at home or the commitment it took to have them made by a dressmaker. Regardless of economic status, most women participated in a wide variety of activities for which they sought a wardrobe that was suitably varied as well as comfortable, practical, and fashionable.[2]

While cheap ready-to-wear had previously been available to working-class women, it was middle-class women who were critical in the acceptance of ready-to-wear as a viable fashion choice. This occurred largely through department stores.[3] They became centers for display and entertainment, allowing women to see and be seen in fashionable clothing, thus changing shopping rituals forever.[4] As advertisements and retail shop displays made high fashion more widely visible, women were influenced to desire more frequent style change and became increasingly interested not only in fashionable clothing but also in owning more of it.

The ready-to-wear fashion industry grew at a remarkable pace in the early decades of the twentieth century, with firms creating new styles at an ever-increasing rate to gain a competitive edge. Initial fashion directions came from French couture designers, but the requirement for enormous numbers of design variations demanded by ready-to-wear manufacturers in order to compete almost immediately became problematic.

The idea of an original design that was in fact intended to be copied began even earlier, with the rise of French haute couture as big business, and in particular with Charles Worth. Charles Frederick Worth, generally credited as the father of haute couture, developed a business model by the 1870s that allowed him to operate on an almost industrial scale. Integral to his plan was a continuous series of design models that could be repeated, not only as variations for his wealthy clients, but also as models sold to department stores for reproduction. This commercial approach was different from that of the traditional dressmaker's practice, whereby a single garment was produced for an individual customer. As the historian Nancy Troy has stated, it also meant "models described as unique creations that were nevertheless subject to endless adaptation and repetition."[5] In addition, a single designer now heavily influenced fashion—one who created an artistic persona and whose name was stamped onto a label inside the dress. Hence almost from the inception of haute couture the distinctions between originality and the various reproductions and adaptations proceeding therefrom were confusing, at least to consumers. An original was quite simply the first version, almost always intended for copy. The idea of a copy was considered an acceptable and indeed natural component in the diffusion of fashion. However, with the rapid rise of the women's ready-to-wear industry, there were more US designers and manufacturers in direct competition with each other. Rather than go to an original French source for design ideas or hire their own designers, American competitors soon realized it was easier and less expensive simply to copy each other. The process of copying became widespread, and design piracy was soon an internalized practice of the industry. Indeed, in one of its initial issues from 1910, trade publication *Women's Wear* described the now pervasive practice as the "copying evil."[6]

Style change became the driving force in the growth of the women's ready-to-wear clothing industry. By the early twentieth century, styles were copied so quickly that any popular fashion was available to all consumers, sometimes within days, and at successively lower price points. While today the ability to see digital images of new designs makes the transmission of copies seem immediate, in the past the industry had mechanisms in place that allowed an almost equally fast transmission of designs. These included sketchers and other design "spies" sent out to factories and showrooms to produce copies. In addition, women who worked in the Paris design houses often sold sketches of designs to US manufacturers—often the same sketch to multiple companies. The industry's ability to quickly reproduce new styles impacted the very nature and organization of the women's apparel industry. As a design was copied at lower price points, the market was flooded with cheap imitations of higher-end goods. Piracy permeated the industry; even copies were copied. According to progressive reformer Ida Tarbell, writing in 1912:

> From top to bottom we are copying. The French or Viennese mode, started on upper Fifth Avenue, spreads to 23rd St., from 23rd St. to 14th St., from 14th St. to Grand and Canal. Each move sees it reproduced in materials

a little less elegant and durable; its colors a trifle vulgarized, its ornaments cheapened, its laces poorer. A travesty, and yet a recognizable travesty.[7]

As the apparel industry realized the influence of mass media on consumers, advertisers began to emphasize fashion as the most important motive to purchase a product rather than reasons of durability.[8] Fashion stimulated sales by encouraging obsolescence and premature replacement of goods. In 1910 *Women's Wear* editors noted:

This feature of the business is a radical departure from the old time system of turning out good, staple styles in quantities, when the idea of "dressing in uniform" as it is now called, was not regarded as objectionable, but contrarily, the more one saw of any special style and color, the more fashionable it was considered.[9]

An atmosphere was created wherein a woman would rather be "caught dead" than wear last year's style or gaze on another woman wearing the same dress. Obsolescence set in, not because a product became worn or unusable, but because it was dated and no longer fashionable. The public desire for continual style creativity, evidenced by the number of styles introduced each season by various manufacturers, was encouraged by the apparel industry.[10] Even if a woman could be satisfied with outdated styles, manufacturers produced and retailers stocked only fashionable goods.[11]

As aspirations to keep up with changing styles increased, a new philosophy evolved that quality was less important than stylishness. While consumers of haute couture and custom-made goods wanted quality and personalization, ready-to-wear consumers seemed more interested in following every whim of fashion produced in prices that they could afford.[12] Rather than purchasing one or two expensive dresses of such quality as would be wearable for a number of years, women sought variety and quantity. Perhaps exaggerating the importance of style to the twentieth-century woman, a writer for *Women's Wear* stated, "The woman of today almost does not care if the dress is put together with pins, if it gives her individuality and the fashionable appearance."[13]

At the same time, the rapid diffusion of new styles at all price levels made purchasing decisions difficult and sometimes bewildering to consumers. The similarity in appearance, if not in quality, could be disconcerting to women accustomed to relating clothing with social station. The home economist and lecturer Bertha June Richardson explained the class confusion of wealthy women confronted with working-class girls in similar styles: "These could not be poor girls, earning five or six dollars a week. They looked better dressed than you did! Plumes on their hats, a rustle of silk petticoats, everything about them in the latest style." She went on, however, to describe the sudden realization that the appearance of extravagant dress represented "girls who wasted their hard-earned money on cheap imitation" in an attempt to "bridge the difference" between themselves and what they perceived as an upper-class way of dressing.[14]

Manufacturers and retailers also faced challenges because of the increased speed and importance of fashion change. As an industry, it continued to be dependent on Paris not only for fashion direction but also for models to copy. Authorized French models were expensive and US clothing manufacturers were slow to develop their own design talents. Moreover, manufacturers that invested in designers or in the authorized purchase of French models to copy saw their product devalued through repetition in cheaper goods. In describing the situation in 1916, lawyer and regular apparel industry commentator Julius Henry Cohen stated that after the expense of "thousands of dollars" to adapt a Parisian design to appeal to the American consumer, copies appeared "within forty-eight hours." The only recourse was "multiplicity and rapidity of design at such frequent intervals" that competitors would "lag behind."[15]

Manufacturers constantly introduced large numbers of new style variations. One manufacturer claimed three hundred "active numbers" at a time, with styles tending to persist for only about six weeks.[16] Much of this production of seemingly unlimited style variations began in the shirtwaist industry. For example, in 1895, V. Henry Rothschild and Co. claimed to have 1,200 styles prepared for the coming season. Fisk, Clark and Flagg planned to show 1,452 different patterns and designs for the spring 1896 season, and the company apparently offered style exclusivity to at least some of the retailers that purchased their goods. This was accomplished by offering a specific style to only one retailer within a specified geographic area. The practice of offering enough style variations to satisfy women's perceived need for exclusivity continued well into the 1930s (Figure 1.1).[17]

For the majority of US ready-to-wear manufacturers it was far easier and cheaper to keep up with style change by copying the successful gar-

Figure 1.1 Advertisements like this one, offering clever variations of similar designs at reasonable prices, were popular promotional motifs throughout the 1930s. "New Showings of Style Protected Dresses," *Women's Wear Daily*, November 19, 1935, sec. 2, 7.

ments of American producers than it was to research the latest trends, hire designers, risk product failure, or even spend the money on travel and customs duties for French goods. Manufacturers copied one another in a number of ways. Submanufacturing firms often produced garments for more than one company. Because they engaged in volume production on short notice, the submanufacturing firms could introduce replicas within twenty-four hours after the introduction of the original garment. Company executives sent spies to factories for purposes of observing and copying the most salable items. Sometimes employees of copyists would visit showrooms of original creators and memorize, take notes, or sketch designs. This practice was referred to by one manufacturer as "sending

• 9 •   Historical Overview

Figure 1.2 It is not clear from this advertisement if the reproductions were authorized from companies such as Mainbocher or if they were copied by the "fashion staff" of Wanamaker's. "Paris Comes to Wanamaker's," *Women's Wear Daily*, April 1, 1936, 7.

scouts with camera eyes," in that supposed buyers would visit manufacturers and retailers and take mental photographs of new designs.[18] Copyists might also bribe employees of original creators to furnish samples of their designs or just steal garments outright from manufacturing firms.

The speed of fashion change and reliance on repetition of ideas at various price points made design protection both difficult and controversial. Moreover, although French couture houses in fact sanctioned and were paid for at least a portion of this type of copying, most retailers advertised their reproductions and adaptations regardless of whether they were authorized (Figure 1.2). For both stores and consumers there was also a veneration of Parisian designers—designers known by name. Thus, the association of a name with a copy, legitimate or not, could increase sales. The US market, by comparison, was very slow to create a personality for its own designers as fashion authorities.

Many manufacturers tried aggressively to protect their merchandise through trademarks or patents, but the physical design was virtually impossible to protect. In a few cases, well-known New York custom design houses adopted the example of the haute couture and offered their originals to other houses and to ready-to-wear manufacturers for use as authorized copies. Some also recognized the importance of branding their lines, thus associating the brand name with quality and style through advertising. None of these measures slowed the rampant design piracy, however. Legally, designers and manufacturers had tenuous success in proving their work "original and novel" as required by US patent laws, and copyright did not apply to apparel design. Arguments both for and against style piracy were (and continue to be) heatedly debated in the trade and popular press, as well as in legal, business, and intellectual property journals.

Attempts to stop or at least control design piracy through legal protection began in the 1910s, with both textile and apparel firms supporting various bills in Congress. There were proponents on both sides of the piracy debate, but the crux of the issue both in the popular press and from a legal perspective often centered on three concerns: what constituted an original; at what point did the original become an adaptation; and when was it a derivative copy. The idea that changes such as different trim or an alteration of sleeve length, for example, constituted a new design made the arguments ambiguous at best, particularly since the law was incomplete in protecting fashion design. Historically, the language applied to copy variations began with terms used to create a connection to French fashions. Thus, in some cases a retailer or design house described an "original" as a garment that was an exact copy of a Paris design. Variations that were produced based on that design were described in a range of other terms. There evolved a complex and confusing vocabulary intended to explain the degree of separation from the "original." Some of this confusion can be seen in Figure 1.3, an Oppenheimer, Collins and Co. advertisement from 1923, as they explain that "all copies or adaptations of Paris models must be made from an actual and intimate study of the original." Their definition of an adaptation was a design that had style variations introduced by their in-house designers, and, while the ad states that they did not produce forgeries, the definition is unclear and their text sidesteps the issue of whether the makers of the Paris originals knew about or authorized any Oppenheimer, Collins and Co. copies and adaptations.

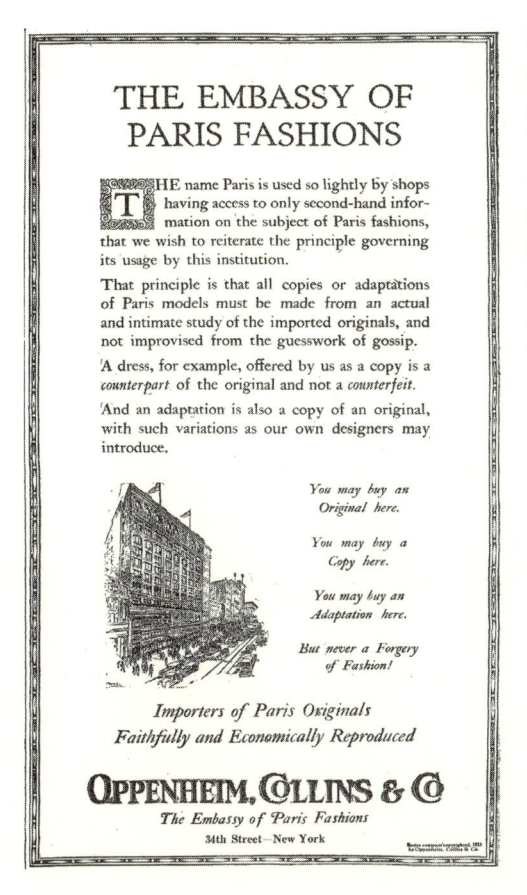

Figure 1.3 Oppenheim, Collins and Co., a women's specialty store based in New York City, asserted that they sold originals, copies, and adaptations but never forgeries. While they explain how a copy becomes an adaptation, it is still unclear what constitutes a forgery. *The New York Times*, March 26, 1923.

Some within the industry wrestled with the validity of original designs at all, believing all garments to be imitative adaptations or variations of those popular the previous season.[19] These industry members believed designers and manufacturers followed the same current trends and ideas in art, architecture, politics, and high society. Culled from identical sources, styles frequently followed a similar idea. An example of this was the widespread use of Egyptian motifs following the discovery of King Tut's tomb in November 1922 (Figure 1.4).[20]

Morris De Camp (M. D. C.) Crawford, fashion editor of *Women's Wear*, maintained the idea that nothing was truly original, despite his strong support for the education of American designers to become independent of Paris for their inspirations. In a 1919 article, Crawford contemplated

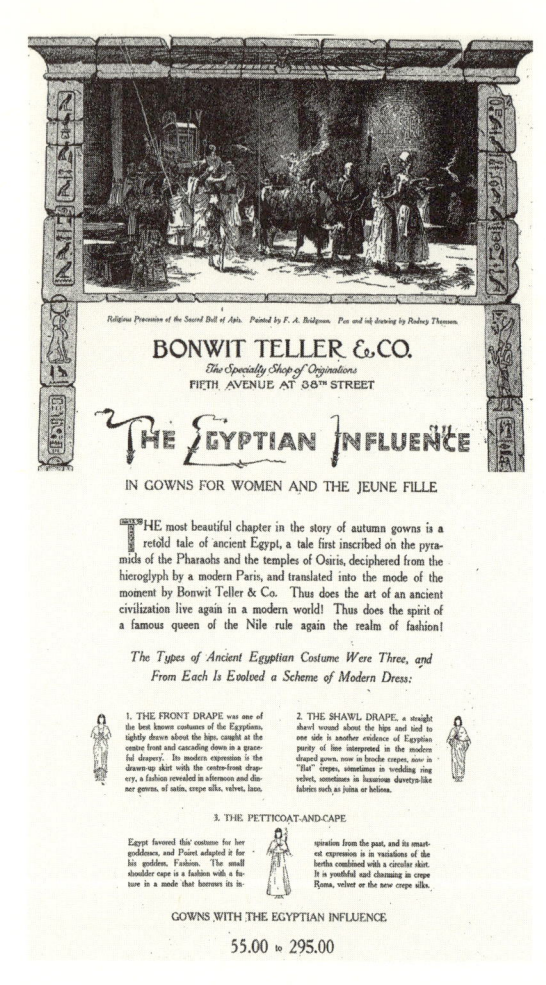

Figure 1.4 An example of supposedly "original models" heavily influenced by Howard Carter's November 1922 discovery of King Tutankhamen's tomb. *Harper's Bazar*, April 1923, 126.

whether any styles were new, since preexisting ideas, styles, and trends were the basis for all garments.[21] Echoing this sentiment, Ben Hirsch, a manufacturer of lower-priced dresses working in the 1930s, stated:

> Every manufacturer in the dress industry . . . takes this sleeve here and the waist there and the neck there and the skirt some other place and a buckle here and a flower there, and a combination here, and put them all together, but we do not have anything that is original, we have simply a compilation of something that has been made many years before. . . . After we have taken these things from these common sources that are open to

everybody, there is certainly nothing that would entitle us or anybody else in the world to a property right in it which would exclude everybody else from making it.²²

In 1940, the legal writer Kenneth Hutchinson concurred: "Practically none of the fashion originators are, in any strict sense, originators."²³ An exact definition of an original design remained ambiguous, particularly when designers and manufacturers used terminology such as "distinctly, original adaptations" to advertise the (supposed) uniqueness of their products.²⁴ Other advertisements also conflated definitions (Figure 1.5). For example, the department store Russeks attempted to legitimize the

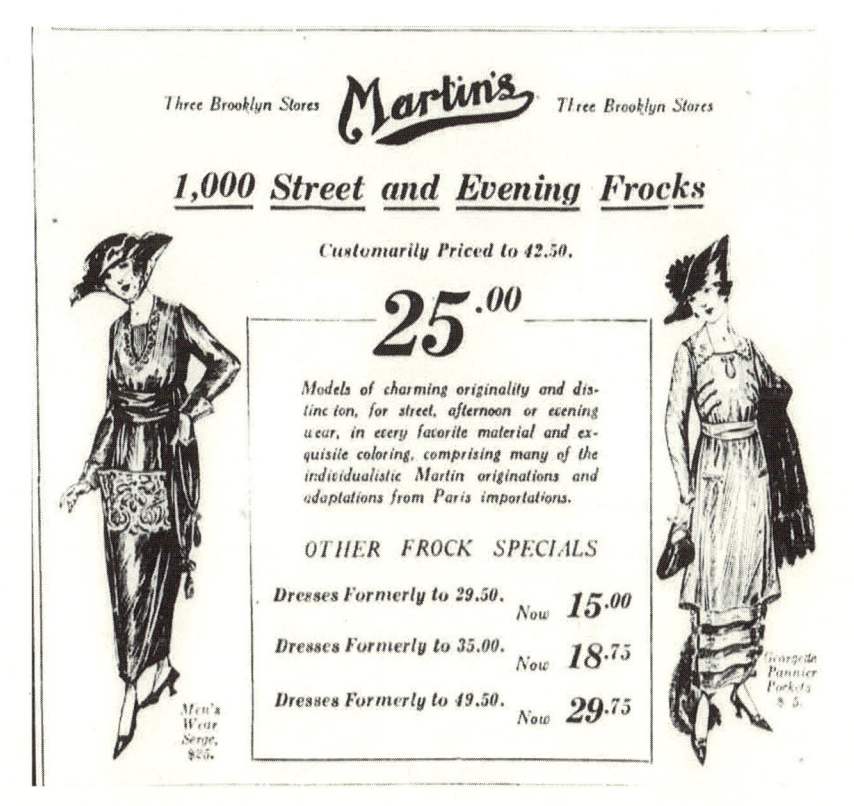

Figure 1.5 Martin's store offered "originations" rather than originals, further complicating the meaning of an original design. *The Evening World*, January 17, 1919, 16.

purchase of copies and at the same time to distinguish between different types by stating: "If your copy fails to express the spirit of the original, then it becomes an imitation rather than a duplication." The advertisement went on to state that "origination is an art—adaptation is a Genius."[25] They offered the public exact copies and "genuine adaptations."

By the early 1930s, with repeated failure of governmental protection, industry groups formed to battle piracy through self-regulation (Figure 1.6). Maurice Rentner, manufacturer and designer of high-priced apparel, along with a group of other manufacturers of better dresses, founded the most successful of these industry groups, the FOGA. Although Rentner himself conceded that "no fashion creator will assert that everything about every dress he offers is new" and that the controversy over design piracy was largely "a conflict of individual interest," the FOGA sought to control copying through retailer-manufacturer collaboration.[26] Described by M. D. C. Crawford as "one of the most unusual, most extraordinary organizations the needle or any other industry ever formed," it sought not only to "cure the evil of design piracy" but also to control problems related to discounts and returned goods.[27] Despite significant accomplishments throughout the 1930s, in 1941 the decision of the Supreme Court was that the FOGA formed a monopoly.

Despite the failure of the FOGA, one fact remained: success within the ready-to-wear apparel industry depended on the combination of stylistic elements that created a fashionable and salable garment. In the 1941 US Supreme Court decision against the FOGA and regarding the inability of the justice system to suppress design piracy, Justice Hugo Black acknowledged:

> Women do not buy hats, they buy fashions. They most certainly do not protect the wearer against rain or snow or cold. Virtually their sole function is to make the wearer happy in the thought that she has a beautiful thing which is in fashion. No matter how beautiful, if not in fashion the hat will not sell. A woman buys fashion, not goods.[28]

Whether that fashion was beautiful or flattering was subjective; ultimately it was the consumer, albeit under the influence of advertising or newsworthy trendsetters, who decided which styles lived and for how long; and whether she was comfortable (and could afford) an original, an adaptation, or a copy.

While the consumers ultimately bought the fashionable goods, it was their collective voice that was most missing from the style protection arguments. And because the US ready-to-wear industry grew and flourished through largely anonymous apparel designers working for named manufacturers, it was usually the manufacturers and not the designers who fought for design protection. Therefore, the recorded voices, whether in newspapers, magazines, or government documents, are largely those of the apparel manufacturers and retailers.

Figure 1.6 *Women's Wear Daily* regularly featured the workings of the various style protection groups, including the FOGA. "Style Protected," *Women's Wear Daily*, November 19, 1935, sec. 2, 1.

Chapter 2

Design Piracy from a Legal Perspective

"No sooner does a new idea or a new design appear upon the market today than it is fallen upon, seized, copied, and mangled by a horde of pirates who crouch in ambush awaiting the opportunity of stealing a ride upon the originality and brains of some enterprising competitor."[1]

This 1913 quote by *Dress Essentials* editor Alphonsus Haire typifies the frustration felt by early apparel industry designers and manufacturers in response to piracy. Intellectual property laws enable inventors, authors, artists, scientists, and musicians to protect the work they create from unauthorized use. United States law is incomplete, however, in that it does not provide protection to fashion designers against copying. In discussing the complexities of protecting design as intellectual property, Ralph Brown in the 1986–87 *UCLA Law Review* suggested:

> The whole body of the law is two faced.... One face recognizes that *Homo sapiens* thrive on imitation and so does the economy. The other looks with distaste on copiers. They reap where they have not sewn; they compete unfairly. Behind the distaste is a more rational concern that easy copying discourages originality and free-riding copiers may diminish investment in socially useful innovation.[2]

The fashion industry is thus an anomaly when it comes to both copying and design protection in that innovation and creativity are highly regarded and encouraged, and yet designers are unable to protect their innovations, even if they try (Figure 2.1). It has been a consistent and frequent complaint of the industry since its earliest days that neither copyright nor patent adequately protects designers of utilitarian objects, as clothing has consistently been defined. While an artist's or illustrator's painting of a dress would be protected, the garment itself is not, as clothing is viewed

• 17 • Legal Perspective

Figure 2.1 This advertisement states, "every precaution is taken to prevent the copying of our designs and to secure their exclusiveness." The consumer is assured that these shirtwaist dresses would not be found in any other New York or Parisian establishment. Alice Maynard advertisement, *Vogue*, May 30, 1901, C4.

in the legal system as serving a function, rather than being merely decorative.

Congress has been slow to act to enforce intellectual property protection for clothing. As noted by the attorney Leslie Hagen, when the piracy of musical recordings reached the $100 million mark in 1971, Congress deemed the problem chronic enough to warrant copyright protection. Likewise, in the face of more than $100 million a year in pirated computer chip designs in the semiconductor chip industry, the United States enacted the Semiconductor Chip Protection Act of 1984, which protects the layouts of integrated circuits. This innovative approach to protection has some aspects of copyright law and some aspects of patent law; it is also different from either. In the semiconductor industry, chip industry representatives asserted that for $10,000, a pirate could copy a chip design that had cost its original manufacturer upwards of $100,000 to design.[3] The apparel industry often points to the extent of pirated goods, yet exact figures for the ensuing profits and losses of offending and pirated companies are not available. One likely reliable estimate of extent, however, comes from self-described "Knockoff King" Jack Mulqueen, an apparel designer and manufacturer who admitted that only 40 percent of his $225 million gross in 1981 was of authorized copies—the rest from knocking off the "cream of the couture" without bothering to ask or pay for permission.[4] However, Congress has never instituted laws to protect fashion design. According to the former Register of Copyrights, Barbara Ringer, the issue of apparel design protection is "one of the most significant pressing items of unfinished business."[5]

Fashion is unique from the forms of art that are protected in that clothing styles change so frequently and these changes are often minute. For example, a slightly different hemline—flared rather than boot-cut—or a different sleeve type—cap rather than short—can make a significant change in the appearance of a garment. These changes occur so frequently that any protection possible to secure them would likely be too late to do any good for the originating designer or manufacturer. Furthermore, the apparel industry relies on and prospers from the practice of creating an original design that is then interpreted into copies for various price points.

Available Legal Protection

Intellectual property protection includes copyright, patents, and trademarks, which will be discussed here, as well as trade dress, which generally refers to characteristics of the visual appearance of a product or its packaging that signifies the source of the product to consumers.[6]

Copyright

Protection of intellectual property was inherent in the origins of the United States, as the founding fathers considered it critical to encourage innovation and commerce. The original Copyright Act of 1790 authorized Congress "to promote the progress of science and useful arts, by securing, for a limited time to authors and inventors, the exclusive right to their respective writings and discoveries."[7] Although originally providing protection to literary works, the scope of protection was expanded to include all sorts of creative works, including sculptures, movies, and even the "funny pages."[8]

Copyright laws generally give the owner the exclusive right to reproduce the work, to distribute copies, and to display the work publicly. Copyright protects an image, but it does not give the copyright holder exclusive rights to the image's subject matter. For example, a photograph of the Golden Gate Bridge could be protected, but this would not prohibit another individual from taking a different image of the bridge. Copyright protection was extended in 1976 from the original fourteen-year term drafted by the founders of the Constitution to life plus seventy years or ninety-five years from publication for works made for hire. Copyrights are registered with the Copyright Office of the Library of Congress.

On the whole, copyright law affords little protection for clothing designs. Some apparel manufacturers and designers have attempted to obtain copyright protection (Figure 2.2), suggesting their work is a type of sculptural creation. However, the courts continue to view clothing as protecting the wearer from the elements and providing modesty, all considered useful rather than applied arts, which would include printed fabrics, quilt patterns, or jewelry designs.[9] According to the legal commentator S. Priya Bharathi, "legislators and courts have a great deal of trouble seeing past the utilitarian function of a piece of clothing."[10]

Patents: Utility and Design

Begun in 1790, patent laws conferred "the right to exclude others from making, using, offering for sale, or selling" a unique invention in the Unit-

Figure 2.2 The Rosen Bros. Company advertised that their "fashion details" were protected by copyright. It is not clear what was protected, as designs themselves are not copyrightable. If the manufacturer named a style, the style name could be trademarked, but not copyrighted. "Rosen Bros. Frocks, Inc.," *Women's Wear Daily*, January 24, 1933, 21.

ed States or "importing" the invention into the United States. Utility patents protect the way a machine, process, device, or object is used or works. Patents are awarded a term of twenty years from date of issuance and are protected by the US Patent and Trademark System.[11]

According to Abraham Lincoln, the American patent system added "the fuel of self-interest to the fire of genius."[12] President Franklin Delano Roosevelt stated, "Patents are the key to our technology, technology is the key to production."[13] Clothing articles that qualify for utility patent protection tend to have underlying technology (functional design) that dictates the outward appearance of the article. Examples of what can be patented include specialized fasteners, high-performance textiles, or protective garments, including hazmat gear (Figure 2.3). Utility patents for apparel products can be very difficult to enforce, however, since there is

• 21 •   Legal Perspective

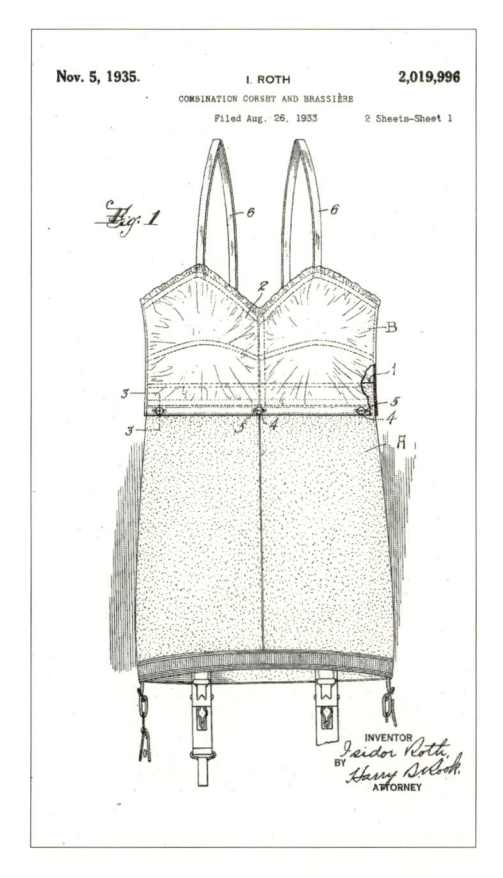

Figure 2.3 Example of a utility patent issued for a combination corset and brassiere. Isidor Roth, Patent No. 2,019,996. (1935).

nothing to restrict a copyist from designing a garment with a similar appearance but using different underlying technology.[14]

Prior to the mid-nineteenth century, no legislative means existed to protect the decorative design of an object. At that time, patent law related only to patents of inventions, or utility patents, while copyright laws related to purely artistic works. In 1842, Congress agreed that the subject of design, as manifested in the appearance of an object, warranted separate legislation. As such, the existing patent laws were expanded to include design patents. Design patents protect intellectual property that falls between purely artistic works and inventions that rely entirely on function. Design patents represent a separate and distinct category of patent protection within the US Patent and Trademark System.[15]

Design patents are governed by the provisions of 35 U.S.C. 171 and

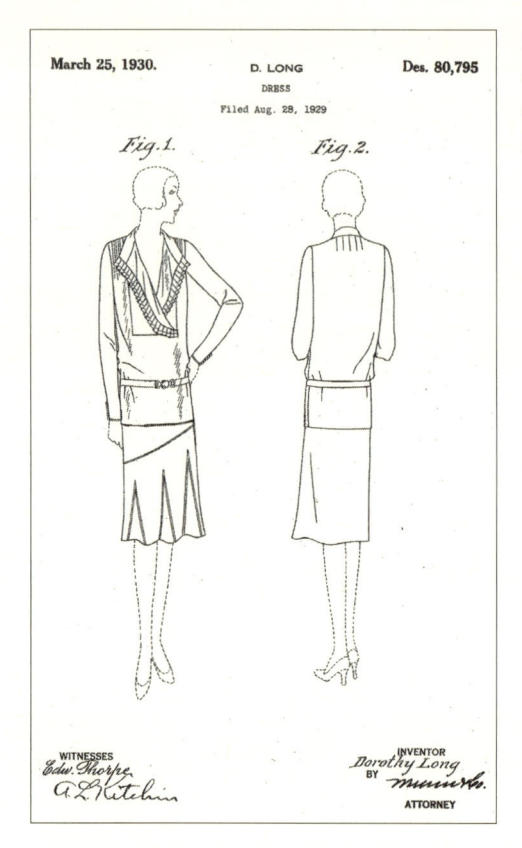

Figure 2.4 Example of a design patent for a dress. Dorothy Long, Patent No. 80,795. (1930).

provide that "anyone who invents a new, original, and ornamental design for an article of manufacture" may obtain a design patent. These patents provide short-term protection to all inventions and designs that meet the requirements of novelty when viewed through the eyes of a hypothetical designer skilled in the art.[16] The term of a design patent, initially set at seven years, was changed in 1861 to three and a half, seven, or fourteen years, to be chosen at the discretion of the applicant. In 1982, the time limit was set to fourteen years. However, patent protection may take up to three years to secure. The inventive novelty of design patent protection resides in the shape, pattern, and decoration (the appearance or visual aspect of the object) and not in the structure or function of the item. Thus, for a dress design patent, only the appearance of the product is protected, such as the placement of the gores, pleats, and ruffles, rather than the un-

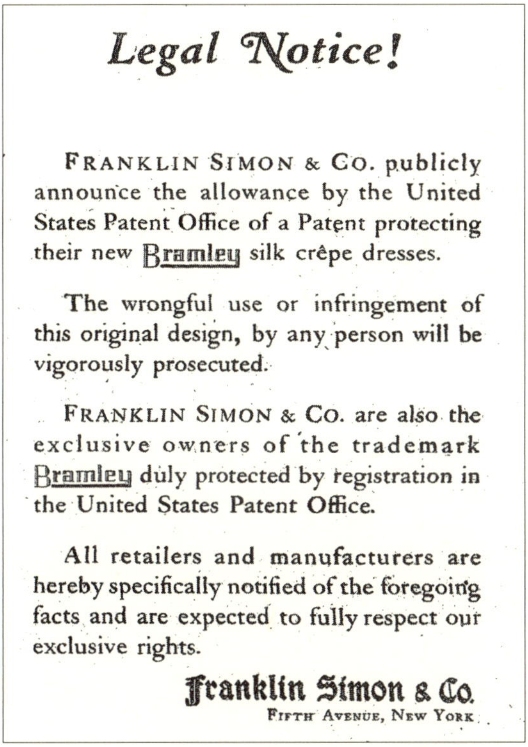

Legal Notice!

FRANKLIN SIMON & CO. publicly announce the allowance by the United States Patent Office of a Patent protecting their new Bramley silk crêpe dresses.

The wrongful use or infringement of this original design, by any person will be vigorously prosecuted.

FRANKLIN SIMON & CO. are also the exclusive owners of the trademark Bramley duly protected by registration in the United States Patent Office.

All retailers and manufacturers are hereby specifically notified of the foregoing facts and are expected to fully respect our exclusive rights.

Franklin Simon & Co.
FIFTH AVENUE, NEW YORK

Figure 2.5 Legal notice warning retailers and manufacturers of the patent protecting the trademarked name Bramley and an original design by Franklin Simon & Co. *The New York Times*, February 18, 1924, 27.

derlying construction techniques (the actual gores, pleats, and ruffles) that create the look of the garment (Figure 2.4).[17]

Because clothing relies so heavily on ornament, design patents may seem to apply perfectly, but there are challenges to their use.[18] Design patents prove difficult to obtain because there is insistence of novelty in the design that is, in a sense, tantamount to invention. It is not enough that the design represents a new, original, and ornamental arrangement of materials; it must also be the result of "inventive gift." As an example of the difficulty in determining talent, the judge in a 1956 patent infringement court case maintained, "It is with some trepidation that I venture to determine what is the ordinary skill of designers of intimate articles of feminine apparel because such skill, at least to a mere man, seems to have no ordinary limitations."[19]

Timeliness was another important factor in the practicality of patent protection. The amount of time needed to determine patentability is gen-

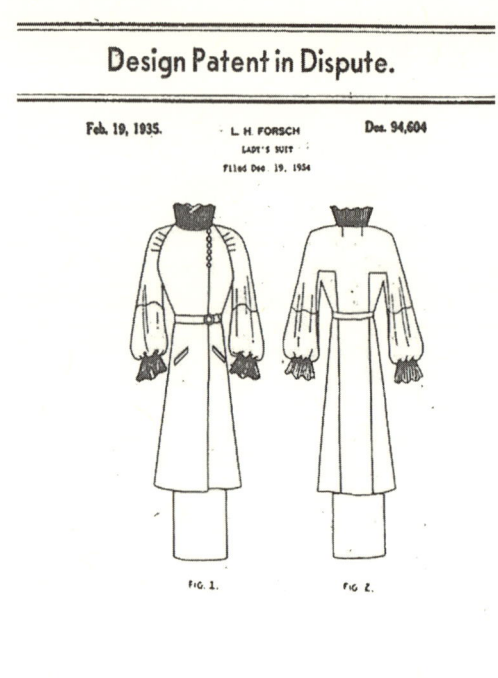

Figure 2.6 Design patent in dispute. The illustration is the patent registration, including front and back views of the garment produced by the Forsch, Benjamin Company. "Design Patent in Dispute," *Women's Wear Daily*, April 3, 1935, 2.

erally slower than the speed of fashion change.[20] By the time a patent is obtained, a design may have already completed its life cycle—created, marketed, sold, and discontinued. Further, the cost of obtaining a patent can be prohibitive. In his congressional report on the registration of designs, committee chairman Martin A. Morrison of Indiana called the American design patent process "slow, tedious, and expensive ... being quite as long as the popularity and value of the design sought to be protected."[21] A final limitation of design patents and other forms of intellectual property protection is that to benefit from them, one must vigilantly sue or threaten to sue anyone who trespasses on one's rights (Figure 2.5).[22]

According to federal judge Robert A. Inch in the 1941 patent infringement case of *White v. Lombardy Dresses, Inc.*, "the obtaining of a patent on simply a new and attractive dress is a waste of time."[23] Even if designers secured patent approval in the Patent and Trademark Office, courts consistently found design patents invalid on the grounds of the design not being novel. According to the US Commerce Department, between 1936 and 1946, federal circuit courts dismissed 85 percent of the patent suits brought before them.[24] From 1930 to 1950, the US Supreme Court reviewed thirty-four patent cases in which the issue of "invention" was raised. Twenty-eight patents (83 percent) were deemed invalid for "want of invention."[25]

Until the mid-twentieth century, it was common to see design patent litigation announcements in *Women's Wear Daily*. For example, in 1935, the manufacturers Forsch, Benjamin Company sued the Morris W. Haft & Bros. Company for infringement on their patented dress (Figure 2.6).[26] The decision of the court was that the patent was invalid. One of the concurring judges did at least acknowledge the need for legislation, stating: "There is a real necessity for some law that will equally protect those who spend a great deal of time and money in giving the public a new and attractive dress, and those who give another portion of the public, who seek a more economical dress, a garment of its own design," meaning that each portion of the industry needed both originality and design idea protection.[27]

The limitations of design patents did not prevent manufacturers and designers from attempting to use them to protect their work, however. Hundreds of designers in the 1930s, including Dorothy Long of Franklin Simon & Co. and Sally Milgrim of Associated Merchandising Corporation, and in the 1940s, including Bonnie Cashin, Nettie Rosenstein, Joset Walker, and Molly Parnis, applied for and were issued patents for their dress designs (Figure 2.7). Nonetheless, attempts to use design patents to protect apparel faded out after World War II, most likely due to a combination of factors, including the failure of patents to actually protect the design as well as a changed environment for US designers after the war—a period when the importance of Paris copies surged. Only in recent years has there been a renewed interest in obtaining patents to provide design protection.[28]

Trademarks

Trademarks, the names, signs, symbols, or devices attached to goods to identify their origin, tend to be the most recognizable representation of a brand. Internationally known trademarks within the apparel industry

Figure 2.7 Example of a design patent for a dress. Nettie Rosenstein, Patent No. 128,561 (1941).

include the double "C" logo of Chanel and Louis Vuitton's signature "LV" logo (Figure 2.8). In the United States, trademark laws provide protection against counterfeiters, who copy the distinctive qualities of famous marks to create look-alike products and pass them off as the original. They do not protect the design of the goods themselves. That means that while trademark law may be used to prevent counterfeiting, it does not prevent pirating. Copyists of designs do not violate trademark laws when they simply copy the design without using the name or trademarks of the works they have copied. Fashion pirates place their own identification on the copies, with even these labels having a striking resemblance to the original.[29]

The trademark practice thrived in menswear. During the late nineteenth and early twentieth centuries, many of the better quality men's shirts manufacturers created brand names and style names that were pro-

• 27 •   Legal Perspective

> **You're Invited to a Party!**
>
> Featuring
> 'Knock it Off'
> Designer Inspired
> Handbags!
>
> 'Knock it Off' handbags feature the latest designs inspired by:
>
> • Louis Vuitton • Gucci   • Prada • Burberry
> • Kate Spade   • Fendi   • Tods   • Brighton
>
> and many more in the season's hottest colors and styles!
> Handbags are cash and carry at time of purchase and they go fast!

Figure 2.8 Invitation to a Knock It Off purse party from 2007. The invitation makes clear that the designs are "inspired by" the latest designs, but do not violate trademark rights because they are not branded as the designer originals. Collection of author.

tected by trademark. The firm of Hutchinson, Pierce & Co., for example, claimed their 1899 Star trademark had been in use for at least fifty years and, in one issue of *The Haberdasher*, warned imitators that they would be subject to court action (Figure 2.9).[30] The value of a trademark was critical in the late nineteenth- and early twentieth-century menswear industry, where company names tended to change frequently, as new partners were brought in, others left, and new family members entered the business. For men's shirts, trademarks also helped in creating an association with quality when there was little to distinguish style differences over longer lengths of time than in women's wear.

Although some men's shirt companies also manufactured women's shirts and thus used their trademarks on these products, the practice did not last long in the women's apparel industry once shirtwaists were no longer the popular garment for women. According to Julius Henry Cohen, as the women's ready-to-wear trade evolved, few if any new manufacturers established trademark identification. Because companies could start a ready-to-wear business with little capital investment, new firms were often very small and relied on contractors and jobbers for part of their production. This did not encourage companies to either spend the

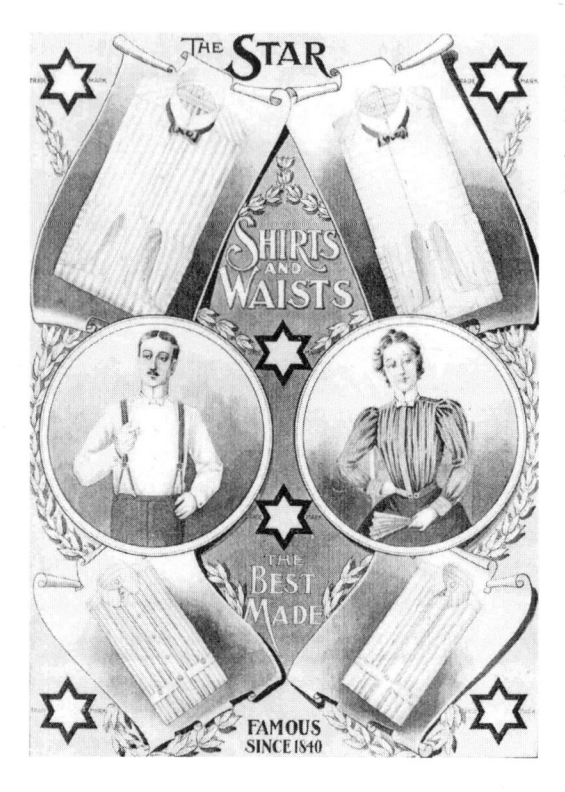

Figure 2.9 Advertisement for Star brand shirtwaists for men and women. *The Haberdasher*, April 1899, 21.

money to create and advertise a brand name, or feel compelled to have a product that could be backed with quality or style guarantees through the name. As competition increased in the women's apparel trade in the early years of the twentieth century, rapid and constant style change, not trademarks, became standard business practice. In hindsight, it is questionable whether women in the early twentieth century would have made purchases based on a trade name. It is more likely that women purchased garments based on style and price considerations and chose to shop in familiar retail outlets.[31]

Bills Submitted to Congress for Design Protection

Due to the inability of intellectual property laws to adequately protect apparel design, the apparel industry has repeatedly pushed for legislation to stop design piracy. Numerous bills have been introduced in Congress to remedy the piracy problem. One of the earliest enacted bills, the 1913 Kahn Act, intended to protect European designers who refused to send their works to the Panama-Pacific International Exposition without first receiving assurances against American piracy. The Kahn Act angered many US designers who argued that it allowed European designers to steal American designs.[32]

The first significant bills to protect American designs were submitted in 1914. Referred to as the Oldfield bills because they were introduced by Representative William A. Oldfield of Arkansas, chairman of the House Committee on Patents, the legislation sought protection against the replication of designs and proposed registration of fashion designs alongside the fine arts.[33] When Oldfield was succeeded by Martin A. Morrison of Indiana as committee chairman, the revised Morrison bill afforded copyright registration to the author of any new or original design, "as embodied in or applied to any manufactured product," including surface designs. Morrison was lobbied by the Design Registration League, a group of manufacturers that produced everything from clothing to stoves to lace embroideries. Created in 1914, the league sought special legislation through Congress to provide a workable, inexpensive, and fast means of protecting or establishing ownership rights of commercial work. The organization argued that many original and artistic designs did not qualify as inventions according to US law, but should still be afforded the same protection as other works of art. Thomas Ewing, the commissioner of patents, favored the bill. Lower-priced manufacturers, for the most part, were against it, as one stated: "We cannot help copying. Infringement depends on how you define a new style."[34] The bill was laid aside and never voted upon.

A 1918 court case, *International News Service v. Associated Press*, provided a flicker of hope to those wishing for design protection in the apparel industry. In this case, the defendants copied news articles from the plaintiff's public bulletin boards and used them in their own publications. The US Supreme Court decided that the defendant's copying of the plaintiff's articles while the facts were still current equaled unfair competition since they were to be reused in rivalry with the plaintiff. Although not related to apparel, the case was used by the Cheney Brothers to sue the Doris Silk Corporation.[35]

Cheney Brothers printed on the selvage of their goods that it was an original design and that they reserved the rights against competitive copies. The Doris Company copied the design and offered their version in competition with the Cheney Brothers. Despite the 1918 *International*

News Service v. Associated Press ruling, the court denied an injunction. Because the patterns were not patented nor were the designs copyrighted, the court found that the Cheney Brothers had no property rights to prevent imitation. The ruling judge, Judge Hand, stated, "It seems a lame answer in such a case to turn the injured party out of court... but judges have only limited power to amend the law; when the subject has been confined to the legislature, they must stand aside, even though there be a hiatus in completed justice."[36] The Cheney Brothers continued to fight in earnest, yet in vain, for design protection legislation.

Another push toward protection came with the Vestal bills, named for Representative Albert H. Vestal, who served as chairman of the Patent Committee during the Sixty-Ninth through Seventy-First Congresses. These bills were introduced and reintroduced from 1926 to 1931 and sought to provide a registration process integrated into existing copyright laws to protect original design. The Vestal bills provided registration of designs in the Copyright Office by anyone "who is author of any design" defined as pattern, shape, or form of a manufactured product. The Vestal bills favored prompt and inexpensive registration of styles (through the Patent Office in the initial bill and through the Copyright Office in later versions), a two-year term for a two-dollar fee, and a right to an eighteen-year extension for twenty dollars. The bills did not require a search for novelty in order to determine the originality of the applicant's design. Secretary of Commerce Herbert Hoover strongly supported the Vestal bills, stating that Paris abounded in styles for textiles, leather, jewelry, and so on, and that with protection the United States could achieve "a larger measure of artistic independence."[37] This statement seems to mean that if American designers were protected, design origination would flourish here as it did in Paris.

Within the Vestal bills, infringement included selling and distributing any product with "a colorable imitation." The National Retail Dry Goods Association, with three thousand stores nationwide, refused to support the Vestal bills because this broad definition of infringement seemed to put the onus of determining infringements on the retailer. Retailers feared the prospect of false claims, intimidation by manufacturers, an inability to reorder because their desired merchandise had been "recalled" as copies, and a fashion monopoly by those who registered their garment styles. When the Vestal bills were argued before the House, Representative Vestal stated that style protection would open the door to greater employment of designers, enable manufacturers to produce larger quantities more cheaply, establish honest competition among manufacturers, and afford consumers a choice of competing designs at competing prices in every range. Amended and re-amended, the Vestal bills were passed by the House in the winter of 1930 to 1931, but Congress adjourned before the bills were presented to the Senate. With Representative Vestal's death in 1932, these specific bills were never reintroduced.[38]

With the failure of the Vestal bills, Professor Karl Fenning, a former assistant US commissioner of patents and professor of law at Georgetown University, envisioned a hybrid plan of style registration. His plan stated that the register of copyrights would establish a searchable file of styles. Garments deemed original and novel would receive a certificate of copyright within seven days with a term of copyright of five years. Fenning's plan was introduced as a bill in 1933 and again in 1935, but it failed to receive approval.[39]

Many of the bills introduced to Congress were ardently fought in the trade press by the "popular price," or lower cost, establishments, especially during the Depression when low-cost dresses dominated the market. In one announcement, representatives of the Popular Priced Dress Manufacturers Group railed against a bill introduced by New York State Assemblyman Meyer Alterman that would establish proprietorship in apparel styles. They stated:

> This proposed bill, if passed, would cripple the progress of all manufacturers of dresses. . . . Like the other restrictions and amendments for style registration that have already been proposed, and on design patents that are now being granted, this bill is not based on creative art, originality or the work of a genius but provides for a franchise to the man or woman who wins the race in the scramble for the registration of styles in Albany.[40] (Figure 2.10)

From 1935 to the end of World War II, there was little governmental action in terms of design registration. The American Council of Style and Design Inc. warned that after the war, with the alleviation of shortages and the return of competitive practices, unauthorized copying would proliferate. In 1946, Henry E. Stehli, chairman of the group, argued, "In-

EVERY DRESS MANUFACTURER IS FACED WITH A NEW STYLE CONTROL MENACE!

You Are Invited to
Attend Our Meeting—Thursday Night—March 14th
Hotel Governor Clinton—8 P.M.

STATE OF NEW YORK
No. 2101
Int. 1882
IN ASSEMBLY
Mar. 1, 1935
Introduced by Mr. Alterman—read once and referred to the Committee on Judiciary

TO PROTEST
AGAINST THE ADOPTION OF
THIS BILL

Figure 2.10 Those organizations for and against design piracy protection used the trade press to advertise and solicit support for their positions. "Every Dress Manufacturer Is Faced with a New Style Control Menace," *Women's Wear Daily*, March 13, 1935, 8.

dustrial leaders who realize the heavy losses suffered under piracy and the consequent increase in production costs, have urged us to revive the American Council . . . and the remedy to the moral and economic wrong done to originators has to be found in legislation."[41] By the late 1940s, designers and manufacturers such as Maurice Rentner stressed that piracy was "rearing its ugly head." Retailers continued to be less concerned regarding the practice, however. Executives at Bergdorf Goodman, Henri Bendel, and Jay Thorpe found piracy "no danger to the business, but a natural consequence of fashion."[42] Congressman Hartley from New Jersey began hearings on bills to protect textile designs by stating, "American styles today lead the world."[43] Despite support from textile manufacturers and the Patent and Copyright Offices, there was strong opposition to the bill largely from the lower-priced manufacturers. The bill was postponed for further study. Renewed lobbying efforts began in the late 1950s under the auspices of the National Committee for Effective Design Legislation.

The opposition by the National Retail Merchants Association ultimately defeated design protection bills during this time.[44]

Industry Efforts

Given their inability to achieve copyright protection through governmental legislation, industry players suggested forming trade unions and associations to support and protect their investments. In 1928, the Silk Association of America established a design registration bureau, later named the Textile Design Registration Bureau, for the protection of print designs. The idea for the clearinghouse of styles came about because print manufacturers, after expending considerable cost to create engraved rollers, would discover the designs were already in use. Fabric designers and manufacturers were encouraged to submit their print designs to the bureau, which saved manufacturers production expense and loss of time in fruitless promotion of an already available print style. The success of the plan was attributable to a number of factors, including a close-knit trade association, printers refusing to process designs not registered, and the very nature of print styles, which may be varied to obtain an almost infinite number of styles. Ultimately, competition between manufacturers and printers stymied the bureau's longevity.[45]

While the Fashion Originators' Guild of America was quite successful (and controversial), other less successful (and less controversial) groups formed to end design piracy included the National Association of Style Creators, Inc., and the American Style Protective Association. The National Association of Style Creators was incorporated in New York State November 16, 1934, "to protect creators and originators of styles in the dress manufacturing industry" through the copyrighting of designs.[46] Taking a different approach, the American Style Protective Association registered original creations with their Design Copyright Service Bureau, Inc., and promoted the interests of American dress, coat, suit, and blouse designers (Figure 2.11). St. Louis had a regionally effective organization, the Style Piracy Bureau, which operated with the cooperation of local retailers.[47] Another organization that appeared briefly in the trade press was the Junior Fashion Creator's League of America, Inc., which refrained from showing or selling merchandise to any but authorized retailers that refused to deal with pirated goods. The first vice chairman of this organization was Ira Rentner, brother of FOGA founder Maurice Rentner.[48]

Figure 2.11 The executive board of the American Style Protective Association included manufacturers Osias Nathanson of the Nathanson Dress Co., William Price of Price-Schlesinger, and Jack Adelman. Their companies, as well as others, are represented in this advertisement. "Exclusive, Registered Fashions of American Designers," *The New York Times*, May 6, 1934, N18.

In 1946, Henry Stehli, chairman of the American Council of Style and Design, Inc., stated, "Designers have no safeguard. No legal barrier stands in the way of brazen copyists."[49] According to a member of the Uptown Retail Guild founded by Andrew Goodman and Adam Gimbel, "The person who is protected is the copyist, the schemer, the sharp guy who sends his designers to showings with sharpened pencils and they run out to the men's room and quickly make sketches. The man whom our laws protect in this guise is the man who preys on the talents of others."[50]

Since 1914, nearly eighty bills to protect designs through copyright or to create a separate "design protection system" were introduced in Congress, the latest in 2012. All of these bills failed, largely because providing such protection to garment designs would extend the law to include utilitarian or useful objects. It was perceived by some in the industry that this extension would allow for monopolies in the apparel industry as one company or designer would hold the rights to a specific style.[51] Further, the definition of an original design has always been highly contested, especially when from its beginnings the language the industry itself evolved included descriptions such as *authorized copy*, *reproduction*, *adaptation*, and *copy*. The debate continues, because as stated by Judge Elisha Brewster, who oversaw the federal district court case brought by Wm Filene's Sons Co. against the FOGA, "[T]he chief value of a quality dress lies, not so much in the quality of the material, as in the smartness and originality of the design."[52] He failed, however, to explain how "originality" might be defined.

Chapter 3

Origins of Design Piracy in the US Women's Ready-to-Wear Apparel Industry

The transition from wearing custom-made clothing created by dressmakers and tailors to purchasing ready-to-wear garments off the rack in retail outlets occurred in uneven and unsystematic stages in the women's apparel industry. Some ready-to-wear clothing for women became available as early as the 1840s. Availability increased by the 1860s with mass-produced corsets, hoop skirts, and cloaks, garments that were at least partially adjustable or did not require the close fit of women's dresses. By the 1870s and 1880s tailored suits began to appear.

The slow development of ready-to-wear has most often been attributed to the need for a personalized fit, the desire for fashion individuality, and a continued identification of sewing and garment making with women's traditional roles in the home. However, many interrelated issues delayed the early growth of women's ready-to-wear. A critical factor in the expansion of the industry was acceptance of these products by the consumer. Women were the primary purchasers and producers of their own and their family's clothing, and as such became active participants in the transformation from custom to ready-to-wear clothing to purchasing clothing off the racks in retail outlets.[1] While income was certainly a determining factor in how much could be spent on family clothing, decisions about how to manage those purchases depended on sewing ability, individual needs, and concepts of fashion. Additionally, dressmakers or seamstresses were relatively inexpensive, with the exception of high-end shops in urban shopping districts. Thus, even women in moderate income brackets occasionally paid a local seamstress or dressmaker to do the complicated fitting and stitching involved in producing more elaborate articles of clothing.

With the exception of outerwraps and undergarments, the growth of the women's ready-to-wear industry remained sporadic until the 1890s. It was the rise of the shirtwaist as a fashionable garment that marked a beginning for significant and long-lasting changes in the industry and gave rise to an organizational structure within women's ready-to-wear that continues in some fundamental ways even today.[2] In the 1890s the women's ready-to-wear industry expanded with remarkable speed. Between 1889 and 1899, it grew three times as fast as any other type of manufacturing, measured by the number of workers and the value of output. According to the economist Louis Levine, writing in 1924, the women's clothing industry more than doubled in "every important item in the balance sheet" between 1890 and 1900, including capital investment, cost of raw materials, labor, and value of product.[3] Between 1899 and 1914, growth of the women's clothing industry in value of products grew from $159,339 to $628,000. In addition, while only twenty-three states had women's apparel factories in 1890, by 1900 there was production in thirty-two states.[4] Such rapid growth in such a short amount of time created challenges and occasionally chaos, as increasing numbers of small manufacturers entered the industry. As we will see in the next chapter, the intersection of cheap labor with increased demand and few barriers to entry for new women's ready-to-wear apparel firms not only led to well-documented labor issues but also laid the groundwork for an atmosphere in which design piracy became a standard business practice.[5]

Women's Ready-to-Wear: Rise of the Trade

The widespread popularity of the shirtwaist style (Figure 3.1), and to a greater degree, the acceptance of it as a ready-to-wear garment by all social classes, marked a critical change in the idea of a democratic fashion that could potentially blur class distinctions. As a *New York Times* columnist observed, it was a garment worn by everyone from the "fat cook in the kitchen to the women who dress upon incomes of millions."[6] As early as 1896, *Vogue* declared it "one of the most democratic of creations."[7] It was also arguably the first article of clothing to seriously encroach on the dressmaker's trade, making it a factor in the decline of custom dressmaking. Indeed, in 1894, R. H. Macy & Co. advertised the advantage of ready-made over custom-made, stating that their lined silk waists were "equal in every respect to custom work" and that "dressmakers would charge double" Macy's prices.[8] Advertisers in this period recognized that customers had concerns about social status and a desire both to be up-to-date and

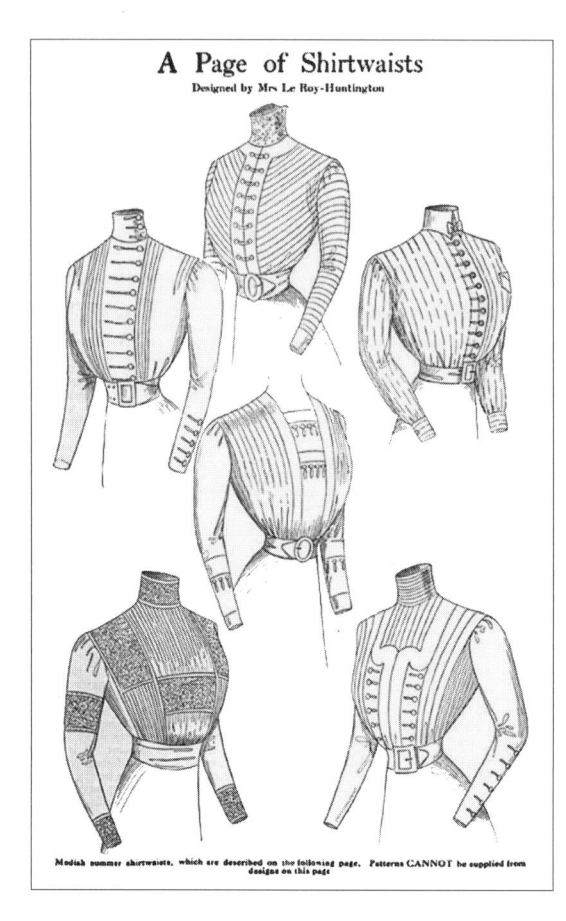

Figure 3.1 A page of shirtwaists designed by Mrs. Le Roy-Huntington, the author of the article "The Shirtwaist Indispensable," *Good Housekeeping* 49 (1909): 83–84.

to imitate those who purchased the higher-status custom-made garments. Thus, whether the waists advertised did indeed meet the same standards as custom-made products, the intent was to draw in the middle-class customer and then hopefully sell her on the ease and quality of ready-to-wear products.[9]

A significant portion of women's factory-made shirt production emerged from the men's ready-to-wear shirt and collar industry. This meant growth initially occurred in a very organized segment of the apparel industry, often in companies with vertically integrated factories and established avenues to consumers through department stores and sales agents.[10] Many of these factories included the entire manufacturing process, from patternmaking and cutting to washing and final starching of the garment. While there was little or no competition in shirtwaist manufacturing at the beginning of the 1890s, by mid-decade, with no sign of decline in demand, an increasing number of companies took up production, despite a concurrent economic slump. There were few barriers to entry into shirtwaist manufacturing. According to Cohen, a potential apparel manufacturer needed as little as $100 to get started producing an enormous amount of goods.[11] For example, in 1895 editors of the menswear trade publication *The Haberdasher* described one unnamed shirtwaist manufacturer with sales of $400,000 in women's shirtwaists. Larger firms such as V. Henry Rothschild and Co. claimed the capacity to produce 150,000 dozen (1.8 million) shirtwaists, while others claimed slightly more modest, but still substantial quantities produced. *The Haberdasher* editors found the rapid shift in production to meet demand for such large quantities of women's shirts significant and began reporting the numbers regularly.[12] Even so, it is difficult to assess total production of women's ready-to-wear waists in this first decade of production, as it was not listed separately in the manufacturing census. However, it was clear that it had become an important business, and store advertisements support that production was considerable. Individual New York City retailers often advertised shirtwaist quantities in the thousands—even as many as twenty-five thousand individual waists—for sale in a season.

The vast majority of new waist manufacturers were located in New York City. While a substantial amount of men's shirt and women's shirtwaist production was taking place outside of the city at the beginning of the 1890s, according to Levine there were only six "well-known shops" in the shirtwaist trade in New York City in 1895, a figure that jumped to 472 by 1905.[13] As a primary port of entry for immigrants, New York boasted a ready supply of both cheap labor and European immigrants with tailoring and cutting skills. It was also the entry port for raw materials, and as such the city was rapidly developing a concentration of fashion businesses from across the industry. As the New York City ready-to-wear industry expanded in importance, a top-to-bottom distribution infrastructure evolved. This included textile suppliers, patternmakers, and trim suppliers, as well as readily available labor for the cutting and stitching processes. In addition, the city provided proximity to other clothing-related manufacturing and retailing firms, as well as a great concentration of wealth among its inhabitants.

Finally, New York offered exposure to critical fashion information. Hotels, theaters, movie and opera houses, concert halls, and other recreational and shopping activities encouraged the city's growth as the natural style capital of America. Large retailers displayed fashionable attire in newly elaborate show windows, and high-end dressmakers brought back samples from Paris to copy, all to appeal to New York's wealthy women. These women also often traveled to the fashion capitals of Europe and returned wearing the latest styles, styles that could be readily copied by astute observers.[14] The importance of New York is even reflected in fashion publications such as *Vogue*, which shifted its focus from covering social life to "what New York stores, dressmakers and milliners were offering and what the smart women of New York were buying."[15] In New York, both consumers and producers were thus exposed to a steady stream of fashion information.

Although the production of shirtwaists expanded and grew elsewhere, with smaller production centers in Chicago, Cleveland, and St. Louis, New York City became the primary center for sales showrooms. Buyers from the entire country came several times a year to view and purchase new styles for the season. *The New York Times* listed the arrival of buyers, often between one hundred fifty and two hundred per season, along with their company and their New York hotel to assist the setting up of appointments with apparel firms.[16] The New York women's ready-to-wear industry was the fastest growing in the nation, and by 1899 the value of its manufactured product had risen to 64.5 percent of American fashion production.[17] This rapid growth continued well into the twentieth century.

By the late 1890s hundreds of large- and small-scale manufacturers were producing thousands of dozens of shirts. Retail store advertisements proliferated, with some stores advertising thousands of shirtwaists in nearly infinite style varieties. While there was a range in prices, most of those advertised in the newspapers were under six dollars, and many were under a dollar. Some retailers began to manufacture shirtwaists in their own production facilities. Macy's, for example, advertised more than two thousand dozen (24,000) shirts of their "own manufacture."[18] And, despite the fact that competition was increasing, manufacturers continued to report "unprecedented sales."[19]

Style Change and Competition

Popularity of the shirtwaist led to the development of other ready-to-wear items of apparel. This included skirts to be worn with the waists, undergarments that supported the shape of the full-front waist styles, and by the early 1900s, the shirtwaist dress, a one-piece version of a waist and skirt. As more and more waist manufacturers entered into production of these other items of women's apparel, and as new companies that manufactured related products joined the fray, they were all forced to find ways to compete and to differentiate their products for buyers. The most frequent route was through rapid style changes and numerous style offerings. The prevailing opinion was that it was essential to show countless styles in order to have a product the competition did not.[20] Technological advances such as the telephone, the wireless, a transatlantic cable, and the first cruise liners made swifter transmission of ideas and apparel styles possible, further accelerating the tempo of fashion.[21]

Exactly what constituted a style variation in shirtwaists or even in dresses is difficult to analyze. In some cases it entailed a simple change in number of pleats, in fullness or length of sleeves, in the shape of a yoke, or in collar height. Shirts were offered with various cuff and collar styles, with and without yokes, with attached or separate collars and cuffs, all in a wide range of fabrics (Figure 3.2). In addition to style details, overall silhouette also changed during the 1890s, particularly in the volume of sleeves, going from relatively narrow to extremely full and back again.

Recognizing the long-held perception that mass-produced fashion denied women garments that were as unique as they were fashionable, firms adopted the strategy of style change and variety to both win women over and gain a competitive edge. Women's fashion discourse supported the notion with concerns about individuality and the idea that no two dresses could look the same. Retailers even advertised "exclusive styles" from apparel manufacturers, suggesting that one objective of the vast number of offerings was to persuade the customer that the style she purchased was in some way individual. The idea of exclusive and original design thus attempted to connect the ready-to-wear product with that of a custom dressmaker. In the long run, however, the shirtwaist seemed to defy these views, as there are scores of images of women wearing shirtwaists with

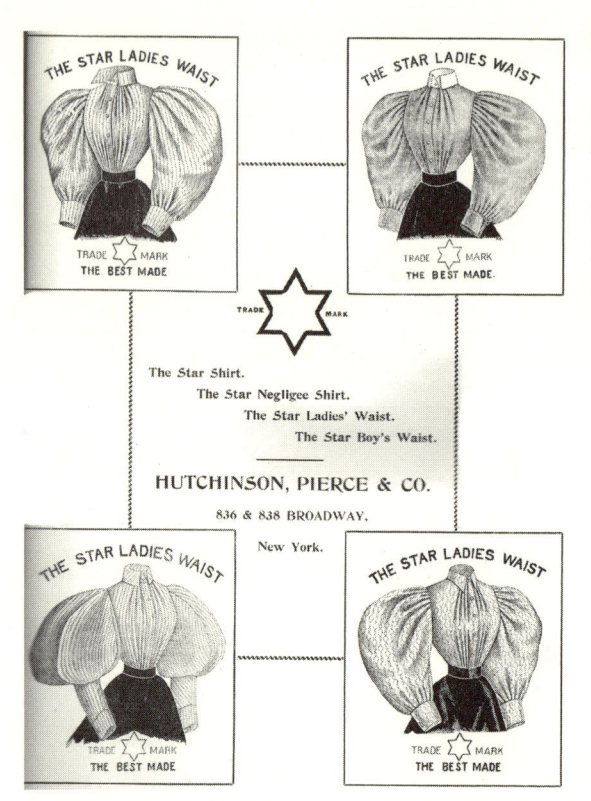

Figure 3.2 An advertisement for Star brand shirts, showing four different styles with subtle variations in fabrics, cuffs, collars, and sleeves. *The Haberdasher*, April 1896, 83.

some obvious but many not-so-obvious differences. These images, as well as the dialogue that occurred in the fashion press and in newspapers, not only demonstrated the seemingly infinite possible style variations but also revealed the overall similarity of the fashionable arrangement of shirtwaist and skirt as the dominant silhouette (Figure 3.3).

As competition intensified, firms began to offer new style variations, not only with each season, but also midseason—changes often demanded by retailers to promote increased buying and not motivated by customer demand. Consumers and producers alike pondered the origins of fashion and the apparently unprecedented changes. In 1894 one writer suggested that producers, not retailers, "manipulated" fashion changes in order to sustain production.[22] True or not, for manufacturers there developed an interrelationship among the speed of change, the most logical and efficient means of designing and producing clothing, and the need to create garments that represented the latest styles. For the latter, questions arose as to

Figure 3.3 Women wearing the many shirtwaist style variations. Class of 1915 senior breakfast. Collection #23-2-749, item RT-S-11, Division of Rare and Manuscript Collections, Cornell University Library.

the ability to identify and then create all the style variations. Ultimately, it was style and fashion change that played a major role in the burgeoning of ready-to-wear clothing production and sales, initiating an escalating cycle of new styles intended to stimulate demand.

A New Industry Organization

The growing importance of fashion and style change had a strong influence on the developing business practices of the clothing industry. Within the men's furnishings industry, many manufacturers performed all of the operations connected with the designing, production, distribution, and marketing of their own merchandise, even when they added women's shirts to their production.[23] By the mid-1890s, however, the structure of the women's industry became increasingly stratified. Profits and longevity of firms in the shirtwaist and dress industry were, to a large extent, due to success in creating numerous style variations and, to a lesser extent, garment quality. This allowed new producers to enter the industry in great numbers, often operating on little capital. However, they needed to find ways to develop many style variations without adding significantly to costs, as well as ways to produce large quantities without additional capital investment.

In their efforts to keep costs down, an increased number of manufacturers dealt with independent agents, or outside shops or contractors, to produce a product, or even part of a product (for example, garment pieces with added trims), for a stipulated price. The manufacturers supplied clothing designs, piece goods, materials, and credit. The contractor rented factory space and machinery, found and hired a labor force, and directed the production process. The manufacturer paid the contractor by the piece. The contractor, in turn, paid his employees either by piece or time wages, often charging them for their use of sewing machines, needles, and threads. So that contractors could make a profit, their contracted labor force often worked for barely subsistence wages.[24] The constant inflow of immigrants, driven by their need for a livelihood and willingness to receive low wages, allowed for the growth of a legion of submanufacturing apparel producers, the prevalence of which removed the need for a new firm to invest large sums in plants, equipment, or even employees.

By the early twentieth century, some of the larger manufacturers required the services of twenty-five to thirty contractors to maintain their production levels. As businesses expanded, they moved from workshops in the Lower East Side tenement districts to established manufacturing sections of the city, concentrating in about a twenty-block area along Seventh Avenue.[25] The stratification and centralization of the apparel industry in New York City meant an increasing number of manufacturing interests involved in the creation of garments located in a close geographical area.

Manufacturers opened new women's ready-to-wear firms on a shoestring and competed effectively with older, well-established firms owing not only to the small amount of capital required to operate factories, but also to the division of risk offered by the contract system. As product offerings increased with the addition of shirtwaist dresses and suits, styling and an effective sales force continued to be critical to sales. Very few advertised their wares other than in product-specific trade publications; however, many maintained a showroom, often next to or within the factory. Despite the importance of fashion, however, if two firms had equally attractive styles, the firm willing to sell at the lowest prices would generally do a greater amount of business.[26]

Contractors were involved in the manufacturing of hundreds of different styles for a multitude of companies at any one time. Submanufacturers and subcontractors felt little loyalty to one specific company, since they often worked for numerous concerns. This also meant that little secrecy existed in the production of clothing, thus creating an atmosphere ripe for design piracy. While copying French fashion was a given, American companies increasingly copied each other. Although some manufacturers spent the time and money to hire designers and to create new styles and product samples, or even to buy samples from French dressmakers, for many the easiest path to adding new styles was to copy those of another US firm. With variety and product differentiation crucial to the ability to sell merchandise, and as copying became increasingly difficult to control, apparel firms began to devise ways to prevent design piracy. For example, in an attempt to control design exclusiveness, owners of the shirt company V. Henry Rothschild & Co. stated in 1896 that they would not publish any illustrations of their latest styles to "counteract the tendency toward imitation" that "constitutes the great part of our present competition."[27] This statement, made in a trade journal advertisement, suggests the new pervasiveness of copying at the time. Trade journals such as *The Haberdasher* or *The Dry Goods Economist* traditionally printed images of the new season's styles. Read and seen by competing manufacturers, it would be easy to copy any published style. A refusal to have images published in a trade journal did not, however, hinder accessibility of samples to store buyers, who saw the goods in showrooms or through sales representatives.

Style variation and change created intense competition among retailers and manufacturers and became a circular problem: as manufacturers offered more and more variety and opportunity for style uniqueness, retailers and consumers became accustomed to demanding product assortment. By 1910, there were calls in trade publications and newspapers for collective action by both manufacturers and retailers to deal with the dual challenges of piracy and the pressure of constant style change. Editors reported sightings of peculiarly similar dresses in even the most exclusive Fifth Avenue shops, such as Henri Bendel and Louise and Co.[28] Those who began to petition for some way to control piracy believed style protection would eliminate, as apparel industry commentator Alphonsus Haire stated, "the ever-present fear which exists today that to create new ideas is only to furnish one's competitors with added material for carrying on their campaign of style piracy and price slashing."[29]

The New Fashion Consumer

By the early years of the twentieth century, more rapid fashion changes, an increased quantity of affordable and stylish ready-to-wear, increased exposure to fashion information, and lower levels of participation in the production of their own clothing permanently altered women's perceptions of fashion. The origination of new styles, traditionally attributed to Parisian dressmakers and designers, meant that both manufacturers and consumers linked the up-to-dateness of fashionable clothing to those sources. However, concepts of fashionable apparel and the process of style and fashion change were always considered enigmatic. Fashion information for the average consumer could come from many sources. These included the local dressmaker who frequently subscribed to various fashion publications, actual Parisian samples purchased by high-end dressmakers and displayed for customers, and, for the home sewer, the paper pattern companies and women's fashion publications that provided fashion information. But, for manufacturers, retailers, and the fashion press, the Parisian design houses were the starting point for fashion change.

Cultural influences such as the changing lifestyles of women as consumers of fashionable products, and especially the changing roles of young, single women in the workplace, transformed routines associated with the purchase and making of women's dress. A part of that transformation included changes in the transmission and communication of fashion information from the traditional sources to new and more varied influences. Clothing became available from new types of retail stores and from more convenient sources, including catalogs and free-standing women's apparel shops. Catalog sales allowed women across the country to purchase garments from such well-known retailers as Macy's, New York; and Charles A. Stevens & Bros., Chicago (Figure 3.4). Even a few men's furnishing stores attempted to add women's departments, with varying success and occasional confusion for their male customers, unaccustomed to seeing women as purchasers for themselves in a men's store.[30]

One of the most important new fashion influences was the department store, especially in urban centers, as it became a locus of fashionable

Figure 3.4 One-piece dresses available by mail-order from Charles A. Stevens & Brothers, Chicago, Fall & Winter 1908/1909 Catalog. Collection of author.

ideas and images. Increased numbers of single women in white-collar jobs in offices and stores created more complex relationships between clothing and class, as opportunities for public display of and interaction with high-fashion images increased. As ready-to-wear became widely available at all price points, fashion as a marker of class distinction seemed to diminish. Young wage-earning women could purchase garments that, if not the equivalent in quality, bore an outward resemblance to the dress of the wealthier classes. Manufacturers sometimes used trims and decoration to hide otherwise cheap construction or material. Although working-class young women could afford these low-priced but sometimes gaudy styles, their appearance produced criticism from commentators who perceived their clothing as extravagant dress that was beyond their means.[31] This was cause for concern from some, who considered their more expensive and often custom-made dress a visible sign of their class (a right and privilege to maintain). Middle-class women in particular viewed fashion as setting them apart from those women who were wage earners, especially factory workers and servants. In 1904, the home economist Bertha June Richardson observed that many of the poorer wage-earning women appeared to dress "beyond their station." In a statement about visiting a settlement house, she went on to comment that the women did not appear to be poor as they "wasted their money on cheap imitation."[32] With the downward movement of fashionable clothing from higher to lower prices, the question of quality and whether or not average observers could distinguish the difference is not clear. However, as ready-to-wear imitations flooded the market, at all price points, and were purchased by women at almost all income levels, one of the enduring arguments for design piracy began to emerge: that design copies offered all women access to fashionable clothing.

Urban department stores also offered opportunities to see fashion in store windows or within store departments, along with a chance for women to display their own fashions as consumers. Shopping became a leisure activity, again altering shopping rituals, as stores became centers not only of fashionable displays but also of entertainment. As the historian Kathy Peiss stated, "The department stores were for and about women, but primarily about women of the middle class."[33] It was the acceptance of ready-to-wear as appropriate fashion by middle-class women that was critical. Mrs. Le Roy-Huntington, a frequent contributor to *Good Housekeeping*, summed up the reasons for purchasing ready-to-wear clothing as well as its consumer acceptance:

> In the past fifteen or twenty years there has grown up an institution in trade of such vast proportions and of such importance to the family life that we may safely say that it has been a sort of stepping stone in the progress of the race. It surely has brought great relief to the busy mother, and saves her both time and money. This institution is the ready-made clothing idea developed to a remarkably fine degree.[34]

While many lower-income women purchased goods from pushcarts or from less expensive bargain stores, the department store was available for all to observe fashion and learn about seasonal styles. Those with limited incomes could observe the upper levels and then shop the bargain counters and the basement level, sometimes called the subway store or the bargain basement.[35]

Competition among manufacturers for the customer who preferred unique designs escalated. Some ready-to-wear manufacturers sold dresses that had the same handwork and fabric quality found in the dressmaker's shop. Specialty stores could even fill their shelves and racks with exclusive-to-them ready-to-wear dresses or waists. *Women's Wear Daily*, for example, illustrated the pressure a buyer was under to provide a selection of unique styles for the season. The editors recommended a practice of choosing "one of a size and color of the best styles from a number of manufacturers, thereby making up their stock with a large variety and perhaps no two suits alike in style and color."[36] At least some manufacturers offered a sense of exclusivity by selling to only one store in a town. This of course put them in direct competition with the dressmaker, whose attractiveness to wealthier clients had been an exclusive and one-of-a-kind garment. Women generally viewed silhouette as representational of the appropriate fashion trend of a given season, including overall fullness, hem and sleeve lengths, and waist placement on dresses. However, other trends in a season might include new colors, changes in the length of sleeves or height of collars, or new forms of surface decoration. There were seemingly infinite variations possible within that distinctive silhouette that might make it unique. Added to this complication was the fact that not all made-to-order dresses purchased from dressmakers were in fact one of a kind. It is impossible to know how widespread the practice was, but at least some women found themselves the purchasers of a "unique," custom-made dress identical to someone else's.[37]

The historian Rob Schorman argues that the ready-to-wear industry continued to use the language of custom-made clothing in their advertisements, especially at the turn of the twentieth century, and indeed many did.[38] But, with or without advertising language that suggested the elements of custom production, for daily wear it was ready-to-wear apparel that women were choosing, not only because of convenience and cost, but also because the industry recognized and responded to the critical

Prices Range from $29.50 up to $125

The three Suits *pictured* are characteristic of the variety of styles in our Salon for Women's Suits. The smart Shepherd Check Suit, bound with white silk braid, with panel pockets and tailored belt, **$29.50**

The French blue Silk Poplin Suit with the quaint upstanding ruffle at the top of the sash-belt, repeated as a finish to the full skirt, **$38.50**

Taffeta Silk Suits, two models, copies of imported suits. Special at **$47.50**

$29.50 $47.50 $38.50

The navy blue Poiret Twill Suit with the ultra-fashionable short jacket with brilliantly striped silk sash and waistcoat, $47.50.

Figure 3.5 Gimbels emphasized the variety of styles, fabrics, and prices available. They also traded on connections to French fashions, although these are American made, to assure the customer that she would be "ultra-fashionable." *The New York Times*, April 8, 1917, 22.

importance of fashion and uniqueness. Women may still have preferred a dressmaker-made gown for evening, but for everyday wear, shirtwaists, shirtwaist dresses, and walking suits provided fashion variety that was welcomed by both wage-earning women and middle-class housewives, with style as the driving factor (Figure 3.5). This was crucial to the widespread growth of the industry, but ultimately it was also a critical factor in the growth of design piracy as a standard business practice.

Cultivating a Style Industry

The increasing rapidity of fashion changes that began in the last decade of the nineteenth century continued into the twentieth century. The issues related to that change permeated women's fashion publications. In 1903, Mary Moss, a writer for *Atlantic Monthly*, argued that it no longer took time for fashions to "permeate the masses."[39] The shop that sold a high-fashion dress at $150 could not stay ahead, at least in terms of style, of the shop selling the same design for "one ninety-eight [$1.98]."[40] A few years later, in *Good Housekeeping* in 1909, B. W. Parker stated that manufacturers offered a vast selection so that women would not be in danger of "annoying duplication of style or fabric on the part of 'that other woman.'"[41]

It also was a concern within the growing home economics field of study and with the National Consumer League, originally chartered in 1899. Numerous articles referred to what one merchant simply called "the style problem" and were directed at shoppers, home sewers, and dressmakers alike.[42] Authors stated concerns over the effects of rapid fashion changes on clothing budgets, especially when it appeared that women purchased just for style and clearly did not wear the clothing long enough to wear it out. In an article on sensible dress in the *Journal of Home Economics*, Pearl McDonald asked the questions: "Who sets the styles? Who forms our fashions? What ends are secured in the striking changes presented every few months?" She went on to suggest that women who "demand the ultra-fashionable" should consider the consequences of "quickly vanishing styles" on both those who produced them and those who wore them.[43]

In addition to broader and more rapid changes in fashion, the number of different styles advertised or sold in a season grew dramatically. To Bertha Richardson, clothing was the consumer good that lasted the shortest amount of time.[44] Women at the time deemed clothing details such a change in sleeve length or height of collar as important for their fashionable appearance. For example, a columnist for *The Ladies' Home Journal* quoted a woman exclaiming in exasperation: "'Sleeves,' she gasped, 'sleeves have changed again this month!'"[45] Retailers began to manipulate what constituted fashion change, advertising even simple changes such as length of sleeve or placement of trim as critical to being up-to-date. It was also clear that styles not only changed swiftly, but also became available to larger numbers of people simultaneously. By the turn of the century, retailers recognized that promotion of fashion change and the importance of being in style provided an incentive to "buy, dispose of and buy again."[46] An Abraham & Straus advertisement, for example, suggested that with the number of styles available combined with the reasonable price, women would want six or a dozen shirtwaists, not just one or two.[47] Advertisers attempted to associate the concept of constant variations and transformations in style with the notion that to be out of style would be unthinkable. They emphasized style and fashion, with little or no mention of the quality of the garment, either in fabric or in craftsmanship.[48]

Department and specialty store advertisements not only showed the latest styles but also created language that associated the latest style with a mass-produced product. This resulted in claims about the up-to-date nature of the clothing, that all the fashion "authorities" had been consulted before the clothing was produced, or that their fashion offerings were "complete," meaning that the selection available included all the styles as shown by the French dressmakers and designers.[49] The ease and availability of ready-to-wear began to impact women's desire to make clothing at home, with a consequent impact on sales in fabric departments. The impression of a widening gulf between fashionable ready-to-wear and not so fashionable made-at-home products also became a focus of advice literature. Author and educator Mary Brooks Picken even went so far as to recommend that women who still made their own clothing take a cue from ready-to-wear and "strive occasionally for effect rather than perfection in workmanship." Ready-to-wear apparel clearly was becoming an important option in women's wardrobe management.[50]

Not all were pleased with the lack of quality of inexpensive ready-to-wear, however. Consumer dependence on style change allowed apparel producers to sell inferior goods, quickly produced, with each season's offerings touted as new and different. In 1914, the General Federation of Women's Clubs attempted to pass a resolution designed to release women from the "tyranny of the ever increasing changes of style" through adoption of simpler styles not completely bound to the latest fashion.[51] In 1919, the need for a "Clothes Administration" to do similar work to that of the US Food Administration was suggested. Some believed rapidly changing styles "impeded rational choice" by taking women's minds off of price, quality of materials, and workmanship. These authors contended that rapid style changes encouraged wasteful buying for the simple reason that last season's clothing was discarded after mere months, never to be worn again.[52] The newly organized home economics programs in high schools and colleges focused some of their teaching on how to make wise purchasing decisions.[53] But, the shift to ready-to-wear and the ability of the ready-to-wear industry to produce fashionable apparel was in place. Even Mary Schenck Woolman, a home economist and director of the Manhattan

Trade School for Girls, evaluated dressmaker and made-at-home clothing as better options in terms of quality, but stated that ready-to-wear offered a better value when it came to up-to-date styling and time savings.[54] As another home economist, Charlotte Baker Gibbs, stated, "As much of the food formerly prepared in the household is now prepared outside, so much of the sewing has passed out and it cannot be brought back, nor is it necessarily desirable that it should be."[55]

The need for fashionable products grew the industry. In New York City between 1900 and 1917 the number of women's apparel companies increased 350 percent, from 1,856 to 6,392 firms. From 1914 to 1919 alone, the value of manufactured women's ready-to-wear clothing rose 255 percent. In 1919, the value of the dress industry in the United States was exceeded only by the food and the iron and steel manufacturing industries.[56]

With fashion and rapid style changes as a focus, and with the industry's striking growth in the first decades of the twentieth century, came all the associated growing pains. The rise of the ready-to-wear apparel industry caused the decline of personal dressmakers and seamstresses and the creation of plentiful factory employment opportunities, a change that offered poorer pay and a change in opportunities and employment for women. Prior to this, many women had made their living as dressmakers, a more-respected job and one that was dominated by women. It was also a job that offered more flexibility, as many worked in their home or traveled to a customer's home. There was very little opportunity to advance as a factory stitcher, who earned far less money and respect. As the apparel industry grew, the types of factories and levels of production also expanded. One more form of production in which the workers were characterized as dressmakers appeared at the end of the century. In this new style of production, manufacturers produced high-end, occasionally one-of-a-kind dresses for a wholesale market. The products of this type of manufacture were usually not available directly to the customer.[57] According to the US Census of Occupations, the number of nonfactory dressmakers and seamstresses declined from 498,000 in the year 1900 to 235,000 in 1920 and 158,000 in 1930. In contrast, the US Census of Manufacturing figures from 1919 placed textile and clothing manufacturing as the number-one employer in the nation. Due to the demand for ready-to-wear, the rate of expansion in factory employment from 1900 to 1920 was faster than at any other time thereafter. Of all of the workers engaged in manufacturing industries in 1919 in the five boroughs of New York City, nearly one in every six was at work on women's clothing.[58]

The transition from shirtwaists to shirtwaist dresses and then to broader dress categories brought the new style industry into more direct fashion competition with Parisian designers. The shirtwaist was not only a widely accepted garment that crossed class lines; it was accepted and demanded as ready-to-wear rather than custom-made. In addition, the shirtwaist and related styles were viewed as American-designed garments. Soon, however, fashionable ready-to-wear shirts and dresses encroached on the traditional fashion realm of the dressmaker and of Parisian designers and dressmakers. American manufacturers of tailored apparel (coats and suits) also competed with European designers, not only in Paris but also in London and Vienna, especially as the ready-to-wear industry was much slower to develop in Europe. Indeed, one of the reasons for the slower development of ready-to-wear in France was that country's system of protection. While the haute couturiers could sell in quantity to US dressmakers and manufacturers for reproduction, they were forbidden to sell to their own ready-to-wear manufacturers. This had the result of suppressing the business.[59]

With rapid and uncontrolled growth of ready-to-wear in New York came challenges. Within the twenty years from 1890 to 1910, the industry had established itself as the primary source of clothing for American women at all but the highest price points. However, many of these women were still convinced of the creative supremacy of Parisian fashion creators. Fashion had rapidly become the driving force in the industry, but there was as yet little development of or support for American design or designers. This pointed up the need not only to educate and support a "homegrown" group of competent designers familiar with the system of mass production, but also to convince the buying public that the United States industry was capable of creating "American fashions for American women." Numerous individuals would provide their input on how best to promote American design talent, and, with the now firmly entrenched business practice of design piracy, also how to protect their creativity.

Chapter 4

Development and Promotion of a United States Design Presence

By 1910, ready-to-wear garments made in the United States represented a significant portion of the American woman's wardrobe at all but the highest price levels.[1] Apparel businesses, both wholesale and retail, struggled to cope with an often contentious industry, one heavily influenced by the ephemeral and allegedly mysterious nature of fashion, and by Paris. Then, as now, the forecasting and management of fashion change was a challenge to the burgeoning number of manufacturing and retailing businesses. Their search for the controlling factors of fashion change mirrored some of the earliest theories about the workings of the fashion system. Both Thorstein Veblen and Georg Simmel, for example, advanced theories of fashion change at the turn of the twentieth century based on concepts of class differentiation and fashion leaders and followers. They described the flow of fashions as beginning in the wealthy and leisure classes and "trickling down" the social structure.[2] Indeed, in one of the first issues of *Women's Wear* in 1910, editors identified sources for innovation for readers, speculating about the roles of influential society women and prominent actresses, as well as clothing manufacturers and Parisian dressmakers.[3]

Fashion Design for the US Ready-to-Wear Market

Paris attribution, whether through a Paris label or an advertisement that suggested Parisian origins, was believed to be a major guiding influence for consumers. American designers employed by manufacturing firms and custom salons in department stores created salable adaptations of prevailing French fashions that were considered more in tune with American tastes. American women were generally considered to have a different physique and temperament, although some argued this was not proven. Others suggested that American women were more individual in their clothing choice, and some even stated that they had "something

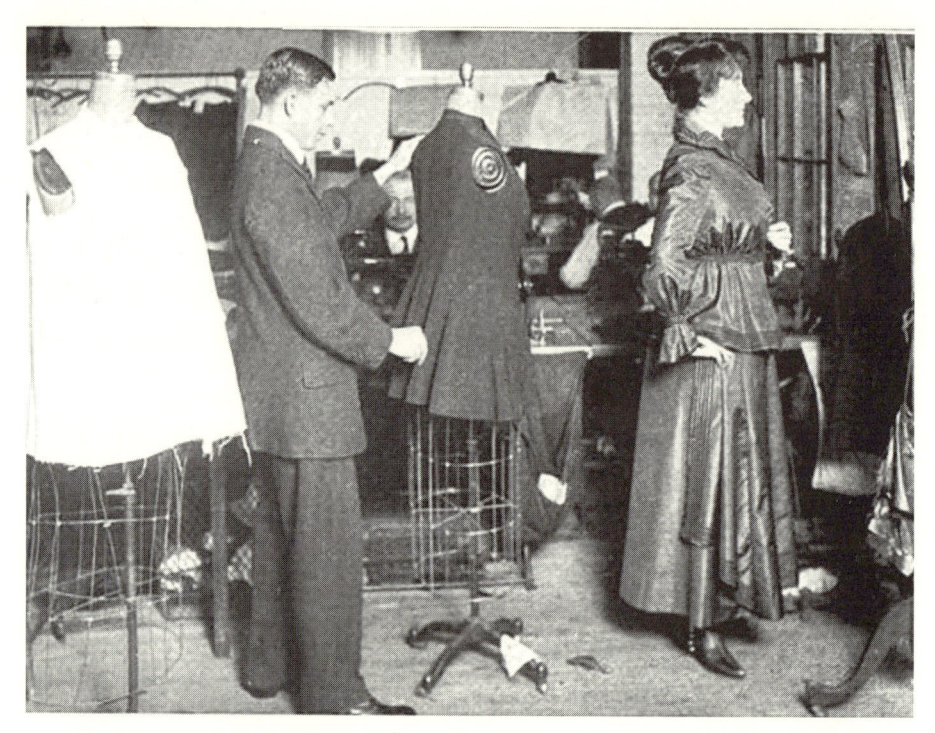

Figure 4.1 Designer working on a tailored suit, with model at right. Edna Bryner, *The Garment Trades* (Cleveland, OH: The Survey Committee of the Cleveland Foundation, 1916).

else to think about besides dress."[4] Thus, the definition was essentially one of impression, rather than specific tastes in silhouettes or fashion details. Undoubtedly, however, the shirtwaist, the tailored suit, and the walking-length skirt were all viewed as "distinctly American products" for their practicality and fashion durability.[5]

Edna Bryner, a social sciences researcher for the Russell Sage Foundation in the 1910s, described the "difficult" role of the ready-to-wear designer/stylist as one of inventing styles that "will sell and that will be economical in the use of material and labor." She went on to explain that "the costumes designed by the great creators of style in Paris are copied by representatives of the leading design houses" in the United States (Figure 4.1). The American designer was charged with determining the season's dominant styles based on the French models and then "varying the standard model with different cuffs, collar, pockets, belts, and trimmings and may evolve 50 to 100 styles to be made in 400 or 500 materials."[6]

Most US apparel manufacturers were slow to develop their own design talents and tended to rely on a growing world of style "commissionaires" who acted as authorized agents for the sale and shipment of French goods to use as design prototypes.[7] Manufacturers presumed these commissioners to have a "thorough knowledge of the American market," in addition to their familiarity with the Parisian dress trade and their ability to expedite transport of goods to the United States.[8] However, American manufacturers and retailers used various methods for obtaining both authorized and unauthorized French designs as models to copy, among them: (1) the authorized purchase of models in Paris that could be sold legitimately in high-end shops as either authorized or exact copies; (2) the importation of French models for exhibition as inspiration for private dressmaking houses, and then sale to other fashion merchants for copying; and (3) the renting out of French models for copying purposes at about $25 for a few hours.[9] Numerous other methods also existed. Some of the commissioners saw an opportunity to make additional (dishonest) profit by allowing freelance sketch artists to make unauthorized illustrations of the gowns before shipping them to the United States. In the latter case, these illustrations would then be sold to other manufacturers or retailers.[10] Smaller manufacturers and designers pooled their resources to purchase Parisian models to copy, a practice that resulted in significant savings on both the initial cost of the model and the amount of the customs duties. Many of these smaller manufacturers then made money on their initial investment by selling both the originals and their models to other firms for copying purposes.[11]

Copying continued from higher price points rapidly downward to the very lowest price points, a process that occurred through often confusing and backdoor practices, aided by independent contractors, retail buyers, and manufacturers. Most ready-to-wear manufacturers recognized the importance of style to create a competitive edge. However, style and style change seemed difficult to control, or at the very least challenging, especially when they needed to gain style information to stay ahead, as well as manufacture the goods in a timely way. Additionally, because of the speed of copying, there were frequently issues between retailers and manufacturers in terms of when and how a design was available to view, how much time elapsed before it was in the stores, and how it was advertised.

Within this frequently contentious environment, there arose numerous fashion organizations and trade associations that tried to predict, to influence, and even to standardize style change. Groups sought to offer protection to various industry segments, and each area of the industry had its own organization, founded to protect its interests, whether it was labor, manufacturing, design, or retailing. By 1910, many sought to promote the value and importance of American design through campaigns such as "American Styles for American Women."[12] The need to develop domestic design talent and to promote and protect it became a continuing dialogue through the 1920s, while the copying of styles, both from Paris and from domestic firms, continued to be the norm.

Industry Organization

While trade organizations and unions existed within the apparel and textile industries prior to 1900, the number grew along with the expansion of the ready-to-wear industry in the early years of the twentieth century. Some emerged out of real or perceived inequities and abuses in terms of labor or fair trade, and they included unions in support of workers, with independent unions for different types of garments, such as shirtwaists and dresses or coats and suits. Other organizations evolved to promote and protect segments of the industry that created and sold apparel. These included manufacturer organizations, retail associations, and designer/creator associations, such as the American Dress Designers' Association, the Associated Dress Manufacturers' Association, the National Garment Retailers' Association, and the National Retail Dry Goods Association. The membership needs of these organizations were often at odds with one another, particularly so when it came to design piracy.[13]

At least initially, many associations focused on managing the timing of production for the ready-to-wear industry rather than on developing American design talent or controlling design piracy. Timing was a critical issue owing to the perceived need to wait for the Paris showings before developing seasonal styles. However, because Paris houses designed for the custom market rather than ready-to-wear, their shows were too close to the actual buying season for manufacturers to plan production efficiently. Thus, dependence on Paris designs for inspiration or for copying hampered timing for mass production. The designs in Figure 4.2, created without benefit of the seasonal French collections for inspiration, were

Figure 4.2 These American designs were introduced at an "American Fall and Winter Fashion Show" prior to the Paris opening, suggesting an early attempt at design independence. *The New York Times*, August 10, 1913, X6.

shown early to accommodate the arrival of buyers who came to New York in July and August from all over the country. This in turn put pressure on factories to produce quickly in order to assure deliveries to retailers.

Associations discussed and proposed a variety of strategies for dealing with the importance of French fashion. For example, at their first meeting, the Cloak and Suit Manufacturers attempted to set standardized coat and jacket lengths for the season, taking into consideration French styles but also perceived American tastes.[14] There was even some discussion of standardized styles, an "admittedly difficult thing to do."[15] They determined that if all were in agreement they might prevent any dramatic changes, such as a sudden trend for longer jacket lengths, which made apparel already in production suddenly out of style. The group recognized and expressed concern that designers could easily choose to ignore any dictum.

Dress and shirtwaist manufacturers were also concerned with a range of style issues, including questions of creativity and originality. Debates focused on the need for a general promotion of American-created styles, and not on support of individual designers. As discussion of design and its promotion evolved, the number of associations that began to focus on a concept of American design increased. Members of the Fashion Art League regularly promoted the work of US dressmakers. Other organizations that held meetings and debates regarding fabric, designs, and products made in the United States included the Waist and Dress Designers' Association, the Dressmakers' Protective Association, the National Association of Clothing Designers, and the Chicago Dressmakers' Club.[16] The National Ladies' Tailors and Dressmakers' Association formulated plans for a Fashion Congress, to create some uniformity in the showing of models throughout the country.[17] Members of this organization believed, however, that the very men most loudly denouncing Parisian ideas at the Style Congress "knew in their own hearts that they must utilize designs which originate across the water."[18]

From the 1910s until the mid-1920s, despite the continued importance of Paris as a style center, the discourse shifted to promotion of a unique American market with distinctive style needs and creative skills. *The New York Times* published articles about American design and even on occasion printed designs that were American made. For example, in 1914 it published illustrations of an American-made society wedding gown that was "absolutely original."[19] However, the balance between praising the design houses of New York and the continued sense of the importance of Paris was often tenuous. While promoting American fashion, editors often credited French fashions as inspiration.[20]

French Fashion Industry Dominance

There were many obstacles to establishing and promoting the United States, and especially New York, as a fashion center with original designs and ideas. Despite arguments for an increased focus on American style, the prestige of French fashion houses and any design that could be labeled as a Paris original design endured through the first decades of the twentieth century. Clara Simcox, a high-end New York dressmaker, in describing New York fashion houses in this period, stated that most dressmakers showed at least some Parisian styles and were dependent on Paris for ideas.[21] While fashion publications acknowledged the leadership of Paris in areas of art and style, some suggested the models available for purchase were too expensive, were not "reliable" (meaning not necessarily the latest style, or even possibly not originals), or were altered for the New York buyers to prevent them from getting the best designs. Indeed, renowned couturier Charles Worth supposedly stated that French dressmakers created different styles for American than for French customers, with the suggestion that American tastes in fact were for much more elaborate gowns than French women wore.[22] It was certainly the prevailing opinion that fashionable customers wanted the prestige associated with wearing the latest Parisian styles, even if they could not recognize specific characteristics of the French style. One US dressmaker described the problem of selling her own designs without the Paris label: "If I had two models side by side, one of my own and one of Parisian make, the customer would choose mine, if she was not aware that it was American made, but, if told, of course would wish the Paris model."[23] Retailers often described fashions borrowed or copied from Paris dressmakers as "authentic" and "authoritative."[24] Thus, they aided in creating a publicized position that it was essential to consult with Paris before purchasing clothing for a season. This seemed to apply to clothing at all prices.

The fashion press in particular maintained a focus on Paris as the epitome of style, and on the assumption that women would be far more likely to purchase a garment if it carried a Paris label or attribution. But with increased acceptance of ready-to-wear, fashion and its production were changing and criticism of Parisian designs and designers began to appear. In 1912 a *New York Times* fashion editor claimed that the French had "lost their art and have put into its place the commercialism of grotesqueness and vulgarity."[25] Throughout 1912, in particular, writers issued a constant stream of criticism aimed at French designers.[26] Contemporaries commented that the dressmakers and designers of France, in an attempt to keep demand continuous, changed styles as often and as drastically as possible. Some writers believed that the French would sell "any old thing" only to change the prevailing style completely later on.[27] They thus were blamed for an increased commercialization of fashion. This was a rather hollow argument, given American retailer and manufacturer insistence on new designs from Paris, the push for timeliness in the mass production process, and the need to produce huge quantities for the US market.[28] Well-known entertainers of the time, such the Russian American actress Alla Nazimova and the opera singer Madame Nordica, as well as average consumers, expressed disappointment in Paris partly because of these real

> **Beginning Monday at 9 A M., in the Dress Salon**
>
> ## Annual Spring Sale of
> # Women's Gowns and Dresses at $25
>
> Many weeks of preparation were necessary to complete arrangements for this important event, the idea being to offer at one price unprecedented values in dresses for all occasions.
>
> As a result of the hearty co-operation received from our dressmakers this will be the greatest sale of dresses ever held in New York.
>
> *Reproductions of and adaptations from designs by these famous modistes are included:*
>
> | Jenny | Agnes | Bertha | Hermance |
> |---|---|---|---|
> | Klein | Beer | Paquin | Doucette |
>
> Some of the dresses are exact reproductions, while others, which we deemed too extreme, have been modified to suit the Saks clientele.

Figure 4.3 Saks and Co. advertised their reproductions and adaptations of Paris styles, but stated that they had "modified" any designs deemed "too extreme" to suit the Saks clientele. *The New York Tribune*, April 9, 1916, 5.

or perceived changes.[29]

While apparel manufacturers and the press generally agreed that Paris would continue to be the fountainhead of fashion innovation, at times the designs were considered too extreme for the supposedly tasteful, commonsense American woman. Those who considered Parisian styles too radical most often turned the spotlight on the designs of Paul Poiret. For example, James Blaine, a designer for New York–based Thurn who had previously worked in Paris, described one of Poiret's early lines as "a lot of queer little girls" wearing "slinky little Greek-line garden party gowns, with their broad sleeves and their ropes about the middle." Poiret's "jupe culottes," which he described as an idea for the future, was singled out for criticism as evidence of the ridiculousness of French design.[30] Poiret, on the other hand, blamed the ready-to-wear industry for vulgarizing his more avant-garde ideas, especially as designs were copied at all prices and in successively cheaper fabrics.[31]

Despite their dependence on Paris, writers, manufacturers, designers, and retailers often expressed anger that American-created goods continued to seem salable only with a Parisian origin, and that women presumably preferred and demanded the cachet of a French label. Whether this was in fact true is difficult to determine. *American Cloak and Suit Review* noted that the emergence of an "American" style of clothing needed to combine the artistic cuts of the haute couture of Paris with the practical designs desired by US women. Consequently, retailers touted original Paris inspirations for American-produced and adapted apparel, occasionally even noting that it had been appropriately adapted for American tastes (Figure 4.3).

The manufacturing company Simpson Crawford Co. was so proud of their adapting skills that they displayed in their store window an original Drecoll imported gown costing $485, reproduced in every detail by their dressmakers for sale at $24.75. By comparing the original Drecoll model with an American-made copy, the company was convinced that fashion-forward American women would realize US dressmakers were the peers of those of Paris, at least in technical skill, if not design sense.[32] They were not the only retailer to make claims about their skills as copyists. R. H. Macy & Co., in a 1913 advertisement announcing a showing of both their new French imported styles and their copied versions (Figure 4.4), declared that their duplicates were so accurate they would be displayed together with the originals so "their effectiveness can be fully appreciated."[33] While the Simpson Crawford Co. dress was copied at a lower price point than many, this was still a substantial amount for a dress in 1912. For example, in the 1910s Franklin and Simon advertised dress adaptations from $20 to $145, while Stewart & Co. listed prices from $16.50 to $169.50.

Much Paris model duplication was in fact authorized by haute couture houses. High-end retailers purchased models for the express purpose of

Figure 4.4 R. H. Macy & Co. advertisement for an exhibition of the new fall fashions for 1913–1914. *The New York Times*, September 24, 1913, 5.

creating copies for their customers. The Paris house was paid for the dress, along with a fee for the right to copy, with the understanding that the design would be copied in quality fabrics and sold for a high price at these stores, therefore not diminishing the reputation of the designer.

The False French Label

While many US firms copied Paris designs, for some manufacturers and retailers the easiest route to a "French" design was to attach a fake designer label. Paris designers had few legal means available to them to prevent the practice, as most did not have trademarks registered in the United States.[34] Both large and small US retailers used these labels, either imported from

Paris or created in the United States, as important selling points to consumers.[35] Some manufacturers felt that false labels were deceptive to the consumer, while others argued that "any American woman knows that she can't get a new Paris hat for twenty dollars. If she doesn't she's a fool, and she deserves to get swindled."[36] Others felt that the producers who used the labels in deceiving their customers were the ones upon whom the legal and/or moral responsibility rested.[37] A leading dressmaker blamed US women for the dependence on Paris. She stated:

> It certainly cannot be that our dressmakers haven't sufficient creative ability to please American women. I believe the fault lies entirely with the women and not with the gown makers. It is a form of snobbery that we should do away with. There are dozens of shops in New York where American-made clothes bear French labels, because American women would not buy them otherwise.[38]

The plethora of false labels led one writer to state, "Paris is very often only a label, and very often, the label is a lie."[39] In 1912, a French house complained that of the one thousand garments found in retail outlets bearing their labels, only two hundred were legitimate.[40] Some Parisian designers struck back through advertising. Paquin and Callot Soeurs ran advertisements in *The New York Times* with lists of the stores that had purchased authorized designs for sale or copy. A Paquin advertisement also stated that new waist belts came with an official registered seal and number, with the hope that it would offer the customer an ability to "discern at first sight the original from a copy."[41]

Poiret was appalled to discover not only the rampant copying of his designs but also dresses with counterfeit labels when he visited New York in 1913. He concluded that "unless something is done to stop the pirating of fashions, there will be no great dressmakers left in Paris in ten years."[42] He initially tried to combat the use of counterfeit labels through ads that showed his authentic label. In one advertisement he claimed to have "no objection" when his designs were copied, if "the label indicates this, as for instance, 'copy of a Poiret Model.'" The ad went on to state, however, that he had registered his trademark in France and had "advised my attorneys to register at Washington my label as a trade-mark and instructed them to

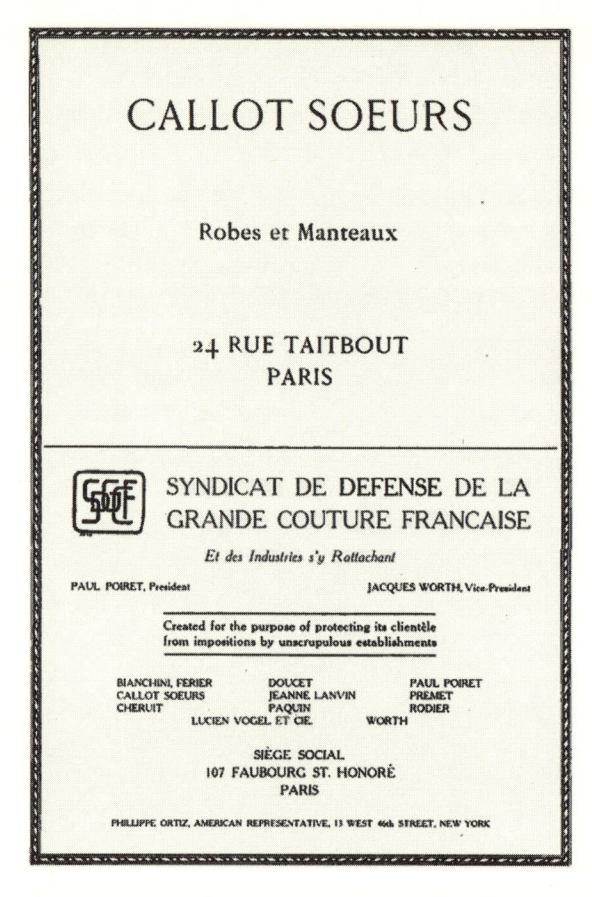

Figure 4.5 Callot Soeurs advertisement with Syndicat endorsement and list of members. *The Lotus Magazine*, April 1913, 265.

protect my interests."⁴³ He also became a vocal advocate for a French organization that would not only protect against copying but also establish new policies related to publication of photographs and, more importantly, the licensing of original designs for legitimate reproduction and distribution by American companies.

In July 1914, Poiret and a group of prominent couture houses founded Le Syndicat de Défense de la Grande Couture Française et des Industries s'y Rattachant (the Syndicate for the Protection of the Great French Couture) under the leadership of Poiret as president and Jacques Worth as vice president. The Syndicat included the haute couture designer members Premet, Doucet, Chéruit, Rodier, Paquin, Callot Soeurs, Lucien Vogel et Compagnie (publisher of *Gazette du Bon Ton*), Atuyer, and silk producer Bianchini-Férier (Figure 4.5).

WEINGARTEN & PEARL

Ladies' Tailors and Importers,
516 Fifth Avenue, Corner 43d Street

150 Paris Models

On Exhibition Tuesday, Sept. 1st

Models will be shown only by appointment.

Tailors and Dressmakers are invited.

THE wonderful collection of 150 Paris Models, purchased abroad by our Mr. Morris Weingarten, arrived yesterday on the steamship Olympic.

This collection represents the very latest ideas of the famous fashion designers, Callot, Paquin, Cheruit, Premet, Drecoll, Bernard and many others, and unlike those shown by other houses, who bought their models prior to August 5th. Original letters certifying to this are in our possession from Callot, Paquin, Bernard, Drecoll and others.

This will be the most important exhibit of Paris Models to be shown in America this Fall.

Copies will be sold at reasonable prices.

You are cordially invited to view the display.

Figure 4.6 Import company Weingarten & Pearl advertisement for an exhibition of Paris designs intended for sale or copying. *The New York Times*, August 30, 1914, 9.

Methods the Syndicat adopted to slow down the unauthorized copying of designs, and thus hopefully to control piracy, included the barring of foreign buyers (particularly Americans) from fashion shows, the prevention of photographers from selling pictures of their newest fashions, and attempts to prevent newspapers from bringing out fashion supplements in which exclusive ideas were broadcast to the world. The Syndicat discussed refusing to show models to any persons except those purchasing them.[44] In addition, licensing would be strictly controlled, with a charge for models lent for reproduction and for every copy that a US manufacturer or retailer sold, along with sale of labels to specify that the design was a reproduction.[45] This would presumably have the effect of increasing profits on authorized copies, a primary goal of the Syndicat.[46] As a way to enforce the new arrangements, the Syndicat members determined to refuse to do business with anyone not willing to follow their rules. With all that, unauthorized copying clearly continued, and in 1915 Poiret wrote what *The New York Times* described as a "diatribe" against the "methods of certain buyers" who continued to buy Paris designs. He asserted that they "haggle and cheapen prices" and steal "buttons or fragments of material in order to have them copied."[47] *The New York Times* argued that while many of the abuses were certainly true, at least some, such as exhibitions of models by the larger stores (where copying could be done by others in the industry) actually helped to make "household words" out of the names of many designers (Figure 4.6).[48]

Syndicat control of copying was certainly going to be more complicated than the members anticipated. The multiple attempts of French designers to limit free access to styles may in fact have bolstered the desire for US apparel industry independence, as retailers and manufacturers grew concerned about cost and accessibility. If the Syndicat itself weren't impetus enough, the impending Great War was already a concern of the US industry and surely pressed home the need for and support of US fashion independence.

Poiret's and other designers' relationship with the New York ready-to-wear industry was increasingly complex and complicated. While Poiret decried copying, he and other French designers also clearly recognized the growing importance of the American mass-produced apparel market to the survival of the Paris couture, as it was American retailers and manufacturers that purchased and promoted many of the designs. Indeed, the couture trade was dependent on the concept of creation of an original design and the sale of authorized copies. In 1915 and 1916 *Woman's Home Companion* published numerous illustrations of Parisian designs supposedly created just for the American market. These included Lanvin, Madame Jenny, and Maison Beer (Figure 4.7). The British designer Lucile also recognized the importance of the US market, arranging to sell her designs through Sears and Roebuck.[49] Although the partnership ultimately was considered unsuccessful for Sears, Lucile nonetheless sold $90,000 worth of dresses.[50]

In describing the possible effects of Paris designers withholding styles in 1913, Francis, a designer working in Paris, stated his position:

> If Paris wants to continue to develop and force the American people to become creators instead of copyists, this is the very best way for Paris to go

• 69 • US Design Presence

Figure 4.7 Garment designed by Madame Jenny especially for the *Woman's Home Companion*. Illustration by Coles Phillips, *Woman's Home Companion*, 1915.

about it. It puts a premium on the development of American designing and it forces America to a much more intense and conscious development than she could possibly have under the old method. If the best French models are withheld from American buyers, America will produce designers, or go elsewhere to procure models.[51]

His statement suggests that perhaps not all French designers were comfortable with the idea of withholding styles, especially if these actions accelerated development of an independent US design presence. The fashion editor Dorothy Dix stated that American consumers were "flocking to American fashions not only because of the merit and real values from a design viewpoint but also because of the so frequent fraud and disappointment of the so-called foreign goods."[52] James Blaine lamented the results of using these false Parisian labels:

America has made Paris and it is a pity. All that time we were sewing in fake labels we were building up the reputation of the Paris houses, and all the time we were killing our own chances. That is what I mean when I say that America has made Paris. We have been doing the same work here with the same materials and the same designers which Paris has had and we have been giving Paris all the recognition.[53]

In all this lively and often overstated debate about American versus French fashion and questions of creativity and originality, the person least consulted or considered was the consumer. A writer for *The New York Times* pointed out that those arguing for and against the need for American design often left out the most important part of the equation, that styles are "made by the women who wear the fashion." The writer went on to describe a process of style adoption: "It is the leader of smart Paris society who begins the popularity of the evening wrap created by Chéruit and copied in a dozen wholesale houses in lower Manhattan."[54] The writer suggested that American buyers "are not sure of their own minds" and feel compelled to be prepared for the "vast variety" of American women, women who on the whole were less inclined to take style risks.

With the rapid growth of the ready-to-wear industry and the difficulty of identifying an authentic design from a copy, the time was ripe for a concerted promotion of the American industry. But clearly, much work needed to be accomplished before American-designed goods with American labels were appreciated and, more importantly, sought after and purchased by consumers, work that would require the efforts of the press, of educational institutions, and of museums, in addition to the development of a system of protection for American designs.[55] Multiple fashion industry players came together to encourage and support American designers, aided in part by the beginning of World War I.

Creating Demand for an American Style

The rampant copying of French dressmakers and designers became central to a new argument for American-created fashion. Although the concept of American design took root almost as soon as women's ready-to-wear began to flourish, it took a combination of very avant-garde French designs and the advent of World War I to add incentive. By 1909–1910, the voices of numerous industry, entertainment, and press personalities began to call for a backing of US ready-to-wear apparel for patriotic reasons. Support for and promotion of a distinctly American fashion sense independent of Parisian dictates became a constant in the popular and trade press in the first decades of the twentieth century and continued through World War II.[56]

By the 1910s, the increasingly strident voices of manufacturers and the press (generally with the exception of the fashion press) began to demand development of an American style. Although the National Ladies' Tailors and Dressmakers' Association claimed origination of a new slogan and advertising campaign, "American Styles for American Women," Edward Bok, editor of *The Ladies' Home Journal*, had already established in 1909 the magazine's Department of American Fashions for American Women.[57] Bok had previously been an advocate for social reform causes, and he used the magazine to support nationalism through fashion. His American Fashions Department sought out and published what were determined to be "American" creations, although an apparent difficulty to find appropriately American designs led him to appeal to the magazine's readers to submit original fashion illustrations. In 1912, Bok also wrote a long editorial in *The New York Times* in support of American fashion and derisive of Paris couture designers. He went on to describe a "charming and artistic" design from an unnamed Paris house that was described in *Vogue* as a "new and shapely waistcoat." His description: "Could anything be more unfeminine, more undress, more inelegant, more slouchy?"[58]

Between 1910 and the late 1920s, a debate over American fashions for American women wore on with advertisements, articles, and letters to the editor celebrating, questioning, and even decrying the possibility of American-created fashion.[59] The popular press occasionally questioned whether American designers could originate their own fashions.[60] The campaign became so ubiquitous that some even poked fun at it (Figure 4.8).

Edward Bok continued at the forefront of the campaign, soliciting women to send in their original designs, which he then published. However, much of his encouragement for American design was in editorials and aimed at women who were making their own clothing (and buying their patterns from *The Ladies' Home Journal*), rather than support for ready-to-wear producers.[61] In addition to his offer to publish readers' designs, he claimed to have hired a "group of good [American] designers"

THE "AMERICAN FASHIONS FOR AMERICAN WOMEN" MOVEMENT

Figure 4.8 A humorous description of American-themed styles for different US cities. *LIFE*, March 20, 1913, 61.

to create the patterns sold by his publication.[62] Editors and advertisers in industry publications continued to express their disappointment in "the freakish, tasteless, and audacious Parisian models," arguing that original American fashions would boost the national economy and promote patriotism.[63] Bok asserted that American women had "told him" that they wanted American fashions. However, the celebration, publication, and copying of French styles continued to be the norm in the leading fashion magazines and in retail stores.

As the European war appeared inevitable, there were concerns that Paris would be cut off from trade, thus limiting the number of designs imported to the United States for copying and inspiration purposes. Other writers viewed the potential conflict as having a positive influence on the creation of an independent US ready-to-wear industry.[64] Soon after war was declared, a *New York Times* columnist commented: "Not the least beneficial result to this country of the European outbreak will be the opportunity for American manufacturers of women's wear to throw off the shackles of custom that have bound them to Paris for so many years and to make the creations of their own minds take the place of copies of the ideas of designers overseas."[65] The very possibility of war strained relations between US retailers and manufacturers and the Paris couture designers. The French were concerned not only about the inability of US buyers to

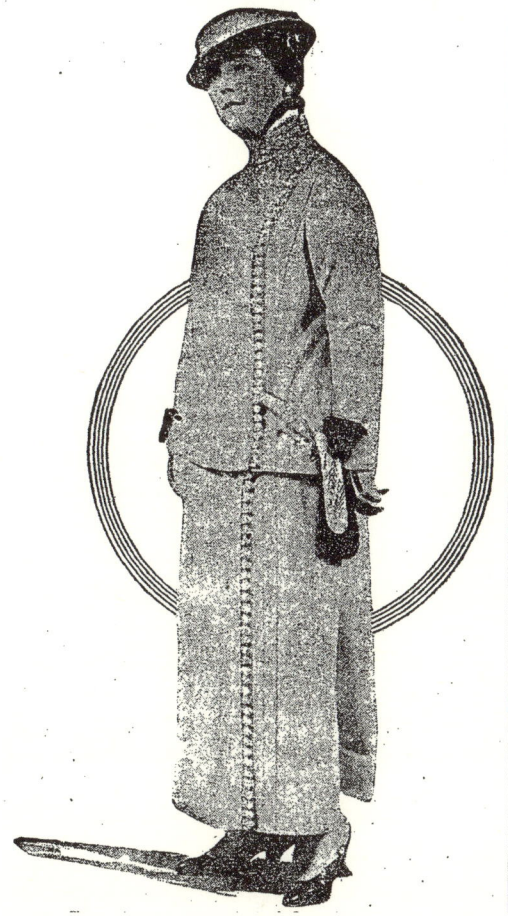

Tailored Suit "Made in America" Wins Much Praise at Society's Fashion Fete

Figure 4.9 A Stein and Blaine suit that received accolades at the Fashion Fete. *The New York Times*, November 8, 1914, X1.

travel to Paris, but also the potential difficulties of shipping apparel across the suddenly dangerous Atlantic Ocean. They also perceived that the situation might become incentive for development of more educated American designers with the ability to truly compete with the French.[66]

Although French fashion houses were ultimately not isolated from the United States during World War I, at the very beginning some couturiers, including Poiret and Worth, joined the military and were thus absentee designers. In addition, many who worked in the ateliers took part in the war effort. There were also shortages of fabrics and other supplies. Fashion editors in particular were alarmed that they would no longer have Paris fashion to fill their pages. In 1914, *Vogue* sponsored a "Fashion Fete" to be held in New York City as a benefit for war relief in Europe. The plan was for it to be supported by American dress designers and socially prominent women.[67] The presentation of American design at the celebration would be an aid to fill the fashion "void" that initially occurred with the beginning of the war. It lasted for three days, was published in the pages of *Vogue*, and was covered by at least some newspapers (Figure 4.9). One of the largest joint showings of American design talent, it would at first glance seem to represent unmistakable support of US designers by one of the leading fashion publications. However, the editors clearly still recognized Paris as the fashion leader, stating that the intention was not "to break away" from the influence of French design, that "American Fashion for American Women" was not part of the purpose, and in fact they hoped "there was no such thing as an American fashion." Their stated purpose was rather to maintain "traditions of smart dress" that war conditions had endangered.[68] While the statement may have in part been an attempt to mollify the Parisian designers they relied on, *Vogue* editors were clearly not ready to deny French designers their preeminence. The show did appear to boost American designers' confidence in their own talents, and it certainly promoted sales of their dresses.

Access to Parisian design continued, if in a slightly modified manner, but the war did trigger changes in business transactions. The danger of making the Atlantic crossing during wartime caused many buyers and dressmakers to stay home, and in some cases, those already in Paris stayed there until the safety of travel could be assured. Indeed, in 1915 the German embassy in Washington placed a warning in New York newspapers that Americans traveling on Allied ships in war zones did so at their own risk. The 1915 sinking of the passenger ship *Lusitania* demonstrated that the danger was real.

In addition, rising wholesale and retail prices of French goods from 1914 to 1927, along with US tariffs, negatively affected the desire for and purchase of French garments by American consumers.[69] In 1919 *Women's Wear* reported that wholesale prices were 300 to 500 percent of previously recorded levels and that luxury goods grew increasingly scarce and progressively more expensive. An editor stated:

The dress that could be bought before the war for 800 francs is 2200 francs and over today. The modest cotton voile blouse of 40 francs of other days is replaced by one for 85 francs today. Before the war 25 francs would buy the fine handkerchief linen chemise adorned with superb embroidery and real *Valenciennes* lace. Today you pay 85 francs for a linen one trimmed with shirred bands of cotton tulle and consider yourself lucky.[70]

Several changes occurred as a result of these economic conditions. The increasing cost of French goods prompted additional techniques for procuring designs for copying. These included saving money through the smuggling of legally purchased Parisian gowns into the United States via Canadian ports to avoid payment to US customs officials.[71] The cost of both goods and customs duties negatively affected US dressmakers and manufacturers that purchased French models. For example, when dressmaker Clara Simcox filed for bankruptcy in 1916 she owed $2,500 in duties.[72] These economic conditions further spurred support for American design independence.

American Designers and Stylists

Simultaneous growth of American nationalism, rapid expansion of the ready-to-wear industry, and a clear market for the products were not enough to stimulate interest in US designers. And, while calls for "American fashions for American women" made good news stories, there were few organizational structures in place to train American designers, encourage American fashion development, or promote the United States as a fashion center. Some existing organizations began to express a need to encourage consumers to purchase American-designed apparel, but these were primarily aligned to support various manufacturing and retailing interests. In 1913, editors for *The Dry Goods Economist* maintained that the US industry did not yet have the resources to take over fashion leadership from Paris.[73] There continued to be lack of a support network for designers and lack of recognition and publicity of US style voices. Other problems included the absence of inspirational and organizational opportunities of the type that had existed in Paris for ages, including museums open to designers for research, and the absence of legal protection of original apparel designs, something the French had made a major priority of the *Syndicat*.

The cost of hiring a designer, the ease with which designs could be copied, and the acceptance of the supposed democratizing effect of design piracy in fashion kept some firms from recognizing a need to hire a house designer. In his 1922 study *Art in Industry*, Charles Richards found that in wholesale fashion houses, the demand for new styles was met by stylists who obtained designs through copying, or "modifying the successful products of the retail houses," both in New York and Europe. Indeed, in six of the blouse firms studied, no designers at all were employed.[74] This was especially true for US companies manufacturing at the lower price points that had always copied the better dress firms, those firms that paid good money for designers and stylists or purchased expensive Parisian designs to copy. Indeed, even as late as 1940, a report to the Fashion Group asserted, "90% of American clothes are adapted, copied or just made somehow, without benefit of designers."[75] In addition, designers' job descriptions varied depending on the type of firm for which they worked. The two broadest categories were (1) dressmaker-designers, who worked primarily on one-of-a-kind garments, although some also had huge workrooms and produced ready-to-wear (or as a Milgrim ad stated "ready-for-service"); and (2) a legion of mostly unnamed designers who worked for larger manufacturers of ready-to-wear.[76] In some businesses these positions overlapped. For example, the designer Harry Collins, who built his reputation on made-to-order dresses, began to sell dresses that he defined as "semi-fitted" or for "immediate wear."[77]

It was the upper and middle price points of the wholesale market that most needed American-trained designers, designers who could be creative but also work within the constraints of ready-to-wear production and pricing requirements. If the "American fashions for American women" campaign was to be successful, how would manufacturers obtain these designers and how were they to be trained? Numerous proposals were offered in the pages of *Women's Wear* and other publications such as *The New York Times* to expand formalized education for nascent American designers, to create museums and style libraries, to publicize American designers in the media, and to support the creation of associations to advance American creative design.[78]

Educating American Designers

Though women had long been working as dressmakers and seamstresses, they were initially discouraged from pursuing careers in ready-to-wear design in the early part of the twentieth century. Not only did the industry require a designer with different skills from the custom dressmaker; designing ready-to-wear in the early years of the twentieth century often meant working in factories, an environment considered less appropriate for women designers.[79] There were also issues of class and ethnicity, as dressmakers and designers were more likely to be US born rather than the legions of immigrant women toiling as stitchers on the factory floor. Dressmaking had always been an occupation that was not only almost exclusively female but also one of the few that was socially acceptable as a career for women. This can be compared to the designers and patternmakers in the women's coat and suit industry, who were more likely to be men. In the first ten to fifteen years of the twentieth century, apparel industry designers were most often referred to as masculine, although women made up a small percentage of designers in the tailored industries. At meetings of organizations such as the Cloak and Suit Designers' Association the membership was always described as male, whether or not there were some women involved in design. In the 1910 US Manufacturing Census, 1,689 out of 1,824 (91.5 percent) of suit, coat, cloak, and overall designers were men, whereas 1,061 out of 1,959 (54 percent) of designers in all other categories were men.[80]

Although the women's ready-to-wear trade began its rapid rise at the end of the nineteenth century with coats, suits, and separates such as shirtwaists and skirts, by the 1910s the dress market began to dominate the trade. With the increased importance of ready-to-wear dresses in women's wardrobes, the demand for women to fill the role of designer increased. The designing and making of dresses had always been considered "women's work," with male designers such as Charles Worth and Paul Poiret an anomaly.[81] Schools such as the New York School of Design (originally the American School of Design, founded 1896) and the Pratt Institute in New York City (founded 1887) were firmly established and training women as designers, dressmakers, and illustrators since their inception. Many schools were created between 1910 and 1925 owing in part to fear that the Parisian fashion industry would be suspended during World War I but also in response to the campaign for American-created fashion. Schools with programs in apparel design included the New York School of Fine and Applied Arts (1906, known today as Parsons, the New School for Design); the Fashion Academy (1912); Metropolitan Art School (1919); the

Traphagen School of Fashion (1923); and Grand Central School of Art (1924).[82] Smaller, lesser known schools such as Professor I. Rosenfeld's School of Designing on Second Avenue in New York City and the Anna Morgan School of Expression in Chicago also advertised programs in the trade press for educating apparel designers.[83]

Artistically minded schools such as the Pratt Institute taught students fashion design, sewing, and drawing as well as pertinent business methods.[84] Typically within commercial vocational schools, students decided between programs in fashion illustration or dress designing, the latter including more hands-on skills. Depending on the talent and needs of the student and the availability of jobs, they were encouraged to consider working in any area within the apparel industry, including manufacturing, retailing, fashion journalism, and even modeling. Prominent apparel industry members recommended young designers take history of textiles, costume design, and artistic courses and urged travel to both domestic and exotic locales.[85]

When Alexandre Grean, chairman of the Society for American Fashion for American Women, spoke to a group of students at the Teachers College of Columbia University in 1912, he stated: "It makes no difference how clever you may become with the pencil. The most important thing is to cultivate your aesthetic taste by observing and studying everything that is beautiful and harmonious in nature and in art."[86] Promising designers were encouraged to analyze fashion tendencies in light of recent events and probable future trends and to recognize important silhouettes that dominated fashionable styles of different periods. Students were also advised to train their powers of observation and analysis by keeping journals and scrapbooks, cutting out illustrations of dresses, suits, coats, hats, and shoes, and recording the popular designs. Grean, a dressmaker and tailor, stated that it was more important to learn artistic drawing than pattern cutting because the United States had enough patternmakers; it needed artists. This was in direct contrast to the vocational programs for dressmakers, which emphasized sewing and patternmaking skills in addition to design. The new attitude to training women for fashion design was that schools needed to train students for "interpretive design creations" and not blatantly copy Paris or even US designs.[87]

A disconnect existed between the fashion schools' curricula and the needs of the ready-to-wear industry. In Richards's 1922 study, his team interviewed designers and company owners from a variety of apparel firms. Most stated that there was a demand for better, more skilled designers, but most schools were not addressing those needs. There existed a tendency to divide the course of study between the technical and the art side, thus those who studied illustration were not necessarily trained in cutting and draping and vice versa. In addition, some students acknowledged that they were still encouraged to copy existing styles rather than develop their own ideas. None of the higher-end establishments surveyed was of the opinion that school curricula were adequate to train the designers of "fine costumes."[88]

As the "American fashions" campaign continued into the years of World War I, other approaches were taken for providing designers not just a formal education but also access to cultural sources for design ideas. While it was acknowledged that the United States did not have the same artistic atmosphere as France, Americans excelled as inventors in science, medicine, and engineering, so why not also in fashion? In the 1910s and 1920s, the Metropolitan Museum of Art, the Brooklyn Museum, and the American Museum of Natural History fostered a relationship with the women's garment industry to create a nurturing and educational environment for designers, manufacturers, and the extended fashion community.[89] The textile industry was one of the first to make use of the museums for research and inspiration. The silk company H. R. Mallinson in particular used museum sources to develop textile prints, claiming that their new approach was to "break away from the general copying" to create American styles that would be "authoritative," a clear use of the word most often applied to Parisian fashion.[90] They openly acknowledged that prior American silk textiles "as expected . . . did not equal the products of the old mills of France."[91] But, as they now considered the quality on par, the primary concern was the lack of recognition for the work of American manufacturers. Initially, they created silk prints that had North American influences, in particular Mexican and American Indian motifs. They also used well-known American actresses and performers such as the opera star Rosa Ponselle and the film star Dorothy Dalton in their advertising. Nevertheless, although their sales were dependent on the American market and on American designers, they did not acknowledge any US apparel or textile designers in their ads.[92]

M. D. C. Crawford was an extraordinary supporter of American de-

Figure 4.10 Dress design examples using the collection of the American Museum of Natural History as inspiration. On the left is a design for John Wanamaker inspired by Ainu coats, on the right an outfit with Russian-inspired embroidery, also for John Wanamaker. M. D. C. Crawford, "Museum Documents and Modern Costume," *American Museum Journal*, 1918, 292 and 293.

sign advancement and education. An editor for *Women's Wear* and a research associate in textiles at the American Museum of Natural History (AMNH), he encouraged a partnership between museums and the apparel industry, with the museum collections serving as inspiration sources. American designers were encouraged to adopt from the same types of historic references that the French designers used, but focused on New York or other domestic resources. According to Crawford, fashion designers of America needed to study not only the trends in fashions, lifestyles, and necessities of the day, but also documents housed in the chief New York City libraries and museums if they were to make beautiful things as were found elsewhere in the world.[93]

Crawford strongly advocated a link between museums and fashion designers that continued from the years of World War I through the 1920s, and even into the 1940s.[94] Crawford and Elizabeth Miner King, a journalist, agreed that the war had "forced the business of the importation of wearing-apparel from Paris to the United States almost to the wall."[95] The quantity of imports from Paris declined during the war, and thus American designers had the opportunity to fill the gap and, as King suggested, to develop an "international reputation." Crawford's columns in *Women's Wear* frequently illustrated techniques for using museum ethnographic collections as inspiration. In addition, he aided the establishment of study rooms as well as lectures and classes at several New York museums. The AMNH in particular supported the efforts to create opportunities for apparel designers. Curators at the museum worked with Crawford, who was the liaison to textile and apparel designers and manufacturers (Figure 4.10). The AMNH curators created a "fashion staff" in 1915 and were instrumental in allowing designers access to their collections.[96] Both textile and apparel companies responded to this creative encouragement. Stehli Silk Co. and H. R. Mallinson & Co., likely finding World War I an additional incentive, also created silk prints inspired by the collections.

Crawford's goals and those of the apparel and textile firms that supported and participated in these activities were aimed at ready-to-wear manufacture, although custom designers also participated.[97] By 1918 Crawford described work by American designers as "the first fruits of what I may term 'creative research' by the American costume industry."[98] In 1919, they mounted an exhibition of the museum objects, especially those from the ethnographic collections, along with the designs that were inspired by the objects. While some of the designs used dress from around the world as inspiration, many of them adopted influences from indigenous art in the Americas. The designers often based both motif and garment characteristics on native North American influences to prove a true American origin of the styles. Although Crawford admitted that such inspirations had, in the past, "suffered" from "snobbish feelings" as not equal to imported designs with European inspirations, his opinion was that through these collaborations and the resulting designs, public opinion was changing.[99] Crawford also worked with the Brooklyn Museum to support a study room for designers, a space frequented by American designers such as Edward L. Mayer, Jessie Franklin Turner, Herman Patrick Tappe, and Harry Collins.[100] Crawford would later articulate: "1914 to 1918 began the greatest era of prosperity and creative design in the costume industries of America."[101]

Promoting American Designers

The "American fashions" campaign tended to focus on promotion of American-created styles in general and not on promotion of individual designers. In addition, there was a clear divide between those designers working for retail or specialty houses and those designing for wholesale firms. Advertising and editorial content in the fashion press highlighted French designers such as Poiret, Doucet, Paquin, and Chéruit among many others, while American wholesale designers mostly worked anonymously. A few became recognized names in the 1920s and 1930s, although not always as fashion designers. For example, Taubé Coller Davis, an in-house designer for Franklin Simon Co., became one of the founders of the fashion service the Tobé Report.[102] Jo Copeland began as a ready-to-wear designer for Pattullo Modes in the 1920s, eventually becoming a partner in the firm in 1938. Occasionally designers were mentioned by name, more often in *Women's Wear Daily* and other trade publications such as *American Cloak and Suit Review*. The latter also published the apparel industry designers and buyers who were sailing to and from Europe, including those usually anonymous designers of wholesale firms. Yet recognition by the trade press was inconsistent at best. In 1922, a columnist stated, "[I]t is a saying trite but true that fashion starts at the top, meaning, of course with the acknowledged designers."[103] Although the author quoted the names of several managers at knit firms, he or she did not go on to acknowledge any American designers by name, and may not have even known the names.

Sometimes names appeared in newspapers or other publications; however, these tended to be the in-house designers for high-end retailers, such as Jessie Franklin Turner, who worked briefly for Bonwit Teller before going out on her own as a custom designer, and E. M. A. Steinmetz, who created custom gowns for the store Stein and Blaine. Designers were also named in store advertisements—again, usually those working in retail design and specialty houses such as Milgrim, where Sally Milgrim designed for both custom and ready-to-wear markets.

The fashion press, for the most part, continued to focus on Paris for style and status reasons, although *Harper's Bazar* sporadically showed the work of New York dressmakers.[104] *Vogue* occasionally showed American designers and high-end dressmakers, or US department store designs, including Harry Collins, Henri Bendel, and James Blaine. In a 1919 article titled "Thus New York Designers Visualize the Mode," the editor stated that such an article would have been impossible five years earlier, as at that time there were "very few original models created in New York."[105] The *Vogue* writer referred specifically to those designers and design houses that catered to higher-end clients and often did custom work, explaining that prior to the war, "practically every large dressmaking house in New York depended entirely on French models."[106] The difference in 1919 was a decrease in availability of models due to the war combined with the fact that ready-to-wear businesses also now specialized in copying French designs. The *Vogue* editorial perception was that this popularized French styles for women of all classes. The specialty houses thus had to design their own if they "wished to offer their clientele anything different from their competitors." However, unable to completely see a fashion world separate from Paris, they did observe that the New York designs demonstrated notable Parisian influences. Whether the women purchasing these dresses, either custom or ready-to-wear, had an eye to discern subtleties of design detail and difference between New York and Paris is unclear.

American designers struggled to achieve recognition in the early part of the twentieth century, not only because of minimal attention from the press, but also because of the type of attention when it did occur. Parisian designers were celebrated as superior creators of exquisite art, whereas American designers were routinely commended for their technical abilities in copying. Even after two decades of the campaign for American fashions, in 1930 *Vogue* published an article on American wholesale designers, clearly stating that they were "interpreters of the mode," and that although their own stamp was on their designs, they remained "in step" with "French arbiters of fashion."[107]

According to the designer James Blaine, the newspapers were to blame for the "bewitching and hypnotizing of women" for all things Parisian.[108] His point was certainly valid—stores advertised Paris fashion, copies of Parisian dresses, and even a loose French attribution for both clothing and fabrics such as "Poiret twill." They also used French descriptive terms in place of English, advertising dresses for the "jeunes filles" or "tailleur" instead of tailored suits.[109] Stores invited "Madame" to visit and to see "authentic" designs as sanctioned by Paris dressmakers. Each season, Parisian design decisions, trends, and innovations filled American department and specialty store ads.

Retailers rarely commented on US-made merchandise, in part due to the system of American manufacturing: many American designers created goods under the labels of manufacturers or department stores, or even used the false Parisian labels. In some cases, stores placed their own label in US-produced apparel. Clara Simcox, one of the few American designers who both advertised her creations and received credit for her designs, stated in an article in *Women's Wear* in 1913, "If we had the support of our own press (who are giving Paris so much free advertising), if they would recognize our talents without fearing that an ad might get lost by boosting our home industries, American women would soon generally realize the great mistake in buying the poorly finished and hurriedly made French dresses."[110]

Unlike the fashion press, *The New York Times* did begin to publish and support New York–produced design more frequently in the 1910s, and it included descriptions of American-made apparel. World War I prompted a few stores to promote American design, especially in the beginning years when the emphasis was on national pride in all things, but most often simply as "American" without a designer name attached. Just a month after the start of the war in Europe, for example, Arnold, Constable and Co. advertised an exhibition of "American Models by American Designers," ironically in their "Louis XV Salon de Robes."[111] At about the same time, *Harper's Bazar* gradually began to publish some New York designer names, again mostly designers who did custom work or a combination of custom and ready-to-wear, such as Clara Simcox, Harry Collins, E. M. A. Steinmetz, and Herman Patrick Tappe. It was these designers, not the wholesale ready-to-wear designers, who produced the high-fashion garments both advertised and editorialized in *Harper's Bazar* and *Vogue*.[112]

Some argued that if the press promoted the work of American designers, stores would be "courageous in advocating and pushing American-made goods."[113] American dressmakers wondered why the US press gave so much space to French and other foreign merchants, especially since these advertisements competed with US-made clothing sold in retail shops.[114] A major consideration in examining the limited focus on individual designers, however, was the organizational structure of the industry. At low-price houses more emphasis was placed on obtaining Paris models to adapt for American tastes. Wholesale manufacturers may have been partly to blame for not advertising and making known their own designers, but in larger ready-to-wear companies there was seldom just one designer responsible for the seasonal collections, thus credit stayed with the company name. Of the seven firms surveyed by Richards, six employed a combined eighteen designers, more in the busy season. In only one of the firms was a single designer, rather than a team, solely responsible for creating the collection.[115]

One way to support American design and designers was to pay them well. Leading proponents of "American fashions for American women" urged manufacturers to pay their designer enough money so that he could "work designs, eat designs, drink designs, and at night he must dream designs or pay a fine for every dream that is alien to the profession."[116] The same year *The New York Times*, in response to "interest aroused" by their American design competition, offered information specifically for girls and women on how to become fashion designers. Their advice explained the two different training options, divided between schools that offered courses on dressmaking, especially design for custom work, and schools that taught "trade" work. The latter focused on technical training on sewing machines and was not intended for the aspiring creative designer.[117]

As the twentieth century progressed, women were not only increasingly encouraged to pursue careers in design; many were in fact well paid.[118] Those interviewed by Richards made anywhere from $35 a week for beginners to $15,000 a year or more for experienced designers, a considerable sum in that period. Alexandre M. Grean claimed that there were at least two thousand first-class designers in New York with salaries that ranged from $1,500 to $15,000 a year. The worth of a good designer was demonstrated by a lawsuit brought against Charles Lang & Parnes, Inc., in 1928. The company was sued by a competing firm for wooing away their designer with a salary increase from $90 to $175 a week. At issue was not just the fact that the designer, Florence Gray, was under contract. The critically important accusation in the lawsuit: the designer allegedly took with her designs as yet unproduced and "exclusive" to the plaintiff.[119]

Design competitions were another attempt to gain recognition for US designers. *The New York Times* conducted the first newspaper contest for

American Fashions for American Women

Nine Cash Prizes for

AMERICAN DESIGNED HATS

AND

DRESSES

TO encourage the designing of American Fashions for Women, THE NEW YORK TIMES offers the following prizes for American-designed hats and dresses:

For a Spring Hat of Original Design

$100 as a First Prize.
$50 as a Second Prize.
$25 as a Third Prize.

For a Spring Dress of Original American Design intended for Afternoon Wear

$100 as a First Prize.
$50 as a Second Prize.
$25 as a Third Prize.

For an Evening Gown of Original American Design

$100 as a First Prize.
$50 as a Second Prize.
$25 as a Third Prize.

The designs submitted will be carefully and confidentially judged, and with absolute impartiality, by a special jury of six judges representing authoritative knowledge of good dressing.

COMMITTEE OF AWARD

MR. EDWARD BOK, Editor of The Ladies'

Figure 4.11 Advertisement for *The New York Times* contest for American-designed hats and dresses. "Nine Cash Prizes for American Designed Hats and Dresses," *The New York Times*, December 18, 1912, 11.

American-designed hats and dresses in 1912 (Figure 4.11). One of the winners of the competition was Ethel Traphagen, eventual founder of the Traphagen School of Fashion.[120] Edward Bok was a supporter of design competitions to identify "American" ideas and earn profit on their designs, if not necessarily to promote the names of those who won.

Other suggestions for promoting American-made goods varied. Some manufacturers and designers suggested development of special departments in stores or even development of special chain stores that carried only American-crafted merchandise. The women's ready-to-wear department of the Bush Terminal Sales Building hired US designers to create "works of art" that were to be produced by the Bush manufacturing department and exclusively sold in their women's apparel department, thus creating, promoting, and selling American-made ready-to-wear clothing.[121] *Woman's Home Companion* and *The American Silk Journal* published several articles as well as illustrations of the apparel created by the US designer Harry Collins. While the fashion press clung tenaciously to French ideas of fashion, these were some of the first US publications to celebrate an American designer.[122]

By the 1920s, various segments of the industry increasingly collaborated to support American design. The textile industry, and in particular silk manufacturers, began to use US designs and designers in their advertising. Shelton Looms and the Associated Garment Manufacturers presented annual exhibitions that featured a competition of the latest models of "over 100 of New York's foremost manufacturers."[123] Penikees Silk used a gown credited to Mayer Chic in their print advertising.[124] Both *Women's Wear* and the textile manufacturer Albert Blum sponsored textile design competitions. The Redfern Corset Company began to promote American designers in their advertisements, with the affirmation that these "recognized" designers "endorsed" their corset.[125] Even the US government supported the sale of silk cloth with claims that the product was "born of Patriotism and the American spirit."[126]

Finally, some designers chose self-promotion. For example, Harry Collins, one of the important custom designers of the 1910s and 1920s, began to advertise his book *Art in Dress* in *The New York Times* and *Vogue*, publicizing the fact that his shop included both custom-made dresses and what he described as ready-to-fit (Figure 4.12).[127] The prices of these designer-labeled ready-to-wear styles were often quite high and demonstrat-

Figure 4.12 Creator of "Art in Dress" Harry Collins. *Vogue*, April 1, 1918, 19.

ed an attempt to trade on the designer or the design house name and reputation. Collins designed for First Lady Florence Harding and maintained a well-established reputation. In advertisements, he described the offerings as originals "of typical Harry Collins distinction," with three set prices of $85, $110, and $150. Hickson, Inc., which advertised itself as "incomparably the greatest in the world," sold dress originals and reproductions for $150 to $165. Retailers, such as Stein and Blaine, also established their designers as "authorities," borrowing language often used in promoting French goods (Figure 4.13).

Despite these efforts, the fashion writer Elizabeth Hawes claimed that most American designers continued to rely heavily on Paris for inspiration and direction. She correctly noted that custom shops such as Thurn, Hattie Carnegie, and Bergdorf Goodman that employed in-house designers also continued to show "French models." Her contention was that it was the designs at the middle price points—the ready-to-wear clothing

US Design Presence

Figure 4.13 Dress design by E. M. A. Steinmetz for Stein & Blaine, *The New York Times*, May 5, 1918, 3.

aimed at the middle class—that were "junked up and tricked out and tawdry." Her contention was that excessive amounts of inexpensive trims and decorations were used to mask poor quality, a response to the need for fast and cheap manufacture and imitation.[128]

True or not, it was clear that manufacturers, designers, and retailers were all beginning to identify benefits to promoting and showing American-made and -designed apparel. To some degree, although Paris was not entirely cut off during World War I, the war did create a perceived need to establish domestic credibility. While before the war many found it cheaper to buy models to copy rather than operate a style department, they admitted it was "unsafe" to completely rely on an "outside source" for styles.[129] Interestingly, Prohibition in the 1920s created an unforeseen challenge to transmission of style ideas, as it potentially limited the opportunities for "fashionable assemblages" in those places where alcohol had traditionally been served.

Although the "American fashions for American women" campaign became less a focus in the 1920s, there was an increased momentum for recognition of US designers. There also continued to be attempts to analyze the origin of various fashions as well as why any given style gained popularity over another. Many of the trade organizations began to sponsor group fashion presentations of members' designs, with industry and especially buyers invited. In 1920 the National Garment Retailers Association put together the first collaborative group style show, held at the Hotel Commodore in New York City. Designers and retailers represented included Henri Bendel, Bergdorf Goodman, Joseph, Nardi, Milgrim, Adolph, and Stein and Blaine.[130] Even into the 1930s, apparel groups such as the American Society of Style Creators sought to develop and foster the ability and talent of American designers, while not wholly turning their backs on foreign couturiers.[131]

Protecting American Design

In an essay focusing on education in American art and vocational schools published in Richards's *Art in Industry*, C. R. Clifford asks, "Why open design schools, why support art societies, why educate designers if the products of their skill can be appropriated by anybody."[132] His inquiry reflected the growing realization that supporting American design and designers

• 91 • US Design Presence

Figure 4.14 A dress and its copy, offered as Exhibit E in the appeal case of Ben Gershel & Co. and Abraham E. Lefcourt against Hickson, Inc., and Richard J. Hickson, Supreme Court of the State of New York, July 29, 1920.

through promotion and education made protection against piracy even more imperative. The push to educate American design talent, and the money spent to hire that talent, certainly made apparel firms determined to protect their investment. Despite the lack of recognition of individual designers by name and a continued reliance on Paris for new styles, rampant design piracy prompted both associations and individuals to take up the cause of design protection. While most were not concerned with their own use of French designs as inspiration or even for direct copies, high-end firms objected to the flagrant reproduction of their in-house designs at the lower price points—a process that happened with amazing speed, sometimes days. At least some of this copying occurred when garments were in the hands of the jobbers, but some was also done by retailers who took purchases to their own factories to reproduce.

The ambiguity of design protection persisted, especially as much of the industry continued to exist at least on some level through copying. Beginning in the 1910s, some New York custom designers adopted the techniques of French couture designers by creating dresses intentionally as models for copying. They then charged other firms, both custom and ready-to-wear, for the right to create an "authorized reproduction," using that company's name. Hickson Inc., considered one of the best custom houses in New York, apparently made a practice of selling these models (Figure 4.14). However, the owners also found themselves in court several times over both the manner in which the rights were advertised and payment for the rights. In one such case they were sued for offering exclusive rights to copy and then refusing to show the complete line of designs to the ready-to-wear firm after the firm paid $25,000 for the rights. In another, they granted rights to more than one firm, each of which advertised exclusivity.[133] In Figure 4.14, the two dresses were both sold to Lord & Taylor, but from two different manufacturers, both of whom had contracted for exclusive rights to the design from Hickson, Inc.

Clara Simcox was one of the first to attempt individual control when she copyrighted her garments in 1912. When each dress was sold, Madame Simcox (who went by the French title) delivered them with legal papers of copyright. *Women's Wear* stated the copyrighting of these designs "stand[s] for more than merely business; it stands for the spirit of patriotism applied to a vast field of usefulness and importance to American welfare."[134] Some designers chose to file patents for their designs. Close to eighty design patents were filed for dresses between 1911 and 1929, even though the ability to actually protect the patent in court was questionable. In the 1910s and 1920s some patents were in individual designers' names, including Harry Collins, but many listed the designer's name with a store or manufacturer as assignor. Franklin Simon & Co. had fifty-six patents in this seventeen-year period, perhaps not surprising as the company was actively attempting to protect its Bramley trademark and associated designs (Figure 4.15).[135]

In addition to patents, by the late 1910s dress manufacturers and stores such as Franklin Simon & Co. began to see benefits to creating recogniz-

• 93 •   US Design Presence

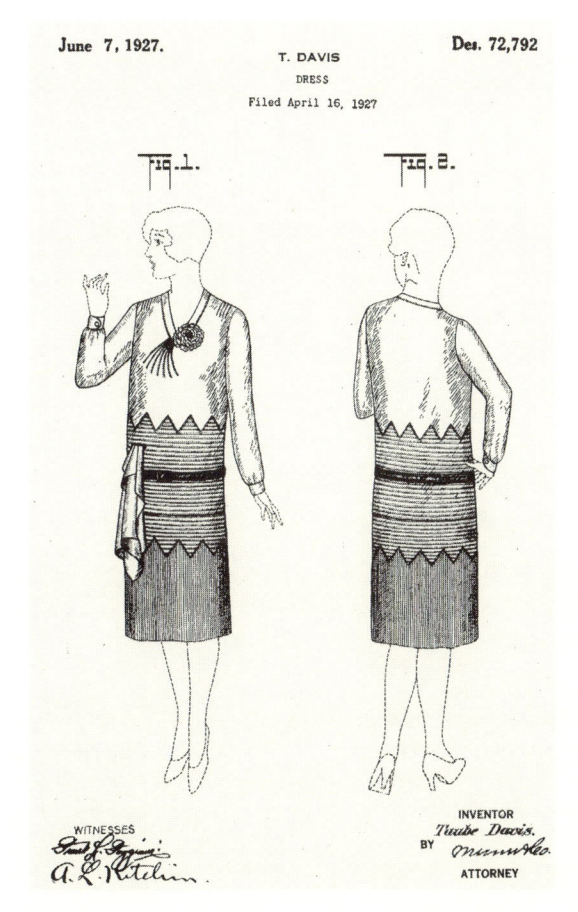

Figure 4.15 Dress patent assigned to Franklin Simon Co., Inc., by designer Taubé Davis. Taubé Davis, Patent No. 72,792. (1927).

able trademarks and brand names that offered consumers a product with associated style and quality. Use of brand names in the dress industry had been slow to develop, with department stores more focused on promoting their name to consumers. In addition, the speed of growth in the ready-to-wear industry, with an emphasis on contractors and jobbers for production, did not encourage companies to create a brand name that could be backed with quality or style guarantees. But the success of a number of trademarked brands, and encouragement from trade organizations, began to lead to creation of recognizable brand images that were also advertised with and backed by guarantees. For example, the Goldman Costume Co. had the brand name and logo of their Betty Wales dresses officially trademarked in 1917 (Figure 4.16).[136] The name derived from a series of novels

Figure 4.16 Betty Wales advertisement. *Vogue*, September 1, 1917, 13.

about a college girl. With its distinctive logo and label, dresses were advertised as "taking the guesswork out of dress buying" and suggested that the consumer no longer needed to "gamble on the authenticity of the style."[137] In addition, the company marketed the line to only one store in a city, thus also projecting some guarantee of style uniqueness. Other apparel companies created distinctive brand names or branded lines within the company, including the Rosemary dress line produced by M&H Rentner, and the Peggy Paige line. The latter was trademarked in 1921, although the company had been using the name for at least five years by then. Advertised as Peggy Paige Dressmakers, or Designed by Peggy Paige, the brand and logo lent the (false) idea that it was a real person, rather than a fictitious name.[138]

There were numerous advantages to creating trademark names for both the retailer and the manufacturer, and the growing use of brand names represented a unique cooperation between them through joint advertising. The brand-name dress manufacturers began to advertise in various women's publications, including *Vogue*, *The Ladies' Home Journal*, and *Good Housekeeping*. This national advertising supported both the brand and the retailers. In a *Vogue* advertisement, Peggy Paige published a list of five hundred stores carrying its dresses. Betty Wales advertisements listed the benefits and guarantees of the brand.[139] The retailers then advertised locally, further promoting the brand. While dresses were still not necessarily protected from piracy, the trademark could be protected. Indeed, in one court case, the Boue Soeurs Company won a case against retailer and designer Hickson, Inc. because the latter had removed their trademark label and then exhibited the gowns as their "importations" or adaptations. While Hickson, Inc. sold copies, they preferred to do it under their own label, customers thus associating the gowns with the Hickson brand. The language in the court case is telling, in terms of the ability to protect apparel designs. The judge explained that "a maker of women's garments has a legal right to copy and sell as its own creations the exclusive models designed by other modistes." The stipulation was that the model was acquired by "fair means." On the other hand, they had no rights if the design was procured through "fraud and deception," which was how Hickson obtained the design in question, when they sent an employee to Boue Soeurs to pose as a customer in order to purchase the gown.[140]

While trademarks and the establishment of brand identity could assist in protecting an apparel producer, it only went so far. In the early 1920s, manufacturer and designer trade organizations began to search actively for other ways to control design piracy. The Association of Dress Manufacturers, directed by Louis Rubin, developed a plan for design registration in 1921 aimed initially at controlling copying by jobbers, rather than retailers. Their plan included establishment of a style registration bureau, stamping the bills of the model provided to jobbers with the statement that the design was "sold on memorandum" and remained the exclusive property of the originator.[141] Others actively sought legal protection through laws submitted for approval to Congress. Because most US apparel production was in New York, an attempt was made by the United Women's Wear League of America to make "the stealing of styles a criminal matter" through the New York state legislature.[142] In 1925 Joseph Bercovici of the Association of Dress Manufacturers, proposed a style clearinghouse controlled by industry representatives, rather than reliance on the government. Members would file their new design sketches seasonally and receive a certificate authenticating originality. Retailers in particular could then do research to verify the originality of designs they were either producing themselves or purchasing.[143] While none of these plans to stop piracy appears to have been effective, they represent both the importance that was attached to the "evil" of piracy and the beginning of discussions that would lead to the industry's longest-lived and most effective effort to thwart design piracy.

The beginning of the twentieth century witnessed an influx of manufacturing and retailing businesses and associations interested in promoting the consumption of American fashion. Although American-made garments clothed the majority of US women, the design inspiration and credit for these garments at all price levels tended to be Parisian. Frustrated not only by lack of credit for their creations but also by an inability to control fashion change, many in the ready-to-wear industry committed to altering the perception of American-made clothing. The campaign of "American fashions for American women" opened the door not only for suggestions but also for actions aimed at supporting and encouraging emergent creative talents in the United States. Although some of the "American fashions for American women" efforts seemed to be personal crusades, this early campaign played a significant role in the beginning stages of development of an American fashion presence. World War I was also instrumental in encouraging US manufacturers to recognize the importance of American designers, if not yet by name. The early US ready-to-wear industry thrived and continued to grow, however chaotically, without recognition of the men and women who created the wholesale designs. Nevertheless, in this early period of the twentieth century, acknowledgment and promotion of American-made garments, attempts to educate and nurture designers, and efforts to protect their creative work were necessary steps. In the 1930s, attempts were made to go beyond just recognition as American, but for many firms, the Depression put an emphasis on sheer survival, particularly for higher-priced dress manufacturers as production of low-end goods increased. With this emphasis on goods that originated in America, concerns over how they might be protected from design pirates esclated.

Chapter 5

Design Piracy and Self-Regulation: The Fashion Originators' Guild of America

The 1930s saw the most attempts to regulate style piracy. This was due, in part, to the damaging effects of the Great Depression on higher-priced manufacturing and retailing interests and on altered consumer buying practices. Support for regulation and protection came primarily from the manufacturers of higher-priced dresses. Neither retailers nor those who manufactured the popular, or lower-priced, merchandise saw a benefit, however, and fought vigorously against attempts to end the practice of copying.[1]

In the early 1930s, a group of twelve manufacturers of high-priced ladies' dresses, located in the New York City area and led by Maurice Rentner (Figure 5.1), began discussions that led to creation of an organization intended to fight design piracy and promote "style consciousness among American women."[2] Called the Fashion Originators' Guild of America, it was incorporated in New York State on March 7, 1932, with the stated objective to protect the "originators of fashions and styles against copying and piracy of styles of any trade or industry."[3] In existence from 1932 until 1941, the FOGA was one of the more successful industry attempts to control design piracy. The guild's administrative program against piracy highlights the controversial debates and the difficulties in regulating fashion's oldest "creative" practice.

Impact of the Great Depression

As unemployment during the Depression reached as high as 25 percent, clothing manufacturers saw a critical change in the shopping habits of women, regardless of income. Comparative shopping became the norm as women evaluated similar articles of clothing across stores to find the best value and quality for what they felt they could afford to spend.[4] Generally speaking, consumers chose to buy less expensive clothing rather

Figure 5.1 Maurice Rentner, chairman of the FOGA. *Women's Wear Daily*, March 6, 1933, sec. 2, 2.

Maurice Rentner
Chairman of the Fashion Originators Guild of America

than cease buying altogether. As stated in 1951 by Florence Richards, the author of *The Ready-to-Wear Industry, 1900–1950*, "Women accustomed to paying $16.95 for their dresses shopped around for one at $10.95, while the $10.95 customer settled for a $6.95 number."[5] Although the number of dresses produced by the manufacturing industry remained about the same, the cost and quality of these dresses decreased significantly. According to published records of the US Census of Manufacturers, the average wholesale value per dress decreased from $5.39 in 1927 to $2.62 in 1937.[6] This 50 percent reduction in ten years caused a fundamental shift in the competitive relationships of the industry. The demand for inexpensive dresses was strong, stimulating manufacturers to produce increasingly lower-cost creations. According to a report of the International Ladies'

Garment Workers' Union (ILGWU), this had a demoralizing influence on the entirety of the garment business: "The crisis . . . has practically revolutionized the main lines of dress merchandise to meet a growing demand for cheaper garments. . . . The production slogan in the New York dress industry has now become not quality but cheapness."[7]

Part and parcel to offering cheaper goods, retail stores began to subdivide by price and type of merchandise and to hire buyers for these individual departments. Expensive, medium, and bargain dress departments were created. As a result, the dress industry was forced into specialized price lines.[8] The increased specialization of the industry meant women could shop in departments that fit their economic means and social status.

The principal adjustment for the dress industry was the increased number of dresses manufactured and sold at the lower price points. While the economic problems of the Depression had minimal effect on the growth of the New York dress industry in terms of overall volume, more high-price than low-price dress companies went out of business. The ILGWU report noted the number of firms manufacturing higher-priced dresses decreased, giving way to those in the $3.75 and $6.75 production lines. According to their report, "As the cost of materials, overhead, and marketing does not vary substantially between firm and firm, this rush for cheapness has been carried on principally at the expense of labor."[9]

One of the ways in which manufacturers reduced costs was through the contracting system. Although it had been around since the beginning of the apparel industry, this method of production increased during the 1930s. Contractors were more able than large companies to respond quickly to fashion and price changes. As opposed to inside shops in which dresses were manufactured from fabric to sewn garments in one factory location, contractors or submanufacturers created clothing in outside locations out of materials consigned to them by the principal manufacturer. Manufacturers often used numerous submanufacturers to create one style of dress. According to some reports, contractors produced 80 to 85 percent of all dresses manufactured in the New York area.[10]

Due to the increasingly cutthroat nature of the business, the apparel industry was besieged with bankruptcies. Studies conducted by the New York Joint Board of the Dress and Waist Makers' Union revealed that 83 percent of businesses formed in 1925 were discontinued by 1933. Further, while customarily about 20 percent of apparel firms went out of business annually, this percentage doubled in 1932.[11] In describing the dress industry in 1933, the dress manufacturer C. Robbins stated, "The dress industry is troubled by an utter absence of security or ease of mind. Every man in it has had a justifiable fear . . . as to what dire developments the next month or week or day might bring forth."[12]

The Fashion Originators' Guild of America

It was in this atmosphere of extreme price competition that the FOGA began to operate. The Guild maintained that women had become so confused by the multiplicity of copied designs that they no longer recognized original design.[13] In a movement to protect and popularize original style, it built its foundation on retailer-manufacturer collaboration. Maurice Rentner, manufacturer and designer of high-priced apparel and founder of the FOGA, contended "everything the mind could conceive" had already been tried in the dress industry, including "specialization of every description, all manner of promotion, copying, debasing, cheapening, but the net result was that no one was pleased." The FOGA was created as "something more constructive" (Figure 5.2):

> To promote cooperation and friendly intercourse in the wearing apparel industry, to establish and maintain uniformity and certainty in the customs and commercial usages of trade, to acquire, preserve and disseminate information and literature which will tend to augment the sale of the commodities manufactured or sold; to advance the trade and commercial interests of [guild] members and to foster the industries of its members throughout America as to promote the sale, identification and recognition of original style and merchandise of the industries of its members.[14]

The FOGA sought to do all of these things through extensive advertising and promotional campaigns in newspapers and trade magazines (Figure 5.3), through the establishment of a registration bureau for original dress designs, and through the issuance of labels to original dress manufacturers.

The FOGA initially targeted the higher-priced manufacturers, wholesaling at $22.50 and up, to join the Guild's program. The guild secured cooperation with local retail guilds such as New York's Uptown Retail Annex Guild, Michigan Avenue Guild of Chicago, Minneapolis Fashion Guild,

Figure 5.2 Fashion Originators' Guild of America inaugural announcement. "To Bring Back the Demand for Good Clothes," *Women's Wear Daily*, March 29, 1932, 9.

and Ladies' Ready-to-Wear Guild of Baltimore, Inc., as the cooperation of retail guilds was considered "essential to an equitable and practical relationship between manufacturers and retailers."[15] In 1933 the FOGA expanded its program to individual retailers throughout the United States.[16] According to the FOGA, cooperating retailers willingly and voluntarily subscribed to the Guild policy of elimination of style piracy. It is to be noted, however, that the FOGA members sold their merchandise only to stores that cooperated with them. Depending on the source, the FOGA members supplied from 12 to 64 percent of the women's garments sold in the New York area. Thus, retailers that wished to carry FOGA member merchandise faced pressure to follow the guild's program.

The guild program operated nationwide, including larger cities such

Figure 5.3 Advertisement promoting exhibition of guild members. *Women's Wear Daily*, March 6, 1933, 10.

as New York, Philadelphia, Washington, DC, Chicago, Boston, Los Angeles, San Francisco, Pittsburgh, Milwaukee, Cleveland, Baltimore, Detroit, St. Louis, Minneapolis, Dallas, and Kansas City. Even retailers in smaller cities such as Troy, New York; Scranton, Pennsylvania; Springfield, Massachusetts; St. Petersburg, Florida; New Orleans; Madison, Wisconsin; and Fresno, California, were included in the guild's program. By 1933, some of the better-known stores that agreed to cooperate with the Guild were Abercrombie & Fitch Co., B. Altman, Bergdorf Goodman, Bloomingdale Bros., Wm Filene's Sons Co., Hattie Carnegie Retail, Jay-Thorpe, Jo Copeland, John Wanamaker, Lord & Taylor, R. H. Macy & Co., and Nettie Rosenstein. Notices of FOGA membership appeared within advertisements for member department stores and labels, such as Amelia Earhart's

Knock It Off • 104 •

Figure 5.4 Amelia Earhart designs registered with the FOGA and the National Recovery Administration, with a listing of stores at the left. *Vogue*, September 15, 1934, 20.

Figure 5.5 The FOGA had its own section in this issue of *WWD*. "The Fashion Originators' Guild Section," *Women's Wear Daily*, March 6, 1933, sec. 2, 1–20.

short-lived aviation-inspired designs (Figure 5.4).[17] Members paid a $250 initiation fee and $10 in weekly dues.[18] The collaboration of the larger and more powerful retail associations, such as the National Retail Dry Goods Association and the Associated Merchandising Corporation (AMC), was avoided as the department store members feared FOGA plans would exert undue control over their products and prices.[19] According to Albert Post, executive director of the guild, these larger groups would not be as interested in the problems of piracy as the original founders and members of the FOGA, designers and manufacturers of "better," higher-priced merchandise.

The FOGA advertised to such a degree in the early 1930s that it was difficult to turn a page of *Women's Wear Daily* without seeing either a pro-

Figure 5.6 FOGA-registered dress worn as a wedding dress by Ann Meany Appleton, October 29, 1938. Courtesy Missouri Historic Costume and Textile Collection, The University of Missouri.

motional message from the guild or the joint advertising of the Guild with fellow antipiracy guilds and member retail and manufacturing shops. In March 1933 *Women's Wear Daily* ran an entire section of more than twenty pages devoted to the Fashion Originators' Guild (Figure 5.5). From 1932 to 1936, the Guild was everywhere within the pages of the trade press, with multiple ads, notices of guild-sponsored fashion shows, and full-page announcements of their work "safeguarding the market's stability."[20] They even sponsored what they termed "Fashion Week," a showing of dresses from member "creators."[21] The guild even permeated regional market reports in such segments as junior wear and evening wear as reported in *Women's Wear Daily*.

The FOGA was divided into the following sections: the dress division, composed of manufacturers of ladies' dresses; the coat division, composed of manufacturers of ladies' coats; the junior miss division, composed of manufacturers of junior miss dresses; and the sportswear division, composed of manufacturers of knitted ladies sportswear (Figure 5.6).[22]

The FOGA also included a textile and fabric division named the National Federation of Textiles, Inc., comprising one hundred textile manufacturers, converters, dyers, and printers of silk and rayon used in making women's wear. The federation maintained a department known as the Industrial Design Registration Bureau. Garment-manufacturing members refused to purchase textiles from manufacturers that did not register their designs with the bureau.

The Protective Affiliate division was made up of nonmember ladies' garment manufacturers that cooperated in the style protective program of the Guild, including the Dress Creators' League of America, which produced dresses starting at $10.50 wholesale. The affiliate members registered their styles for design protection with the FOGA, but were in lower price points than what the FOGA protected. The FOGA did not initially encourage extension to lower prices, as Albert Post maintained it would have been too complicated to have too many members in different branches of the industry. Rentner even tried to encourage Parisian couturiers to draft a code with the FOGA to "minimize harmful and cheap copying as well as premature exploitation of adaptations of Paris." The cooperation of the Wholesale Fashion Trades Association of London was also sought.[23] Neither of these attempts at international cooperation was successful.

To facilitate a program to "confront the demoralizing and destructive practice in the trade, known as style piracy," the Guild's design registration bureau included submission of sketches (Figure 5.7).[24] Registration of original designs was an easy process. Manufacturers submitted a slip of paper with a sketch and brief description of their design, and signed an affidavit of originality. The design was assigned a serial number by the guild, stamped with the Guild's logo, and dated to establish priority so that the originator could have exclusive retail rights. Sketches were not cross-referenced or compared with other registered designs, and sketches were

Knock It Off • 108 •

Figure 5.7 Herbert Sondheim sketch registered with the FOGA. Courtesy Special Collections, Gladys Marcus Library, Fashion Institute of Technology.

returned to the manufacturer. Any alleged copies identified in stores were dealt with by an arbitration committee. Protection lasted for six months, in effect closer to three months as it generally took no longer for anything new to go out of style. The Guild estimated that members and affiliates registered forty thousand to fifty thousand styles a year, and about half of these styles were in the price range of $16.75 and up.[25]

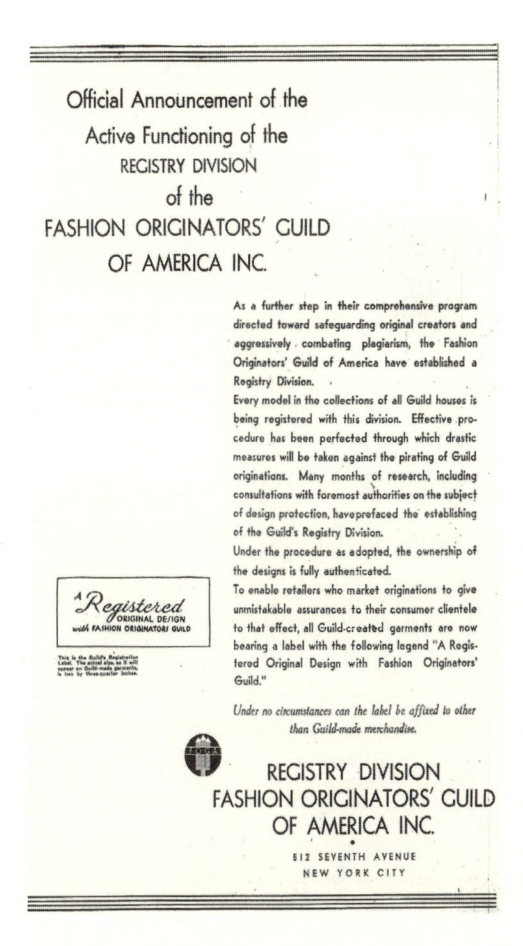

Figure 5.8 Announcement of the Registry Division of the FOGA with a sample label. Note the label is slightly different from the one appearing in Figure 4.6. "Official Announcement of the Active Functioning of the Registry Division of the FOGA," *Women's Wear Daily*, August 3, 1933, 3.

Foreign models and licensed copies of foreign designs were not subject to registration. The Guild maintained that there was a difference between the use of Paris importations as a basis for adaptations and the copying of designs of a dress created by members of the Guild. Albert Post, executive director of the guild, maintained Paris couturiers made it a business to create dresses for the specific purpose of showing their ideas to the manufacturers of the world that paid a fee for the privilege and right to adapt the design themes to an American clientele. Style pirates, on the other hand, without authorization or consent or payment of any fee, copied in detail the original designs of Guild members. While most higher-end designers frequented Paris for inspiration, others agreed with Elizabeth Hawes, who stated there was no need for her to consult with Paris "for her next move."[26]

Once registered, manufacturers obtained labels for their designs that read, "A Registered Original Design with Fashion Originators' Guild of America" or "An Original Design Registered by a member of the Fashion Originators' Guild" (Figure 5.8). These labels cost fifty cents each. An August 1933 report indicated more than eight thousand labels a day were ordered; in 1936, the Guild maintained that sales of labels averaged five hundred thousand to 1.1 million per month.[27] In a later court hearing regarding the Guild's practices, the presiding judge stated, these labels "came to have a definite significance as indicating that the dresses bearing the label represented quality merchandise manufactured according to original designs by skilled workers."[28]

To protect original designs, the Guild enacted a set of agreements known as the Declaration of Cooperation between manufacturers and retailers. This statement read in part: "This order is placed upon the seller's warranty that the above garments are not copies of original styles created by members of the Fashion Originators' Guild of America."[29] The Declaration of Cooperation was a signed agreement that retailers would not knowingly or intentionally purchase copied merchandise and that the retailer would return to the manufacturer any copies bought through misrepresentation or error. The Guild employed secret investigative shoppers who searched member and nonmember stores for supposed copies of merchandise. Alleged copies were removed from retail stores and evaluated by a mediation board named the Impartial Retail Arbitration Committee on Style Piracy, which consisted of one person chosen by the FOGA, one by the alleged copyist, and the third agreed upon by the two. Potential panelists were buyers, retail store owners, and merchandise managers.[30] Those retailers that refused to remove items deemed copies from the sales floor were "red-carded" by the Guild. Red-carding, not dissimilar to blacklisting, was a system for labeling stores that promoted copying, failed to protect design, or were found consistently in violation of FOGA policy in some other manner.

Once a month, the Guild sent a list of all noncooperating, red-carded merchants to member retailers and manufacturers. Guild members were instructed to show, sell, and ship merchandise only to those department and specialty stores that acted in full collaboration with the signed Declaration of Cooperation. Rentner maintained that to curb plagiarism and to restore consumer confidence, the unprecedented yet "thoroughly feasible step" of red-carding was necessary.[31] It was estimated that by February 1936 more than $500,000 worth of orders were held back by manufacturing members and that more than four hundred retailers had been red-carded by the FOGA, with more than one hundred manufacturers also stigmatized.[32] Red-carded retailers operated in states from New York to California, from Wisconsin to Texas. Some of the red-carded retailers included Abraham & Strauss, New York; Bloomingdale Brothers, New York; Filene's of Boston; Dayton Company, Minneapolis; Ed. Schuster Company, Milwaukee; J. L. Hudson Company, Detroit; R. H. White and Co., Boston; Strawbridge and Clothier, Philadelphia; and The Hub, Baltimore.[33] Violating members were fined from $100 to $5,000 and were not allowed to return to the FOGA for a period of six months. Repeat offenders were expelled from the guild. In a move to counteract the impact of the red-card ban by the Guild, the AMC made a collection of thirty imported models together with supplemental fashion sketches available to AMC retailers, including R. H. White and Co. and Strawbridge and Clothier. While the AMC had imported models in the past for the use of manufacturers, the executive director of the organization considered this a more extensive collection and an experiment in inspiring AMC-related manufacturers. There were no restrictions on the sale of the garments created from these models.[34]

The timing of the FOGA's programs brought it under the scrutiny of the National Industrial Recovery Act, passed in 1933. Title I of the act led to the creation of the National Recovery Administration (NRA), which gave the force of law to any "code of fair competition" set up as a trade association.[35] Under the NRA, the design piracy problem was worked out in the code of each separate industry, and no uniform design code was established. Participants of the NRA's Hearing on the Codes of the Dress Industry included key FOGA proponents, such as Maurice Rentner, chairman of the FOGA; Samuel Zahn, chairman of the Dress Creators' League of America; and Irene Blunt, executive secretary of the National Federation of Textiles and sometimes called the "first lady of design protection." Although the Supreme Court found the National Industrial Recovery Act unconstitutional in May 1935, the diverse perspectives concerning the concepts of originality, adaptation, and copying relative to design piracy brought the problem to the national stage and provided critical insight into the attitudes of leading apparel insiders, as well as the arguments for and against control of piracy.

Chapter 6

Design Protection Arguments

As the FOGA began to exert an influence on and attempt to control the copying process, arguments both for and against style piracy were heatedly debated in the trade and popular press, as well as in legal, business, and intellectual property journals and at the National Recovery Administration's Code of Fair Conduct hearings.[1] Supporters of design piracy regulation believed the practice detrimentally affected all individuals involved in the production and consumption process. As long as a design remained exclusive (protected against imitations), its creators and sellers would reap the profits of innovation.[2] According to Maurice Rentner, the "devastating evils growing from the pirating of original designs" destroyed the interests of manufacturer, retailer, consumer, and laborer.[3] Success in marketing clothing, especially some styles of women's clothing, had become so speculative as to be comparable "to playing the stock market," a damning sentiment, particularly so soon after the stock market crash of 1929.[4] Proponents such as higher-priced dress manufacturers believed style protection would eliminate "the ever-present fear which exists today that to create new ideas is only to furnish one's competitors with added material for carrying on their campaign of style piracy and price slashing."[5]

Those industry members opposing style protection argued that the entire fashion industry would be hurt by style protection and that regulation against piracy was in the best interest of only the higher-priced manufacturers. They contended that frequent turnover of styles, caused by copying, accounted for the sizable volume of business achieved by the ready-to-wear apparel industry. Manufacturers opposed to style protection were concerned that it would destroy their ability to create fashionable garments at cheap prices. It was, after all, their purpose to turn the latest high-fashion, high-price styles into garments that lower-income consumers could afford.

Figure 6.1 Advertisement "shouting value" for the price-conscious consumer. *Women's Wear Daily*, November 1, 1932, 9.

Arguments both for and against piracy were often contradictory and generally fell into one of two broad areas: enforcement and cost-benefit perspectives. The former hinged on the logistical matters of determining which garments were originals, adaptations, and copies. The latter perspectives were multifaceted, as they raised issues that involved price, quality, consumers' access to fashion, and the relationships between manufacturers, workers, and retailers. One thing was clear: piracy accelerated during the Depression as women looked in earnest for "value" (Figure 6.1).[6]

Enforcement

The matter of enforceability was the most fertile field for criticism of the FOGA. Those in opposition contended that a broad plan for style protection would be so burdensome as to be wholly impracticable, the enforcement of property rights near impossible. In the dress industry alone there could be more than one million styles registered as original each year. Even if a dress design could be declared an original, an adaptation, or a copy, there was no proof that exclusive rights given to a design would result in greater profit than if piracy "killed" a design.[7]

Supporters of copying asserted that protection would cause greater industry problems than allowing piracy to continue unchecked. If designs were protected, manufacturers would be slowed down in the creative process trying to prove originality and avoid possible infringements. Further, violations would be innumerable, some deliberate, but others innocent because of simultaneous origination of styles by different individuals. Those in the industry who supported piracy worried that the complexities of the arguments concerning original garments versus adaptations would be lost in design protection legislation. Ultimately, they feared, the fair determination of original goods would be as "unworkable as liquor prohibition."[8]

Cost-Benefit Perspectives

The cost-benefit perspectives regarding design piracy frequently revolved around the topics of price and quality. In the 1937 appeal within the US Circuit Court of Appeals, *Wm Filene's Sons Co. v. FOGA*, Justice Wilson ruled in favor of the FOGA, stating, "Copying destroys the style value of dresses which are copied. Women will not buy dresses at a good price at one store if dresses which look about the same are offered for sale at another store at half those prices. For this reason, copying substantially reduces the number and amount of reorders which the original creators get."[9]

As copies inundated the various price lines of the dress industry, higher-priced merchandise was knocked off and "killed."[10] The "pernicious practice of piracy" was said to contribute "substantially to the bankruptcy of many concerns engaged in original style creation."[11] Copies of successful lines could be sold at lower prices than the original dress lines because copyists saved money on research and development and avoided the pitfalls of producing unsuccessful lines (Figure 6.2). This led to loss of incentive to create and invest in designing original goods. Many manufac-

• 115 • Design Protection Arguments

VIONNET'S collarless coat for spring
•
a replica by CAROLYN

Vionnet—in an unusually inspired creative mood—designs a coat of unmistakable spring importance. The Carolyn committee of over 65 nationally known stylists has been traditionally exacting in making this Carolyn copy follow the original in every detail, since its charm is determined by its detail—by the width of the lapels with their rows of stitching, the choice of patent leather belt and flower, the subtle line of the silhouette. Carolyn keeps faith with Vionnet even so far as to import a beautiful cloth for it.

CAROLYN MODES
ARE CONSERVATIVELY PRICED
Frocks and Gowns, $29.50, $39.50, $49.50. Coats, $39.50, $49.50, $69.50. Ensembles, $25.00, $39.50, $49.50. Junior Frocks, $25.00. Junior Coats, $39.50, $49.50. Hand bags, $5.00 and $7.50. Carolyn Underwear and Hosiery in a range of prices.

Send For Style Booklet: National Modes, Inc.
128 West 31st Street, New York City

Carolyn

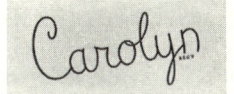

Figure 6.2 This advertisement for a replica Vionnet collarless coat contends it follows "the original in every detail," from the silhouette to the width of the lapel and patent leather belt. Even the fabric was imported. However, the prices were "conservative" and undoubtedly much less than the Vionnet original. *Vogue*, February 15, 1931, 14.

turers did not want to spend money on design costs when copying was so easy and profitable.[12]

In addition to saving money on the cost of designers, those who sold pirated designs often used fabrics and trims of poorer quality than those used by the higher-priced manufacturers. According to Irene Blunt, director of the Textile Design Registration Bureau of the Silk Association, copyists saved on production costs through cheap fabrics, "by making it [the garment] of less satisfactory construction, by using cheaper dyers, and printers."[13] F. Eugene Ackerman, president of the Forstmann Woolen Company of New Jersey, went so far as to say that design piracy had made it necessary for textile manufacturers to make cheaper merchandise to meet the prices dictated by style pirates. He indicated that piracy had so ruined the textile industry that "legitimate manufacturers and merchants today are obligated to advertise and guarantee against shoddiness."[14]

Speaking tangentially about pirated goods in 1934, Ruth O'Brien, chief of the Division of Textiles and Clothing of the Bureau of Home Economics within the US Department of Agriculture, commented on the quality problem in the 1930s apparel industry. She stated,

> One fact which seems to stand out clearly is that many consumers have money and need to buy but are very skeptical about getting their money's worth. It is chiefly because consumers have no measure of quality that they are misled into buying inferior products, often with the result that inferior goods drive superior goods off the market.[15]

Supporters of piracy regulation, such as New York dress manufacturer John Keating, believed that if manufacturers competed in terms of quality rather than the chiseling of prices, retailers would "have a more decent existence, [make a more] legitimate profit by changing a dress design a little so he does not kill the sale of the other man, and will not have to sweat his labor."[16] The protection of designs would eliminate rapid design changes, which in turn would lengthen the seasons of operations and avoid wastes resulting from the fast turnovers.[17] The assumption was that if styles were protected, women would once again purchase higher-quality (and more expensive) garments. In addition, women would save time, money, and energy purchasing goods less sensitive to fickle fashion change. According to supporters of style protection, great waste resulted from the purchase of poor-quality merchandise because women had to replace their clothing more often. And, rather than purchasing expensive goods of high-quality materials that might not sell to consumers, retailers ordered cheap imitations of the popular, expensive garments. Even when buyers took quality of the garments into consideration, consumers often "drifted away from quality original merchandise" due to price.[18]

In interesting counterarguments, some retailers believed women purchased lower-priced goods not because of the ability of pirates to mimic current designs at lower quality, but because there were actually few differences between higher-priced and lower-priced garments. Ernest Siegel, general merchandise manager for B. Siegel Co., declared that the increased bankruptcy of higher-priced firms was caused not by piracy, but rather by the general quality of merchandise. During the 1920s, better quality goods were often made of silk and lesser-quality merchandise in rayon. In the 1930s, more dresses in all price ranges were made of rayon. Thus many began to place blame for the consumer's choice of lower-cost dresses directly on the better quality manufacturers. Nathan Ohrbach of the Ohrbach Department Stores stated, "This store is glad to return merchandise which the Guild adjudges to be copies, but I feel I ought to point out that in certain cases recently I liked the copies better than the originals."[19] Bina Patterson, better dress buyer at the Ernst Kern Co., also blamed the higher-priced manufacturers for their own problems. She declared there was a "need for more value built into the higher priced merchandise and faster production so the manufacturer of the cheaper merchandise will not be able to get his line ready for shipment before the better dress manufacturer."[20] H. Stanley Marcus, executive vice president of Neiman-Marcus Co., argued that the better dress houses had a responsibility to improve the intrinsic value of their products. Stating that fashion was the lifeblood of the garment trades, Marcus believed that better materials needed to be used in garments from $22.50 and up. Dresses made of the same fabric in several different price ranges discouraged consumers from buying higher-priced garments, more so than piracy alone.[21]

Consumers' Entitlement to Fashion

Although styles changed rapidly in the twentieth century, the very concept of fashion encouraged women to dress in a similar manner. No silhouette or style detail could be fashionable if it weren't copied and imitat-

Figure 6.3 An illustration demonstrating the economic essence of Ida Tarbell's statement showing the high-cost "original" down to lower-cost derivatives. "Piracy on the High Fashions," *Vogue*, July 1, 1933, 28.

ed (Figure 6.3). Improvements in the technical proficiency and the rapid adoption of ready-to-wear apparel tended to create clothing with "gross similarity and subtle differences in fashion."[22] Even when style variations were numerous, only a few garment trends would become fashionable. This idea was supported by a 1930 estimate by authors Roy Sheldon and E. Arens that of the thousands of models presented by the Parisian haute couture in one season, about two hundred found acceptance in the United

States, with only twenty copied by US manufacturers in all price ranges.[23]

Scholars have stated that stylistic similarities in fashion during the early twentieth century were attributable in part to the culture of consumption. The historian William Leach described the availability of fashion to consumers of all economic levels as a key feature of the success of department stores in this period. The vast availability of ready-to-wear clothing was the primary reason for what Claudia Kidwell and Margaret Christman defined as the democratization of fashion, a process that tended to blur class lines. But, while social class was perhaps more fluid in the United States than in Europe, there was still a clearly demarcated leisured society in the United States that showed their wealth through possessions. For the middle class attempting to present the appearance of success, there was also a desire for stylish apparel. In addition, a growing contingent of women who worked outside of the home also wanted fashionable clothing.[24] With the availability of similar styles at all price points, women were more able to afford and had more opportunities for participation in fashion exchange.

Design piracy allowed reproductions of goods to diffuse to all economic levels. This presumably led to the democratization of style by allowing women of all classes to wear the latest fashion, even if it wasn't in the highest quality. It was also assumed that piracy provided women of lower income fashionable clothing that did not set them apart from their wealthier sisters; thus, it served a "socially useful form of business competition."[25] According to those who opposed style regulation, if piracy were prohibited, class differentiation would become visible, and dress could become a "badge of class distinction."[26] By contrast, the rapid dissemination of styles in all price ranges allowed sometimes uncomfortable comparisons between the dress of wealthier women and that of working women even in the early years of the ready-to-wear industry. As one 1906 observer exclaimed, "How these working girls do dress! Why the children uptown dress no better than that!"[27]

Those opposed to protection stated that consumers had a legitimate interest in obtaining copied merchandise. They pointed out that in 1934, about 80 percent of the public purchased in the "popular priced" departments—that is, the lower price points.[28] It was assumed that with style regulation, current fashions would be unavailable to lower-income consumers until the fashion's popularity was exhausted by more wealthy citizens. Opponents feared that women accustomed to purchasing stylish merchandise at cheap prices would rebel against purchasing lower-priced merchandise not exactly in fashion, especially if it were indeed a "badge" that distinguished them from their wealthier sisters. Some worried that women might revert to the practice of home dressmaking with consequent damaging effects to the dress industry.[29]

According to Kenneth Hutchinson, writing in 1940 in *The Harvard Business Review*, "Those who complain about copying fail to realize that without the social process of imitation, the lucrative business of fashion could not exist."[30] He continued, "Desirable styles, must, of course, be imitations." The entire fashion cycle meant that there were originators and followers that copied the leader. Styles that became popular soon became commonplace and were then abandoned. The entire process of fashion necessitated new, or at least slightly new looks. The fashion writer Elizabeth Hawes expressed in her 1938 book *Fashion Is Spinach*, the irony of yearning for new items differentiated from past offerings only in the smallest detail:

> All the filling in is done on the same basic patterns. . . . It is the proud boast of some wholesalers that they make up a whole line with only three dress patterns. The newness, so loudly called for, is new trimming, new collars and cuffs, new glass buttons, new flowers, and all of this, not too new, please.[31]

For discriminating consumers, piracy prevented them from purchasing original designs with any assurance that the garment would not be copied and the uniqueness immediately ruined. Those who favored protection believed women who could afford better quality would become dissatisfied with the original when they saw copies and would be frustrated with the retailer that sold her the design.[32] Consumers would return the original higher-priced garment to the retailer and thus lower the net profit and decrease the number of reorders the original manufacturer would receive. According to Clay Meyers, a manufacturer, the optimal retail situation in terms of profit was to have a dress sell so well that a reorder would be placed. If retailers had to survive the "constant turnover in styles with the odds and ends that are left, the markdowns which we take to meet competition on the next corner, in the next block," they would be unable to compete.[33] The belief of manufacturers of higher-priced goods was that more expensive, yet original garments would prove unsalable if cheaper imitations were available. Some consumers were grateful to be able to purchase the cheap imitation in their price range, but others would not want the higher-quality original garment if cheaper variations were also available. This was primarily because quality was becoming less of a factor in many women's buying decisions, in favor of newness.

Samuel Zahn, chairman of the Dress Creators' League of America, a group of ladies' dress manufacturers with wholesale prices from $10.75 to $16.75, represented a midpriced group of manufacturers that supported regulation (Figure 6.4). In testifying before the NRA on its Code of Fair Practice and Competition in the women's dress industry, Zahn was asked whether he or members of his league "ever considered the fact of design piracy from the consumers' viewpoint, that is, why should not the stenographer or the shop girl wear a dress just as beautiful as the society leader?" Zahn replied, "Dresses of a $3.75 design and style or $2.85 can be prettier than a dress that sells at $10.75." He continued that members of the Dress Creators' League of America

> came to the conclusion that the people who buy $3, $4, $6, $7 merchandise are entitled just as much to originality as the people who buy $50, $60, or $100 merchandise.... There is no reason why a woman of limited means should not have originality in her dress as well as the woman who paid a large amount of money.[34]

Zahn also stated that the stenographer should not feel embarrassment if met in the street by a women wearing the same dress as she, but bought in a different price bracket, either higher or lower. Indeed, women who bought lower-priced dresses probably did not want to see other women wearing the same exact design any more than did those women who purchased higher-priced apparel. However, inherent in the dynamic of fashion transmission is the natural desire to emulate women of higher socioeconomic classes. Samuel Hartman, legal counsel for the Popular Priced Dress Manufacturers Group, stated that any legislation against piracy:

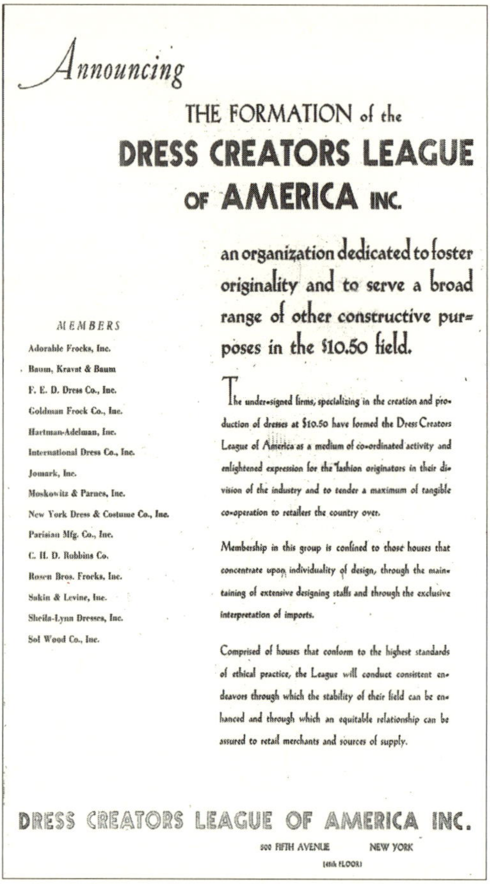

Figure 6.4 Announcement of the formation of the Dress Creators' League of America, Inc. *Women's Wear Daily,* December 1, 1932, 14.

Would spell death. . . . The masses of American women have always demanded and received styles that are comparable with those worn by their richer sisters. [Legislation] is seeking to deprive Judy O'Grady of her just right to dress as well for little money as does the colonel's lady. Passage of style registration would create a monopoly for a handful of stylists who cater to women of means. It must be defeated in the interests of progress and in consideration of the 93 out of 100 who have little money to spend for clothes.[35]

Much of the commentary throughout these arguments about what the consumer did or did not want was based on supposition. There appeared to have been few attempts to actually determine consumers' true desires in regards to pirated merchandise.

The Industry Perspective

Both supporters of the copying process as essential to the industry and opponents who considered it design piracy fervently voiced their opinions regarding piracy's impact upon the apparel industry. These included apparel manufacturers, retailers, and those in the apparel labor force. Within each group, opinions existed on both sides of the debate.

The Industry: Manufacturers

Apparel manufacturers may have had the most strident voices in the design piracy debate. Apparel manufacturing was not like that of other goods. Firms entering the business of dress manufacturing could lack all of the necessary ingredients for success except one: the hope of the owner that the firm could create a popular style, or "number," that captured the public's imagination. In other, less fashion-oriented manufacturing industries with standardized products, capital requirements were much greater. These firms needed to maintain large production plants and consistently seek improvements in technical efficiencies.[36]

According to supporters of design protection, "originating" companies spent money to develop, produce, and experiment with the salability of original goods. Because styles were quickly copied, original manufacturers needed to constantly revise their creations, generating slight variations of previous models. Piracy promoted the production of small inventories of ever-changing merchandise. In their 1936 study of design piracy and its treatment under the NRA's codes of conduct, A. C. Johnston and Florence Fitch stated, "Manufacturing became a series of sprints between originators to make and sell their dresses and pirates to quickly copy the style of each popular dress, followed by slack periods in which all waited for another popular style to be developed."[37]

The practice of piracy afforded manufacturers and designers at all price levels the opportunity to profit from others' work. Those who spent the time, effort, and money to create original garments would see their profits diluted when imitators created similar goods in lower prices. One pirated manufacturer asserted that only about two out of the one hundred dresses in a sample line were successful and that when these styles were copied his business was damaged. Furthermore, he needed these two dresses to sell to have any hope of recovering the research and development across the board for all one hundred garments.[38] According to Zahn, original manufacturers needed approximately twenty to twenty-five new styles per week in order to stay ahead of design pirates, seeming to indicate that all business models were calculated on the practice of piracy.[39] Other manufacturers described a work environment that demanded as many as fifteen hundred new models a year, causing dependence on copying for "sources of design."[40] Of the thousands of styles created, perhaps only a few would prove successful. Herbert Sondheim, FOGA vice president and women's dress manufacturer, claimed that the fast-moving tempo of the fashion world and "excessive acceleration of style will very often kill the goose that lays the golden egg."[41]

Supporters of protection argued that copyists caused unfair trade practices, that they profited from the hard work of originators and then undersold these same originators. According to New York State Assemblyman Meyer Alterman, who introduced a style protection measure for the women's dress industry in 1935,

> Very often a great many styles and designs are created and are then discarded by the manufacturer for a style that would meet with wider approval, and after all of this experimental stage has been completed and great expenses incurred, the manufacturer finds that some irresponsible concern has pirated this particular design or style and floods the market with a very cheap grade of merchandise, thereby greatly reducing the value or demand for the original design.[42]

According to members of the Dress Creators' League of America, "Devotion to high ethics and maintenance of finest merchandise standards must be accepted as the only safeguard to longevity in this industry of tremendous turnover of firms and individuals."[43] Rather than frantically producing new style variations, manufacturers could rely on the merits of their production and extensively reproduce successful styles. Sondheim contended, "Nothing can kill consumer interest in fashion more than a too-rapid descent in price in too short a period of time. Your customers and salespeople almost simultaneously lose an essential enthusiasm when a trend of fashion finds itself featured in basement departments before your customer upstairs has even had a chance to look at it."[44] The protection of original goods could decrease the number of firms that relied on copying to survive, and save the better, higher-priced firms from insolvency.[45]

Critics of style protection stated that the growth of the fashion industry was in fact due to the ability of lower-price manufacturers to supply affordable, fashionable merchandise to consumers. It was further argued that copyists did not destroy markets for apparel but rather created them, since the demand for new goods stimulated the fashion cycle. Hutchinson argued, "There must be copies if there are to be fashions, and as long as there is a strong consumer demand among those of lower purchasing power for styles, there will be someone ready to satisfy it."[46]

Lower-price manufacturers also pointed out the economic infeasibility of employing designers to create original merchandise. As stated by one *Women's Wear Daily* fashion writer, Chas Call, originals in lower prices "would be nice," but the main purpose of these firms was "to bring out some nice copies of slightly higher priced dresses." He contended that when manufacturers attempted to "be original" at the $4.75 level, their retailers weren't interested; they just wanted "some good copies that could be sold at a generous markup."[47]

The Industry: Retailers

Retailers, like manufacturers, were not in unison on the issue of piracy, split largely according to the price point of their merchandise. According to those who desired protection from piracy, copying was a heavy burden on retailers. Primarily, style piracy encouraged retailers to adopt a hand-to-mouth buying approach from manufacturers. Orders were small and many retailers hesitated to reorder garments, as anything fashionable would be quickly copied in lower price levels. If retailers did stock a number of dresses in a particular style, there was always the risk that copies would saturate the market. If retailers could not sell their merchandise due to piracy (nor return them to the manufacturer), prices were marked down at an economic loss. In a speech in honor of Maurice Rentner's leadership of the FOGA, Boston department store president P. A. O'Connell stated piracy cost the department stores 9.6 percent of their net sales and cost specialty stores 11 percent. While it is difficult to know what the expected rate of loss would be without piracy, O'Connell indicated that "if we can curb the copying and bootlegging of styles, we shall have removed a very substantial part of the markdown loss."[48]

Piracy also caused problems for retailers if consumers who had purchased an original garment later viewed a copy of it at another store at a lower price. In the circuit court appeals case, *Wm Filene's Sons Co. v. FOGA*, Justice Wilson, ruling in favor of the FOGA, stated,

> Reputation for honesty, style, and service is an important asset of retailers. Copying often injures such a reputation. A customer who has bought a dress at one store and later sees a copy of it at another store at a lower price is quite likely to think that the retailer from whom she bought the dress lacks ability to select distinctive models and that she has been overcharged. Dresses are returned and customers are lost.[49]

Even within one department store, individual sectors complained about piracy. A buyer in Pittsburgh stated that in her high-fashion division a linen suit was selling for $29.95, when in the sportswear division an almost identical copy was offered for $14.95. Ultimately, the sportswear buyer returned the remainder of the merchandise to the manufacturer, leaving the item to be promoted exclusively by the better dress buyer. This did not solve the problem entirely, however, since other stores also carried the lower-priced option at an even lower price.[50] Sometimes before a "quality store" could receive merchandise, copies would appear at lower-priced stores. Indeed, piracy did not impact just the original creator of the garment, for other manufacturers copied the copy and the garment traversed the entire gamut of price ranges very quickly.

Those who wanted style protection believed that if garment designs were protected, retailers would be able to anticipate and order larger amounts of goods, thus saving time and money on cancelled orders, marked-down merchandise, and returns. These proponents argued that piracy caused cheap imitations of goods and that protection would eliminate inexpensive knockoffs, restoring customer loyalty and purchasing habits. The prohibition of copying, according to proponents, would allow for a greater diversification of products because manufacturers would have to create their own style ideas in garments. In light of the business failures caused by the Depression, supporters of protection argued that the diversity of garment styles created for specific price points would permit retailers ample opportunities to become more specialized, presumably creating niche markets less susceptible to business failure.[51]

Retailers who opposed style protection believed they would bear the burden of responsibility for enforcement. In most proposed style protection plans, including the FOGA's, retailers were required to discern pirated from original goods, purchasing only the novel ones. Irving Fox, counsel for the National Retail Dry Goods Association, stated the organization would only support proposed legislation or programs that included adequate methods to ascertain whether alleged originals were really originals and regulations that protected the rights of the retailer.[52]

The Industry: Labor

According to supporters of protection, piracy negatively impacted the interests of labor, from the most to the least skilled workers. It was argued that as price became the primary selling point to consumers, piracy proliferated, causing employees to be exploited. To save costs and to undercut other manufacturers and retailers, employees, when working, were paid minimal wages for long hours. Proponents of protection asserted that if piracy was stopped, manufacturers would need a more constant supply of goods and thus a more consistent labor force, rather than producing garments with only minor style variations and short bursts of seasonal employment.[53] This would result in better working conditions, including higher pay, for employees. Even New York City Mayor Fiorello H. LaGuardia stated, "The mistakes of the past have encouraged style piracy, which has resulted in an irregularity of employment among the skilled labor groups of New York City."[54]

According to the FOGA, twice the amount of labor was required to produce a garment retailing at $25 as one retailing at $15. They also contended there were six to ten more hours of actual workmanship in the preparation of a $75 dress than in one selling for $25. Therefore,

> The destruction, through plagiarism, is in reality, an attack upon labor's means to a livelihood. The manufacturer who engages in style thievery is wresting hours of needed employment from the workers in the trade. And the retailer who buys copied merchandise is aiding in thwarting the

efforts ... to reduce idleness and augment earnings.... It is a direct and serious loss to labor, when a consumer, who would otherwise buy a fifty dollar garment, is induced to purchase a fifteen dollar copy.[55]

According to Rentner, protection would afford employment to many thousands of dress workers in the United States apparel industry.[56]

Pirates utilized the products of a relatively small number of designers because companies copied established fashions rather than hiring designers to create new modes. With protection, it was asserted that the competent designers trained in vocational schools and colleges would find profitable work, and protection would reward creative expression.[57] Without the emphasis on stealing, copyists would be encouraged to create their own designs, stimulating the domestic fashion industry. Dress manufacturer Clay Meyers suggested piracy hurt designers and aspiring designers. He stated, "We have three colleges in Pittsburgh that are developing stylists, designers, technicians. Those girls will all be looking for something to do. The most pitiful thing in my experience is the great number that are coming in and looking for work, capable, excellent, clever people. I think piracy is narrowing down this field."[58]

The number of designers hired in the mid-1930s increased, which the writer Helen Everett Meiklejohn suggested was the direct result of design protection measures, as the lower-priced firms were forced to hire designers.[59] Conversely, some firms purchased designs from freelance designers, a practice that left the latter open to victimization. According to one unidentified designer, "Once seen, style ideas are so easily stolen that few free-lance designers are ever paid for all the creations they show to manufacturers."[60] With that said, the Design Creators' League of America, organized in 1934, issued a call to the FOGA that if so consulted they, the designers, could actually do something about eliminating design piracy. How they intended to do this they never made clear, nor were they heard from again in the trade or popular press pages. This perhaps speaks to the instability of employment evident in the apparel industry during this time, as workers frequently moved from firm to firm.

Others believed that piracy actually benefited labor by inducing a more rapid turnover of fashions and additional sales.[61] In stating the common arguments regarding piracy, Meiklejohn commented, "Imitation means the rapid obsolescence of design which stimulates invention, assures to the designer a market, and brings to the industry accelerated business all along the line."[62] The problem with this thought, however, was that a new idea might not be as popular as an established "hit." As stated by Ralph Brown, "a head-start confers an advantage" only to those who succeed and is "perceptible only by hindsight."[63] In other words, even if every firm in the industry originated its own designs, some firms would still go out of business.

The growth of American garment manufacturing meant firms copied other American companies rather than relying on the adaptations of the Parisian designs. With the advent of the Depression, this issue accelerated as the demand for lower-cost apparel rose. The creation of the FOGA meant an organization actively working to curb design piracy, leading to an increasingly determined and vocal group of industry professionals debating who benefited and who lost out from such practices. While some within the industry felt piracy was detrimental to all involved, from manufacturers to consumers, others felt piracy was the cause of rapid economic growth and development. The arguments both for and against piracy were contradictory, complex, highly subjective, and not easily resolved.

Almost no one in the apparel industry was without an opinion on the topic of design piracy, even if their opinion changed with time or was based solely on anecdotal evidence of personal experience. Piracy unarguably sped the transmission of fashion. To meet consumer demand for new goods, manufacturers were on a constant cycle of create, copy, create. Retailers stocked small amounts of goods, rather than carry large amounts of potentially unmarketable merchandise. Copying allowed style reproductions at all economic levels, thus women of vastly different economic means were able to wear similar styles. Within the lower price ranges piracy allowed diffusion of garment styles. In the higher price ranges, however, piracy prevented style exclusivity. In short, either piracy provided the public service of making the latest fashions available to all consumers or it destroyed the chance for style distinctiveness to be enjoyed by the relatively few who could afford it. Ultimately, all these arguments were used in both defending and decrying the practices of the FOGA when it sought to extend its influence in 1935.

Chapter 7

The Fashion Originators' Guild of America: Controversy and Defeat

By 1936, manufacturer membership in the FOGA numbered approximately two hundred and twenty-five, and retailers numbered twelve thousand individuals and corporations located throughout thirty-two of the United States. Most members clustered principally, however, in the major cities of New York, Chicago, and Boston, as well as in St. Louis.[1] According to Maurice Rentner, by 1940, the number of cooperating retailers reached an all-time high of twenty-five thousand.[2] While this would seem to indicate significant success for the Guild, there were also problems.

Despite their announcements and advertisements stressing protection of original goods, the Guild in 1935 faced claims that it did not adequately protect designers and manufacturers from piracy. When the FOGA filed a $120 injunction against the children's dress house Nathanson & Beck, Inc., for alleged refusal to pay the Guild dues of $10 a week, the company made a counterclaim of $570 in the Manhattan municipal court that the FOGA failed to protect them from style piracy and had "acted with intent to deceive and defraud the defendant."[3] The children's dress firm asserted that numerous complaints were made to the FOGA that others were pirating styles that it had designed, manufactured, and registered, but that the guild refused to take any steps to stop these actions. The FOGA won its suit with the counterclaim dismissed.[4] However, legal challenges against the Guild were just beginning.

New Regulations and Controversial Policies

Inspired by their successes, in April 1935 the Guild expanded its oversight over design piracy to include moderately priced lines wholesaling from $10.75 to $16.75. This change was supported by the Dress Creators' League of America, a group of ladies' dress manufacturers with wholesale prices in this targeted price range. Beginning in September 1935,

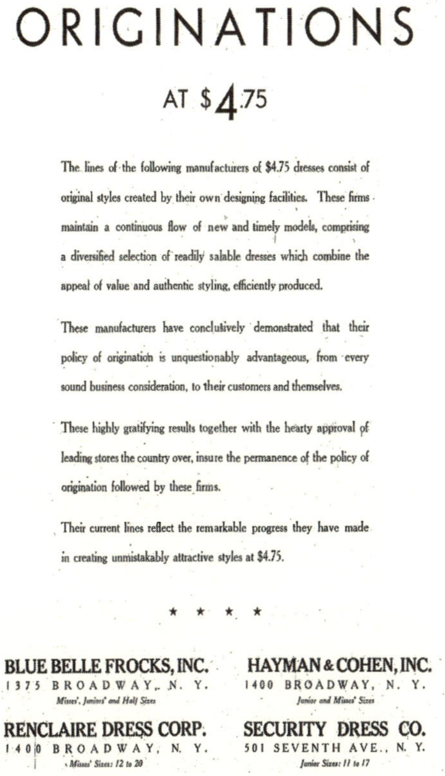

Figure 7.1 The extension of FOGA protection into the $4.75 field was adopted by few dress manufacturers. *Women's Wear Daily*, November 7, 1935, 5.

ORIGINATIONS
AT $4.75

The lines of the following manufacturers of $4.75 dresses consist of original styles created by their own designing facilities. These firms maintain a continuous flow of new and timely models, comprising a diversified selection of readily salable dresses which combine the appeal of value and authentic styling, efficiently produced.

These manufacturers have conclusively demonstrated that their policy of origination is unquestionably advantageous, from every sound business consideration, to their customers and themselves.

These highly gratifying results together with the hearty approval of leading stores the country over, insure the permanence of the policy of origination followed by these firms.

Their current lines reflect the remarkable progress they have made in creating unmistakably attractive styles at $4.75.

★ ★ ★ ★

BLUE BELLE FROCKS, INC.
1375 BROADWAY, N. Y.
Misses', Juniors' and Half Sizes

HAYMAN & COHEN, INC.
1400 BROADWAY, N. Y.
Juniors and Misses' Sizes

RENCLAIRE DRESS CORP.
1400 BROADWAY, N. Y.
Misses' Sizes: 12 to 20

SECURITY DRESS CO.
501 SEVENTH AVE., N. Y.
Junior Sizes: 11 to 17

---

changes in the Guild's policies raised alarms with retailers and low-price dress manufacturers, as the Guild extended protection to the $6.75 and $8.75 wholesale price lines. In October it expanded to lines as low as $4.75 (Figure 7.1). The Guild argued that because copying was rampant in all price divisions of the apparel trade and each successively lower "rung of the price ladder is attuned to await the launching of the next higher level before proceeding with its own collections," the FOGA was justified in extending its protection program.[5]

In late 1935, the FOGA issued new pledge cards, which asserted retailers would not purchase any copies regardless of price, including lines down to $1.75. The continued extension into lower and lower priced merchandise caused an uproar from nonmember manufacturers and retailers, buying syndicates, and others in the dress industry. The primary objection was that these firms existed to copy and adapt the designs of higher-priced dresses for the mass market. Further, the copies made in the lowest price brackets did not compete with the higher-priced goods due to changes in materials and production that made them adaptations and not necessarily exact copies.[6]

A decision to oppose the style registration system of the Guild on the basis that it was "monopolistic and illegal" was reached by members of the Popular Priced Dress Manufacturers Group, Inc. (PPDMG), an association of more than four hundred manufacturers of dresses wholesaling below $4.75. In an announcement in *Women's Wear Daily*, PPDMG stated, "This Association will continue to protect its members against any and all invasions of their moral and legal rights; [and] to safeguard their business investments against undue restrictions."[7] According to Ben Hirsch, a popular price manufacturer and the PPDMG chairman, the FOGA advocated "plain, pure and unadulterated boycott, intimidation, and duress."[8] The PPDMG issued a Declaration of Policy against the methods of the FOGA. The declaration stated, "whereas the FOGA improperly, ruthlessly, and with a total disregard of the public interest" brought about "grave injustices to the manufacturers of lower priced dresses," the PPDMG "resolved to unite and cooperate in preventing and resisting the FOGA in an attempt to foist upon the dress industry, such un-American trade principles as monopoly, boycott, price fixing, and other unfair methods of competition."[9] They refused to accept orders from retail merchants bearing the FOGA stamp (Figure 7.2) and pursued litigation against the FOGA. These steps would ultimately bring about the end of the guild.

Other groups such as the Merchandising Division of the National Retail Dry Goods Association, the Retail Dry Goods Association of New York, the Uptown Retail Guild, and the Associated Merchandising Corporation, as well as buying syndicates in St. Louis; Chicago; and Columbus, Ohio, also opposed the FOGA's "invasion" into the dress field priced below $10.75. These groups argued that agreement with the Guild's policies restricted trade. They suggested that the Guild's program would force businesses to gravitate away from New York to other manufacturing centers in Cleveland and Los Angeles, which did not have large FOGA memberships.[10]

Other changes that outraged industry groups included the Guild's attempts to formulate a code of fair trade practices that went beyond its

WE CANNOT AND WILL NOT ACCEPT ORDERS BEARING THE F.O.G.A. STAMP

We Believe Their Method Is Detrimental To Retailer and Manufacturer Alike

•

Popular Priced Dress Mfrs.' Group, Inc.
1440 BROADWAY, N. Y. C.   LOUIS RUBIN, Exec. Dir.

Figure 7.2 Popular Priced Dress Manufacturers Group, Inc., announcement that they will not go along with the FOGA protection plans. "A Statement by the Popular Priced Dress Mfrs.' Group, Inc.," *Women's Wear Daily*, February 27, 1936, 14.

initial objective of eliminating style piracy by "giving protection, support, and counsel to every group within the industry who honestly and competently creates designs."[11] The new regulations included the prohibition of members from conducting trade with any company not supported by the guild. Restrictions extended to include participating in retail advertising and selling at retail, as this extended business beyond manufacturing; and selling to businesses conducted in residences, residential quarters, hotels, or apartment houses, as these places of business were not originally included in the FOGA policy.[12] The Guild also sought the eradication of unwarranted returns and cancellations of merchandise. Further, the Guild employed auditors to inspect members' books to ensure they were not selling to red-carded retailers or violating any of the other regulations.[13]

Most retailers considered the Guild's activities an attempt to regulate and restrict trade practices in operating their stores. They argued that if they had to return $6.75 dresses copied from $10.75 models, it would be practically impossible to produce and sell low-priced dresses, since many manufacturers of these lines could not afford to pay designers or to buy original designs. Retailers contended that in the bitterly competitive apparel industry, protection could only mean ruin.

Lower-priced manufacturers further maintained that some of the cooperating retailers used the guild pledge as an excuse to return merchandise even if no copying was involved. The PPDMG claimed returns increased from 4 percent to 11 percent due to allegations of copying. The FOGA stated approximately twenty thousand dresses were returned to copyists during a three-month period in 1935, but that this figure represented an "infinitesimal" amount compared to the total number of dresses shipped.[14] The guild responded to the return complaint by devising a system that would make available a complete record of the returns of copied merchandise to guard against groundless returns of merchandise. In reaction, the PPDMG created a Dress Control Returns Bureau to act as an arbitrator between manufacturers and retailers regarding unjustifiable returns.[15]

The FOGA provisions, including the extensions into both lower-priced lines and fair trade practices, were viewed by an ever-broadening segment of the industry as "trampling upon the rights of others."[16] A 1936 report prepared by the National Retail Dry Goods Association found that 88 percent of the surveyed retailers believed the Guild should confine its activities to style protection only. Seventy-five percent of respondents indicated that the FOGA activities and original style protection program should be confined to merchandise costing $16.75 and more, and those dresses retailing for less than $10.75 should not be regarded for design protection.[17] The Guild reasserted that its fair trade practices were designed to protect the ethical retailer and manufacturer and rejecting its "stabilizing policies on discounts and returns and the question of style piracy regulation in cheaper goods is just a smoke screen."[18] It is probable that manufacturers and retailers were responding to the demand for cheap clothing and felt threatened by any actions that would limit their ability to supply those goods. Sylvan Gotshal, a longtime proponent of style protection, believed the Guild's principles of voluntary cooperation between manufacturers and retailers were sound, but predicted the attempts at coercion through red-carding amounted to "suicide" and would lead to the eventual collapse of the FOGA.[19]

Legal Battles

The Guild's extended efforts to put teeth into its campaign against piracy caused industry watchdogs, large retail associations, and the federal government to take notice. The FOGA was continually brought to court. In a typical case, the retailer Wolfenstein argued that under New York's Donnelly Act, the guild made unlawful contracts creating a monopoly in the manufacture or sale of goods. The FOGA countered that its tactics were necessary to restore order to the industry and that it did not create a monopoly: it never set prices for manufacturers or retailers, nor controlled or regulated the production of members, nor directed members with respect to the quality of materials used. The New York appellate court agreed with the guild that it had not intended to regulate prices or to control production, but had endeavored solely to stabilize and eliminate abuses within the women's dress industry.[20]

In March 1936, the US District Court of Massachusetts decided *Wm. Filene's Sons Co. v. FOGA*. Filene's maintained that the company reserved the right to copy styles that were already being so widely copied that its business would be impeded if it could not meet demand.[21] After Filene's was red-carded by the FOGA, orders the company had placed were not delivered due to Guild regulations. A Filene's representative stated in court that the red-carding prevented merchandise deliveries, which then led to a $90,000 decrease in sales over a two-month period. Further, the Guild program "had a severe effect on the morale of our people, not only the buyers, but to the selling force."[22] The red-carded retailer sought an injunction against the Guild under the Sherman and Clayton antitrust laws. The court found that since members were perfectly free to compete against themselves on price and were able to resign from the Guild, the FOGA was not in violation of federal antitrust acts. Although the red-carding limited the number of manufacturers from whom Filene's could buy, the court found there remained "substantial and reasonably adequate markets to which it could resort for the purchase of ready-to-wear dresses."[23] The

Guild's practices were upheld in three different courts: the New York Supreme Court, the United States District Court of Massachusetts, and the United States Circuit Court of Appeals, First Circuit. In the ruling of the court of appeals, Justice Elisha Brewster stated, "The object of the Guild and its members and affiliates was beneficial, rather than prejudicial, not only to the interests of the dress industry but as well to the interests of the public."[24]

In April 1936 the Federal Trade Commission (FTC) began hearings on the FOGA's practices. The FTC charged that the Guild suppressed competition and created a monopoly through combination and conspiracy. In theory, the guild did this by requiring members to register their designs with the Guild Registration Bureau, confining dress sales to retailers affiliated with the Guild, and coercing retailers into refusing to handle copied garments distributed by non-FOQA members. These tactics were reinforced by fines and boycotts, which the FTC claimed resulted in "the establishment of a virtual dictatorship . . . with serious hardship on members of the industry refusing to fly the Guild flag and has substantially increased the prices of ladies' garments."[25] After hearings held in New York, Massachusetts, Maryland, Pennsylvania, Michigan, Ohio, Illinois, and Minnesota, the FTC ordered the "combination known as the FOGA to cease and desist" from its monopolistic practices.[26] The verdict was bitterly contested and the fight was carried to the United States Circuit Court of Appeals, Second Circuit. Rentner cautioned that the ruling would have "a vital bearing on the fate of the style industries and whether the New York market will become the style center of the world or relapse into the chaos of unrestrained copying and piracy."[27] In deciding this case in favor of the FTC, Justice Learned Hand stated, "It may be unfortunate, it may indeed be unjust that the law should not therefore distinguish between 'originals' and copies; but until the Copyright Office can be induced to register such designs as copyrightable under the existing statute there was little that the courts could do to ensure design protection."[28] The Guild was found guilty of unfair practices: while the Guild's intention to suppress style piracy might be justifiable, it was determined that the means used were illegal. The FOGA regulations that were independent of the fight against copying were found to be most detrimental to participating retailers.

The FOGA petitioned the US Supreme Court in 1941 to review the decision of the US Second Circuit Court of Appeals. Rentner asserted the court would rule on two basic questions:

Is the right to employ ingenuity and skill in the pirating of styles given precedence by the Constitution over the right to utilize ingenuity and skill in the creation of original designs? Is the license of predatory parasitic elements to thwart progress and precipitate chaos in an industry more sacred under the nation's laws than the privilege of constructive factors to devote their talents and resources to the fostering of industrial decency and progress? We shall ask the Supreme Court to determine whether the welfare of a great industry shall be demoralized to make a style pirate's holiday.[29]

On March 3, 1941, Justice Hugo Black delivered the opinion of the court, agreeing with the decision of the FTC that the "purpose and object of the combination, its potential power, its tendency to monopoly, the coercion it could and did practice upon a rival method of competition, all brought it within the policy of the prohibition declared by the Sherman, Clayton, and Federal Trade Commission Acts."[30] He continued, "The power of the combination is great; competition and the demand of the consuming public make it necessary for most retail dealers to stock some of the products of these manufacturers. And the power of the combination is made even greater by reason of the affiliation of some members of the National Federation of Textiles, Inc."[31]

Justice Black declared,

> [The FOGA] narrows the outlets to which garment and textile manufacturers can sell and the sources from which retailers can buy, subjects all retailers and manufacturers who decline to comply with the Guild's program to an organized boycott, takes away the freedom of action of members by requiring each to reveal to the Guild the intimate details of their individual affairs and has both as its necessary tendency and as its purpose and effect the direct suppression of competition from the sale of unregistered textiles and copied designs. In addition to all this, the combination is in reality an extra-governmental agency, which prescribes rules for the regulation and restraint of interstate commerce, and provides extra-judicial tribunals for determination and punishment of violation, and thus "trenches upon the power of the national legislature and violates the statute."[32]

With that, the cease-and-desist order against the FOGA was upheld.

The FOGA outlined a new protection plan following the Supreme

Figure 7.3 Label from FOGA dress that indicates "U.S. Patent Applied For." Courtesy Missouri Historic Costume and Textile Collection, The University of Missouri.

Court's ruling. Albert Post, the executive director of the Guild, announced the plan at the ready-to-wear session of the National Retail Dry Goods Association summer convention. The new plan revoled around the idea that each member should secure patents on his or her designs (Figure 7.3).

These designs were to be limited to those that manufacturers and designers were sure were original, although how they would determine originality was never stated.[33] By basing protection on garments that were protected by the government, the FOGA believed it had "fairly and properly overcome former objections" regarding the originality of designs. Samuel Zahn patented hundreds of designs in the 1940s (Figure 7.4), while others patented few if any.

The new plan called for speedier adjudications of cases involving infringements of patented designs. The Guild program proposed prompt referrals of cases to court-appointed arbitrators or to an independent agency such as the American Arbitration Association. The FOGA envisioned cooperation of retailers through participation in a voluntary agreement to remove infringing copies from sale. The boycott provisions, or "red card" system, which ran afoul of federal laws, were eliminated from the new plan. However, the system of using the FOGA shopping staff to find infringements would continue. Nonparticipating stores that carried

Figure 7.4 Samuel Zahn dress patent, Patent No. 138,869. (1944).

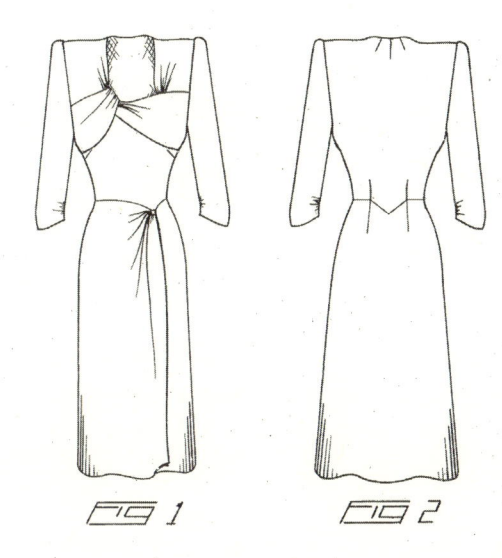

infringing copies of patented garments would be subject to suits seeking redress. To avoid legal troubles, Post stated the new plan would take into consideration retailers, and steps were being taken to "determine its complete legality in the eyes of both the Department of Justice and the Federal Trade Commission."[34]

The vagueness of this new plan carried none of the bite of the original protective measures of the FOGA. However, Herbert Sondheim, women's dress manufacturer and FOGA member, stated support:

> If we do not succeed collectively in reasonably protecting the rewards of fashion origination, so that trends may become fashion, and fashion in

turn may realize a profit, our entire ready-to-wear manufacturing industry will disintegrate and your retail ready-to-wear departments, which you have always said should be the backbone of your store, will be reduced to the status of those minor departments which are already a headache in retail.[35]

Others believed the new plans would be ineffective due to the limitations of the patent laws. Ernest Siegel, general merchandise manager for B. Siegel Company, stated:

Certainly there should be some sort of arrangement by which better dress departments are protected against cheap copies but it is very doubtful whether . . . any feasible solution of the problem can be found. I don't see how registration with the U.S. Patent Office would help. For at best it would take too long for patent protection to be granted to be of any use in the dress industry where a week may make all the difference in the world.

Nevertheless, numerous companies filed patent infringement suits with little success in the courts. While many were dismissed or settled out of court, some cases went to trial and some went further and were eventually settled on appeal. A significant problem, one that had been an issue from the beginning, was the difficulty in determining what constituted an original design. Issues arose when judges were forced to make decisions about minor changes in trims, decorations, and seam lines to determine what constituted "newness." In the end, judges frequently agreed with plaintiffs that their design had been copied. However, one of the critical issues raised was validity of the design patent in the first place, and many were determined to lack invention (Figure 7.5). Judge Inch, in the case of *White v. Lombardy Dresses, Inc.*, observed that the designer Syd Novak turned out "several hundred dress designs a year" and stated, "I believe that skilful [sic] dressmakers . . . cannot possibly find true invention, week after week, in considerable numbers, in the dressmaking industry, despite the fact that frequently a dress is produced . . . that is unusually attractive and is successful for the season for which it is made."[36]

With the difficulty of determining what constituted an original, even legal experts argued that legislative statutes were needed to help fashion designers. In one case, in which Flora Dress Company argued that Lea-

Figure 7.5 Design patent by Syd Novak for Flora Dress Company, determined to not meet the requirement of invention by Judge Inch. Patent No. 121,448. (1940).

nore Frocks manufactured and sold dresses that infringed upon the plaintiff's patents, Justice Learned Hand stated:

> There is little chance that valid design patents can be procured in any such number as to answer their demand. What they [original creators] need is rather a statute which will protect them against the plagiarism of their designs. . . . [A]s the law now stands, [it] is not likely to help them. If their grievance is as great as they say, Congress may yet be able to help them; but short of that, an effective remedy seems open.[37]

Despite the importance of the FOGA throughout the 1930s, the group struggled to remain relevant after the 1941 Supreme Court ruling. Mentions of the FOGA as a group were seen in *The New York Times* through

1952; however, these listings largely related to announcements of seasonal openings and rarely to design origination and protection.

Did the FOGA Monopolize the Industry?

In handing down the Supreme Court decision, Justice Black was clear that violators of the Sherman Act did not have to achieve a complete monopoly, "for it is sufficient if it deprives the public of the advantages which flow from free competition."[38] The Guild's effective control over the dress industry is somewhat unclear. The Guild stated that in 1935, the value of the total dress industry was $708 million, with guild members contributing 12 percent, or $87 million.[39] In the ruling of the US Circuit Court of Appeals, First Circuit case, *Wm. Filene's Sons Co. v. FOGA*, the aggregate total of dresses manufactured by Guild members was numbered at 55 percent. However, Guild members stated that they accounted for only 130 of the 2,130 dress manufacturers in New York, and produced only 6 percent of the total 84 million dresses manufactured in 1935.[40] The Supreme Court estimated their contributions as much higher, and in the case of *FOGA v. FTC*, found that in 1936, Guild members sold more than 38 percent of all women's garments wholesaling from $6.75 to $10.75 and more than 60 percent wholesaling at $10.75 and above.[41] Total percent of the industry is thus unclear.

The effectiveness of the Guild's actions is also subject to opinion. According to its own tally, its program reduced sweatshop labor, increased wages, reduced slack seasons, and created more continuous labor. Further, the Guild maintained the public at large benefited in that women relied with greater confidence "upon the integrity and the quality of the dresses which they purchase, and have been provided with a market for what they wish to purchase."[42] Nonsupporters of the Guild indicated that the FOGA's programs became less and less representative of the industry as a whole, particularly as they reached into the lowest price ranges. The difficulty of identifying and controlling copies at the lower price points may have ultimately become insurmountable even without the legal problems the Guild encountered.[43]

The Guild's program of self-regulation against design piracy was short-lived. While the case of *FOGA v. FTC* is still considered a pivotal design copyright case in legal proceedings, it has ultimately become a footnote in the history of the design piracy debate within the apparel industry itself.

Following the court's decision, the FOGA struggled to remain relevant in the news. Particularly during World War II, more efforts were made to promote American design rather than insistence on antipiracy measures.[44] In June 1940, the month Germany occupied Paris, Maurice Rentner stated, "Stirred by their profound sorrow over the catastrophe to their fellow originators abroad, the American creators will scale new heights in the exercise of their designing genius."[45] In August 1940, when asked, "Is New York prepared to become the style center now that the couture is no longer functioning?" Rentner replied, "Certainly. The New York designers are fully equipped and ready to carry on. People seem to forget that we have been dressing millions of women in this country very successfully for twenty-five years. Now that the Paris workrooms are closed we have not ceased to create. On the contrary, the garment center has never been more active." He concluded by stating, "All American design needs is the opportunity."[46] This sentiment was echoed by Paula Neiman, one of Maurice Rentner's stylists and representative of the FOGA when she stated in 1940, "The style industries in this country are doing an annual volume of well over a billion dollars, and employing about half a million persons, which proves that although France's contribution . . . has been of incalculable importance to us, we are not destitute without French leadership."[47]

While individual designers and manufacturers affiliated with the FOGA continued to create popular "best-sellers" and achieve great successes in the apparel industry, few discussed fashion origination or design piracy.[48] During World War II, the focus shifted to support of New York City as a design city, rather than enforcement of design piracy measures. In a 1944 article with *New York Times* editor Virginia Pope, Maurice Rentner declared,

> Don't confuse creation with design. We have many designers and but few creators. There are about eight in the city. The creator is one who has basic style ideas that are widely adaptable and make trends; the designer is one who makes variations on them. We have enough creators and designers to make New York a great fashion center.[49]

In this quote, Rentner is belying his formerly extremely forceful position against piracy during the 1930s. His claim clearly states that there is an opportunity for both original design and those who interpret and adapt it.

Rentner's son-in-law, Arthur Jablow, remembered Rentner going to Paris in 1945 with a young lady who secretly created sketches of garments. Jablow also reminisced, "Maurice made the best copies of [Dior's] 'New Look.' He made a tapered waistline in a suit that 90 percent of them couldn't do in New York City. . . . [A]ll the retailers bought those suits. He out-Diored Dior."[50] Jablow conceded that the FOGA was wonderful publicity for the manufacturing business in New York and "put the crimp in a lot of places. Los Angeles was trying to come to the fore. Well, they didn't have a chance. . . . The FOGA was definitely a New York thing . . . and Maurice was the genius who thought it up and who directed it and he did a wonderful job of it."[51]

Chapter 8

Original, Adaptation, Copy, Reproduction?

"Fashion should slip out of your hands. The very idea of protecting the seasonal arts is childish. One should not bother to protect that which dies the minute it is born."[1] This quote attributed to Coco Chanel has become ubiquitous in the current dialogue on fashion copyright and protection, cited by those on both sides of the argument.[2] The wool tweed suit for which she is perhaps best known has been copied and adapted in various fabrics by innumerable designers and knockoff houses and at almost every price point. In the 1950s and 1960s Chanel also authorized copies of the suit, along with other couture designs, to be reproduced in New York and other large fashion centers. Her suit remains a style that is connected with Chanel, although one that even the Chanel designer, Karl Lagerfeld, may or may not be able to recognize as an original or a copy.[3] Perhaps, although the style continues to be identified with Chanel, it has over its sixty-year history become what might be termed a fashion classic, one so copied and recognizable that, while Chanel still gets credit for the original, it has in fact become virtually impossible to identify an original that might qualify for protection. This is not the case for many designers as the very definitions of an original, a copy, or an adaptation have a seldom agreed-upon history, and the difficulties of identifying the arrangement of specific design elements of apparel that constitute originality have thwarted design protection efforts from the beginning of the twentieth century.

The question of whether fashion can or should have a right to protection from design piracy has largely been argued in the legal press, with passing references to the history of the US apparel industry. Most frequently cited in legal documents is the *FOGA v. FTC* Supreme Court case as a pivotal decision against design protection. However, it is important to recognize that the history of design piracy is also a history of the American women's ready-to-wear apparel industry, and that the work of the

FOGA was in response to an already thirty-year dialogue on fashion piracy, as well as to the economic times in which it operated. Indeed, the copying of designs from both foreign and domestic sources fueled the growth of an industry that evolved through efficient production but anonymous designers. Rapid style change and the infrastructure of the New York market, with its available fabrics, labor, and technology, meant fashions were copied so quickly that any popular garment was available to all consumers virtually immediately, at successively lower price points.[4]

After the FOGA was told to "cease and desist," the process of copying continued unabated, and in the late twentieth and early twenty-first centuries, the speed of the design piracy process has seemingly accelerated through newer technologies and global communication networks. For example, in 1947, a New York bridal-gown manufacturer claimed to have reproduced an exact copy of Princess Elizabeth's wedding gown eight weeks prior to the wedding, choosing not to offer it to buyers until the wedding day "in order not 'to create an international incident.'"[5] In 1981, Jack Mulqueen gloated that he could copy twenty styles in a day, reproduce patterns, have the garments produced in Asia, and within ten days ship fifty thousand garments around the world. Interestingly, the then Bloomingdale's president suggested that carrying both the original and the copy in the store helped sales, noting that the women who purchased the copy would never be able to afford the $4,000 original, but would happily "plunk down $150 for a nearly identical Mulqueen."[6]

Perceptions continue that copies seem to appear almost simultaneously with the original, as evidenced in 2011 by countless designers' and manufacturers' near identical reproductions of Kate Middleton's wedding dress just twelve hours following the ceremony (Figure 8.1).[7] Although technology has certainly increased the speed at which fashion images are available, it is unclear what the differences in production time might be. Perhaps what has changed is less the time it takes to copy and more the increased consumer connection to designers and designs with brand identities and the instant sharing of fashion information by all, both on the runway and on the street. An increased tenacity of pirates was expressed by Jean-Jacques Picart, one of the world's most influential fashion consultants and a founding member of the Christian Lacroix couture house, when he said, "In the old days, there was copying; now people are hijacking the very identity of designers. Copies are like mosquitoes. One bite

Figure 8.1 A worker in China preparing a copy of Kate Middleton's wedding dress. Courtesy Adam Dean/Panos Pictures.

doesn't matter, just an irritation, but 100 bites gives you a fever that can kill."[8] Indeed, fashion bloggers such as shoppingwithKyle.com and phone apps such as Instagram and Snapchat help to speed the fashion information process, as nearly anyone with a smart phone can create, post, and share images for others, perhaps to adapt or straight-out copy, but most certainly to create customer demand. That demand is often for the copies of original designer apparel, something many customers assume they are entitled to wear.

The problems of apparel design protection have been acknowledged, argued, and written about for more than a century, and although some of the organizations have changed, much of the rhetoric has remained the same. While the importance of design originality, and the value of the work of a designer, was and is often at the center of the discourse, of equal and often more importance is an American concept of democratic fashion.

Consumer desire for new styles has always been encouraged by the apparel industry.[9] Whether that average consumer was historically concerned with the identity of the designer of her clothing is debatable, especially as the industry grew to provide clothing to most women at most prices. However, as American designers gained confidence and the press began to support their efforts, they sought ways to protect their designs. Bills submitted to Congress for legislative approval as well as trade association efforts to limit piracy were persistently offered as solutions to the copying epidemic. Through the twentieth century, nearly eighty bills to protect designs through copyright or through a separate registration bureau were introduced in Congress. These bills were largely lobbied by the apparel industry and ultimately failed to win approval because of concerns by other facets of the industry or because of concerns regarding the logistics of design protection. One of the paramount issues has always been determining what constitutes an original design, especially in an industry where "original" could also mean the first faithful and legitimate copy based on a purchased couture dress and where there were then constant multiple adaptations. Even today, when it would seem easier to register and search databases of designs, the determination of what changes separate an original from a copy seems insurmountable.

In addition to seeking governmental legislation, industry members developed trade associations to protect their investments. The FOGA represented one of the best efforts to stop piracy and also highlighted the ethical, economic, and social considerations of a program of industry-wide self-regulation. The guild was built on a foundation of retailer-manufacturer collaboration to protect and popularize original styles. Through advertising and promotional campaigns and the creation of a registration bureau for original dress designs, the FOGA established a presence in thirty-two states.[10] However, its practices, particularly those related to fair trade, led to their downfall. The Supreme Court ordered the FOGA to cease and desist and the organization was effectively ended as a force in design piracy protection.[11]

With the failure of legislative solutions, some designers have tried to beat pirates at their own game. In the 1980s designers such as Anne Klein introduced diffusion lines of garments (eponymously but distinctively named Anne Klein II) with less elegant tailoring, less expensive materials, and at reduced prices.[12] In the 1990s, this practice continued and grew with bridge lines from Emanuel Ungaro (Emanuel), Donna Karan

(DKNY), and Ellen Tracy (Tracy). Bill Blass believed that his $1,950 pearl-strapped black cocktail dress would be an easy target for knockoff firms, so he concurrently created a $150 copy for his lower-priced dress collection.[13] Indeed, savvy designers have created a demand for their label in nearly every price range. In the 2000s, designers ranging from Isaac Mizrahi to Vera Wang to Viktor & Rolf created lower-priced goods to be sold at big-box stores such as Kohl's and Target and at fast-fashion retailers H&M and Zara.

While these diffusion lines have certainly created cults of personalities around some designers and their brand, other designers find different ways of protecting their work. In 2007, the *Wall Street Journal* reporter Cheryl Lu-Lien Tan discussed the efforts of designers such as Carolina Herrera and Graeme Black, the chief women's wear designer at Ferragamo, both of whom created goods so complicated that they were difficult to copy.[14] For instance, Black created cocoon-shaped coats and jackets with draped collars and puffy sleeves to limit possible mass-market imitations.[15] In February 2015, the *Wall Street Journal* reporter Meenal Mistry also noted that designers were attempting to develop new textile technologies that would make copying difficult to impossible. For example, Nicolas Ghesquière, in his work for Louis Vuitton, created easy-to-wear pieces such as T-shirts and baby doll dresses but with experimental fabrics, including a sequin-embroidered georgette silk trimmed with lambskin and eel leather.[16] Writer Mistry also quoted the British designer Mary Katrantzou as saying that these details make it difficult, if not "impossible [for mass-market chains] to come close to the quality and the craftsmanship," and that it is a way to "build a luxury brand" today.[17] However, it is to be noted that some designers remain either ambivalent or accepting of the copying practice. According to evening-wear designer Carmen Marc Valvo, "Fashion is more evolutionary than revolutionary—you're always inspired by something else. Besides, I don't think anyone copying me would be able to do it the same way."[18]

As the importance of brand identification increases, some design houses strive for unique and recognizable elements that can become a signature, such as the red soles of Christian Louboutin shoes.[19] Other designers, recognizing the limits of intellectual property protection and the costs of pursuing legal action, have waged battle with copiers through social media campaigns. In September 2015, New York–based designer Maryam

Nassir Zadeh accused breakthrough accessories label Mansur Gavriel of mimicking her exact shoe design, even providing receipts that showed the shoe in question was purchased by Rachel Mansur and Floriana Gavriel. Even if evidence supports the exact copying of the shoes, for designers like Zadeh, the cost of legal action "may not outweigh the benefits." Thus, they have turned to social shaming as a remedy, in order to disgrace the copyist.[20]

Design patents have increasingly surfaced as a means to provide design protection, even with their limitations.[21] While the patenting process can take well over a year, something that clearly works against fashion, the US Patent and Trademark Office (USPTO) is making an effort to streamline the process to ten to twelve months. It may also be possible to reduce the time to six months, if the patentee is willing to pay additional cost by using the USPTO's expedited procedure called the "rocket docket." For a design patent to be of value, the company also must be willing to pursue any infringement through the courts. In 2012, Lululemon Athletica Inc. took on Calvin Klein in a patent infringement case over unique features of its yoga pants. They settled out of court, so it is unknown whether the patent proved to be a critical component to design protection in this case. Other designer brands, such as Raf Simons for Christian Dior Couture and Frances Howie for Stella McCartney Limited, have also obtained design patents to protect specific features of their designs. Meanwhile, as legislative solutions remain stalled in Congress, other industry initiatives are increasingly pursued. These include a "You Can't Fake Fashion" campaign launched in collaboration with the Council of Fashion Designers of America on eBay that advertises the importance of original and authentic design (Figure 8.2).[22]

The practice of piracy seems only more complicated because of the rate at which designers protest, yet continue to knock off each other's designs. In the 1980s, Oscar de la Renta complained about Victor Costa stealing his work, yet de la Renta very closely adapted Yves Saint Laurent's (YSL) ready-to-wear embroidered tulip jacket. The tuxedo dress patented by Raf Simons bears a strong resemblance to an Yves Saint Laurent tuxedo dress, one that YSL sued Ralph Lauren for copying in 1994. Because the case was pursued through the French court system, where fashion copyright is recognized, YSL was able to win a verdict against Lauren, but many questioned whether the Lauren dress was a true copy, with its different buttons and lapel design.[23] The fashion press seems either to support the practice

Figure 8.2 Bag designed by Diane Von Furstenberg as part of the "You Can't Fake Fashion" campaign to raise awareness against counterfeit goods and celebrate original design. Courtesy of CFDA.

through publication of copies that represent a good buy or to look the other way when a couture designer is the copyist, such as when Nicolas Ghesquière's Balenciaga work was found to have closely copied the work of San Francisco designer Kaisik Wong.[24] The venerable House of Dior was accused of knocking off the design aesthetic of the famous Chanel quilted bag in 2009. Chanel, on the other hand, lost a copyright infringement suit in 2012 for a crochet vest that the courts deemed a "slavish copy" of the design of a French knitwear company.[25] With the practices of borrowing and adapting of other's creative work, designers would sometimes seem to be on thin ice as proponents of design copyright legislation.

While designers and manufacturers continue to argue the costs and benefits of the piracy practice, consumers seem to embrace the ability to purchase knockoff goods that resemble higher-priced lines at a fraction of the cost. According to self-appointed copycat king Allen B. Schwartz, design director of A.B.S., "Gaultier or Galliano will put their spin on it, I'll put my spin on it, but fashion isn't anything unless everyone is buying it."[26] Consumers indeed are the ultimate adjudicators in whether or not the practice of piracy continues. In the "Ethicist" section of *The New York Times Magazine*, author Randy Cohen was asked if a consumer should stop buying counterfeit handbags from street vendors in New York City. Cohen replied, "You are right to shun counterfeit handbags, but you may buy knockoffs, which are not the same thing. A knockoff apes the appearance of the original but does not present itself as other than what it is." He continued, "Drawing on other people's work—in fashion, in art, in literature—is how ideas spread through culture."[27] This sentiment, that piracy is good for consumers and for the fashion process, was repeated by Joan Kaner, who observed that "today's knockoff houses provide good value and style," making it a better buy than "overpriced" designer houses that spend a lot on advertising and fashion shows.[28]

In a 2005 conference called "Ready-to-Share: Fashion and the Ownership of Creativity," which explored "the fashion industry's enthusiastic embrace of sampling, appropriation and borrowed inspiration," Lear Center managing director Joanna Blakely encapsulated the "right to fashion" argument, that piracy has caused "an unprecedented democratization of fashion. More people have more access to more innovative clothing design than ever before."[29]

Whatever the belief regarding the practice, it seems certain that the fashion industry remains dependent on the various practices of copying, adapting, borrowing, and pirating designs. Fashion is certainly as important to the economy as semiconductor chips and musical recordings, which have received legislative protection against piracy. Clothing provides protection to the wearer, modesty, decoration, and pleasure. It can symbolize a person's interests, dreams, and aspirations, yet it remains largely unprotected against copyists. Perhaps this is because fashion is so ephemeral, it changes so very quickly, that any protection would be a moot point. Or, perhaps it is because clothing is the most democratic of all consumer possessions, and thus trying to prevent someone from acquiring the latest fashion goes against the very spirit of being American.

Appendix

FOGA Officers and Members, 1936

Officers

Maurice Rentner–President and Treasurer
Herbert Sondheim–First Vice President
Charles Gumprecht–Second Vice President
J. A. Livingston–Treasurer
Albert M. Post–Executive Director
James M. Golby–Executive Division

Dress Members

Aldrich & Malvin
Milton Altmark
Charles Armour & Bros
Arons, Berstein & Arons
Joseph & Ben Barnett, Inc.
Rose Barrack & Lahm, Inc.
William Bass Dress Corp.
Herman Beispel, Inc.
Bender & Hamburger, Inc.
Blotta & Conti, Inc.
Brenner, Joseph, & White
Brenner, Morris, Inc.
Hattie Carnegie, Inc.
Clifford Salkin, Inc.
Lewis Cohn, Inc.
Jo Copeland, Inc.
David Crystal, Inc.
Eta, Inc.
Feigenbaum & Adelsohn

Pauline Fields, Inc.
Herman Floersheimer & Bro
Louise Barnes Gallagher, Inc.
Henry Ganz, Inc.
Gardner & Schwartz, Inc.
Ed. Garrick & Co., Inc.
A. Goodman & Co., Inc.
Joseph Greenberg-Bettina, Inc.
Charles Groden, Inc.
Julius Grossman & Fred Greenberg Dress Co., Inc.
Joseph Halpert, Inc.
Max Heit Dress Corp.
Myron Herbert & Charles Cooper, Inc.
Jack Herzog & Bro., Inc.
Virginia Hume & Gold, Inc.
E. A. Jackson-Bienard, Inc.
Kallman & Morris, Inc.
Kaplan & Moskowitz, Inc.
Samuel Kass Gowns, Inc.
Kiviette, Inc.
Charles Kondazian & Papaz, Inc.
Kornhauser Gowns, Inc.
Charles Lang, Inc.
La Rue Dresses, Inc.
Lenkowsky Modes, Inc.
Marry Lee Frocks, Inc.
Mary Liotta, Inc.
M. A. Litvin, Inc.
H. Milgrim & Bros., Inc.
Germaine Monteil, Inc.
Jennie Moskowitz, Inc.
Nanty Frocks, Inc.
Nomis Dress Co.
Paul Parnes, Inc.
Pattulo Modes, Inc.
Perles & Gilbert, Inc.
Ben Reig, Inc.
Maurice Rentner, Inc.

Nettie Rosenstein, Inc.
Nettie Rosenstein Gowns, Inc.
James J. Rothenberg, Inc.
Rudolf Gowns, Inc.
Ruffolo Bros., Inc.
J. M. Silverman Dresses, Inc.
Somay, Inc.
Herbert Sondheim, Inc.
Spectator Sports, Inc.
Frank Starr Friedlander, Inc.
Straus-Miller, Inc.
Suttre-Fox, Inc.
A. Traina Gowns, Inc.
John Traina, Inc.

Affiliated Members

B. G. Garment Co., Inc. (Chicago)
Fred A. Block, Inc. (Chicago)
S. Eisenberg
H. N. Fried (Chicago)
Junior Guild Frocks, Inc.
Lang-Kohn Mfg. Co.
Matthews-Kadetsky Co.
Robinson Bros., Inc.

Coat and Suit Members

Carmen Bros., Inc.
Dartmoor Coat Co., Inc.
Deitsch-Wersba & Coppola, Inc.
Del Monte Hickey Co., Inc.
Ben Gershel & Co., Inc.
Ben Ginsburg, Inc.
Aaron Goldstein Co., Inc.
Louis Goldstein Company, Inc.
Grossman & Spiegel, Inc.
Philip Mangone & Co., Inc.
Monte, Sans & Pruzan, Inc.
Zuckerman & Kraus, Inc.

Appendix

Junior Miss Members

Louis Kallish and Max Rosenbluth
Ashley Frocks, Inc.
J. H. Horwitz and Joseph M. Duberman
Jane Junior Dresses, Inc.
Joanna, Jr., Zinn Bros., Inc.
Junior League Frocks, Inc.
Louise Mulligan, Inc.
Ira Rentner-Miller, Inc.

Textile Associates

Amrein, Freudenberg & Co., Inc.
Bianchini, Ferier, Inc.
Bloomsburg Silk Mill, Inc.
Sidney Blumenthal & Co.
Brueck & Richards, Inc.
Case & Co., Inc.
Chantillon, Mouly, Roussel, Inc.
Cheney Bros., Inc.
Combier & Co.
Coudurier, Frustus, & Devigne, Inc.
Descours, Genthen, Inc.
Croydon Fabrics, Inc.
Silk Guide of American, Inc.
F. Ducharne Silk Co., Inc.
Empire Silk Co. Inc.
Cohn Hall-Marx Co., Inc.
The Forstmann Woolen Co., Inc.
Frank Associates, Inc.
Theodore J. Gallagher, Inc.
Hess, Goldsmith & Co., Inc.
L. J. Hyams & Jane Hyams
Kandelaft Silks, Inc.
Lace Net Importing Co., Inc.
Maginnis & Thomas, Inc.
H. B. Mallinson & Co., Inc.
Menke Kaufman & Co.
Onondaga Silk Co., Inc.

Wm. C. Openhym
Remond-Holland, Inc.
L & E Stirn, Inc.
Stunzi Sons Silk Co., Inc.
Susquehanna Silk Mills Inc.
Schwarzenbach, Huber, Inc.
J. A. Wagenbauer, Inc.
Wahnetah Silk Co., Inc.
Wechaler Silk Corp.
Zellinger & Schreth, Inc.
J. J. & N. Blackstone, Inc.
Dutschler, Trull & Justin, Inc.
Ellen Lace & Embroidery Co., Inc.
L. H. Hollander
Ikle Freres & Co., Inc.
Herbert Lehman, Inc.
Lido Embroidery
Maison France, Inc.
Record Lace & Embroidery Co., Inc.
Swiss Novelty Embroidery Co., Inc.
Walter Tobler & Franz Hoenig
Sol Wolfman, Inc.

Sportswear Members

Adler & Adler, Inc.
Davidow, Inc.
David M. Goodstein, Inc.
Kane Weill, Inc.
Joseph Levay, Inc.
J. A. Livingston, Inc.
David N. Lowenthal & Son, Inc.
Mutual Rosenbloom Corp.
Charles W. Nudelman, Inc.
Zoltan Rosenberg & Theodore Rosenberg
Sport Kraft, Inc.
Star Maid Dresses, Inc.
Sam Steinberg & Co., Inc.
Townley Frocks, Inc.

Protective Affiliates

Aywon Dress Co., Inc.
L. & D. Beilinson, Inc.
Daytime Frocks, Inc.
F.E.D. Dress Co., Inc.
Harry Frank
Friedman Dress Co., Inc.
Goldman Frocks Co., Inc.
International Dress Co., Inc.
Jomark Dresses, Inc.
Joe Levine Dress Co., Inc.
Parisian Mfg. Co., Inc.
C. H. D. Robbins Co., Inc.
Rosen Bros. Frocks, Inc.
Sheila-Lynn Dresses Inc.
Silver Dresses, Inc.
David S. Westheim Corp.
Witlin & Schneider, Inc.
Anderman-Bob Burns, Inc.
Bernard Appel, Inc.
Grace Ashley
Bon Ray Dance Frocks, Inc.
Capri Frocks, Inc.
Casino Dresses, Inc.
Cohen Turnick, Inc.
Dalton Frocks, Inc.
Sam Davidson, Inc.
Dresden Dress Co., Inc.
Fashion Wear Dress Co., Inc.
Franklin Dress Co., Inc.
Ginsburg & Abelson, Inc.
Alexander S. Gross, Inc.
Lee Claire Costumes, Inc.
Lyla Modes, Inc.
Lyttle Bros., Inc.
E. N. Marcus, Inc.
Matty Moskowitz, Inc.
Parnis-Levinson, Inc.
Patricia Perkins, Inc.
Radiant Dress Co., Inc.
Reich-Goldfarb & Co., Inc.
L. C. Rosenblatt, Inc.
Schultze-Zuch, Inc.
Stern & Goldberg, Inc.
Will Steinman, Inc.
Valroy, Inc.
Phil Zahn & Co., Inc.
Bretter & Sussman, Inc.
Campus Modes, Inc.
Flo-Frocks, Inc.
George Hess Co., Inc.
Junior Fashion Guild, Inc.
Michael Kaplan & M. Kaplan
Wein Frocks, Inc.
Abbate Swift, Inc.
Argosy Dresses, Inc.
Cecele Dance Frocks, Inc.
Garland Dress Co., Inc.
B. Tobias, Inc.
Samuel Lipman, Herman Lipman, and Julius Lipman
Marie Lynn Dance Frocks, Inc.
Rosenthal & Kallman, Inc.

Notes

Introduction

1. The level of protection in the United States is far different from that in Europe. The current French copyright system makes specific provisions for fashion works. This protection dates to the Copyright Act of 1793, which classified fashion as applied art. Under the laws of the United Kingdom, a garment design is protected as long as it can be related back to a copyrighted drawing. Silvia Beltrametti, "Evaluation of the Design Piracy Prohibition Act: Is the Cure Worse than the Disease? An Analogy with Counterfeiting and a Comparison with the Protection Available in the European Community," *Northwestern Journal of Technology and Intellectual Property* 8 (2010): 147–73; Christine Magdo, "Protecting Works of Fashion from Design Piracy," *LEDA at Harvard Law School* (2000); Rob Walker, "The Acceptable Knockoff," *The New York Times Magazine* (December 12, 2004): 46; James Surowiecki, "The Piracy Paradox," *The New Yorker* (September 24, 2007): 90.
2. Bernard Roshco, *The Rag Race* (New York: Funk & Wagnalls Company, 1963), 25; Sara B. Marcketti, Kate Greder, and Heather Sinclair, "Is Anything Ever New? Fashion Design Students' Perceptions of Piracy," *International Journal of Costume and Fashion* (2014): 17–28.
3. Testimony of David Wolfe, creative director, the Doneger Group, before the US House Subcommittee on Courts, the Internet, and Intellectual Property, Legislative Hearing on H.R. 5055, Washington, DC, July 27, 2006.
4. Roshco, *The Rag Race*, 25. Tobé Coller Davis patented designs under the name Taubé Davis. She appears to have begun using the spelling "Tobé" around the time she began her style service in 1927. See "Presenting Tobé," *Delineator* (April 1937): 24.
5. Narciso Rodriguez testimony before the Subcommittee on Courts, the Internet, and Intellectual Property of the committee on the Judiciary House of Representatives, 110th Cong., 2nd Sess., February 14, 2008. These are his estimates of the number of copies sold.
6. Constance C. R. White, "Patterns," *New York Times*, January 14, 1997.

7. Narciso Rodriguez testimony.
8. Roshco, *The Rag Race*, 54.
9. "Wally Dress," *LIFE* magazine, August 9, 1937, 56–58.
10. In 1994, a French commercial court ordered Polo/Ralph Lauren to pay $383,000 to Yves Saint Laurent for plagiarizing a tuxedo dress design. Ironically, nine years earlier, in 1985, Saint Laurent was fined $11,000 for copying a toreador jacket from designer Jacques Esterel. Teri Agins, "Fashion Knockoffs Hit Stores before Originals as Designers Seethe," *The New York Times*, August 8, 1994, 1.
11. See, for example, Tracy Doyle, *Patterns from Finished Clothes: Re-Creating the Clothes You Love* (New York: Sterling Pub. Co. Inc., 1996); Lee Hollahan, *How to Use, Adapt, and Design Sewing Patterns: From Store-Bought Patterns to Drafting Your Own* (Hauppauge, NY: Barron's Educational Series, 2010); Norma R. Hollen and Carolyn M. Kundel, *Pattern Making by the Flat-Pattern Method* (Upper Saddle River, NJ: Prentice Hall, 1993); Ruth E. Glock and Grace I. Kunz, *Apparel Manufacturing: Sewn Products Analysis* (Upper Saddle River, NJ: Prentice Hall, 2004).
12. The most recent bill, the Innovative Design Protection and Piracy Prevention Act (ID3PA), would offer three years of copyright-like protection for "new" and "original" fashion designs ranging from dresses to eyeglass frames to suitcases, handbags, and belts. It would not cover everything in the fashion world, but rather "those original articles, which are so truly unique that they come closer to art than functionality." The ID3PA did not include a searchable database as part of its proposal, due to potential confusion with the Copyright Office. If approved, a designer would indicate protection by marking designs using the words "Protected Design," the abbreviation "Prot'd Des.," or the letter "D" with a circle. Kristi Ellis, "Design Piracy Bill Returns," *Women's Wear Daily*, September 11, 2012, 1, 15.
13. "The IDPPPA—Is the Third Time a Charm?," *Columbia Business Law Review* online, vol. 2015, no. 2, http://cblr.columbia.edu/archives/11357.
14. Kurt Courtney, speaking as manager, government relations for the American Apparel & Footwear Association, on July 15, 2011, to the Subcommittee on Intellectual Property, Competition, and the Internet, House Judiciary Committee, 2.
15. Alexandra Steigard, "The Copycat Threat," *Women's Wear Daily*, September 9, 2010, 1, 18.
16. See, for example, Susan Scafidi, "Intellectual Property and Fashion Design," *Intellectual Property and Information Wealth* 1, no. 115 (2006); "Is the Fashion Commons at Risk?" *On the Commons: Commons Magazine*, August 19, 2005,

http://onthecommons.org/fashion-commons-risk; Kimberly A. Harchuck, "Fashion Design Protection: The Eternal Plight of the 'Soft Sculpture,'" *Akron Intellectual Property Journal* 4, no. 1 (2010): 73–118; "Catwalk Copycats: Why Congress Should Adopt a Modified Version of the Design Piracy Prohibition Act," *Journal of Intellectual Property Law* 14, no. 305 (2006–2007); Linna T. Loangkote, "Fashioning a New Look in Intellectual Property: Sui Generis Protection for the Innovative Designer," *Hastings Law Journal* 63, no. 1 (2011–2012): 297–322.

17. Aspects of this manuscript derived from the doctoral work of Sara B. Marcketti, "Design Piracy in the United States Women's Ready-to-Wear Apparel Industry: 1910–1941" (PhD diss., Iowa State University, 2005).

Chapter 1

1. Claudia Kidwell and Margaret Christman, *Suiting Everyone: The Democratization of Clothing in America* (Washington, DC: The Smithsonian Institution Press, 1974); Margaret Walsh, "The Democratization of Fashion: The Emergence of the Women's Dress Pattern Industry," *The Journal of American History* 66 (1979): 299–313; Jane A. U. Funderburk, "The Development of Women's Ready-to-Wear, 1865 to 1914: Based on *New York Times* Advertisements" (PhD diss., University of Maryland, 1994); Katherine Cranor, "Homemade Versus Ready-Made Clothing," *The Journal of Home Economics* (1920): 230–33.
2. William Leach, "Transformations in a Culture of Consumption: Women and Department Stores, 1890–1925," *The Journal of American History* 71 (September 1984): 333; Blanche Payne, Geital Winakor, and Jane Farrell-Beck, *The History of Costume* (New York: Longman, 1992).
3. See Kathy Peiss, *Cheap Amusements: Working Women and Leisure in Turn-of-the-Century New York* (Philadelphia: Temple University Press, 1986): 62–67.
4. Leach, "Transformations."
5. Nancy Troy, *Couture Culture: A Study in Modern Art and Fashion* (Cambridge, MA: The MIT Press, 2003), 21.
6. *Women's Wear*, October 29, 1910, quoted in Bernard Smith, "A Study of Uneven Industrial Development: The American Clothing Industry in the Late 19th and Early 20th Centuries" (PhD diss., Yale University, 1989). *Women's Wear Daily* was originally titled *Women's Wear*. On January 3, 1927, the name was changed to *Women's Wear Daily*.
7. From the turn of the century through the 1930s, the American dress industry was highly concentrated in and around New York City. The predominance of New York as a leading style center was largely due to the ample supply of

skilled and unskilled labor, the prevalence of transportation facilities, and the proximity to fabric markets. Ida Tarbell, *The Business of Being a Woman* (New York: The Macmillan Company, 1912).

8. James D. Norris, *Advertising and the Transformation of American Society, 1856–1920* (New York: Greenwood Press, 1990), 104.

9. *Women's Wear*, November 30, 1910.

10. Richard Martin, "Fashion in the Age of Advertising," *The Journal of Popular Culture* 29 (1995): 235–54.

11. Paul M. Gregory, "Fashion and Monopolistic Competition," *The Journal of Political Economy* 56 (1948): 74.

12. John Keating, speaking on November 15, 1934, to the National Recovery Administration, *Hearing on the Code of Fair Competition for the Dress Manufacturing Industry* (Washington, DC: Government Printing Office, 1934), 21 (hereafter cited as NRA Hearing with date and page number).

13. "Style vs. Quality," *Women's Wear*, December 13, 1912, 1.

14. Bertha June Richardson, *The Woman Who Spends: A Study of Her Economic Function* (Boston: Whitcomb & Barrows, 1904), 78.

15. Julius Henry Cohen, *Law and Order in Industry: Five Years' Experience* (New York: The Macmillan Co., 1916), 88.

16. Richardson, *The Woman Who Spends*. See also Emma M. Hooper, "Remodeling Last Year's Gowns," *The Ladies' Home Journal*, June 1893, 26.

17. "The Woman's Waist Department," *The Haberdasher*, November 1895, 57; *The New York Daily Tribune*, May 26, 1895, 4.

18. "Dress Style Piracy Evils Scored in Suit," *Women's Wear Daily*, February 24, 1933, 1, 13; "How to Discourage Scouts of Copying," *Women's Wear Daily*, August 17, 1936, 14; Rudolf Callmann, "Style and Design Piracy," *Journal of the Patent Office Society*, August 1940, 557–86.

19. Kenneth Hutchinson, "Design Piracy," *Harvard Business Review*, 1940, 191–98.

20. There are numerous articles in *The New York Times* related to attempts to copyright designs based on tomb images and artifacts and even attempts to gain trademark of Egyptian names. "Pharaonic Styles Set New Fashions," *The New York Times*, February 3, 1923, 3; "They Watch Egypt for Fashion News," *The New York Times*, February 18, 1923, 3; "Tut-ankh-amen Bag First to Seek Name," *The New York Times*, February 23, 1923, 15.

21. M. D. C. Crawford, "We Need Interpretive Creation—Not Copying," *Women's Wear*, June 28, 1919, 3. In a later article from 1933, Crawford stated, "The world is weary of the false doctrines of price, of the cheapness of tawdry imitations. How can producers and retailers keep faith with their customers, if

every new and acceptable idea, the result of creative energy and constructive intelligence, immediately is cheapened into caricatures of the originals?" M. D. C. Crawford, "Courage, Intelligence Mark Guild's Work," *Women's Wear Daily*, March 6, 1933, 3.

22. Ben Hirsch, testimony, Supreme Court of the United States, October Term, 1940, *FOGA v. FTC*, pp. 419–20.
23. Hutchinson, "Design Piracy," 198.
24. *Women's Wear*, June 24, 1919, 21.
25. *The New York Times*, September 9, 1923, 14.
26. Maurice Rentner, November 15, 1934, NRA Hearing, 113.
27. M. D. C. Crawford, *The Ways of Fashion* (New York: Fairchild Publishing Co., 1941), 179.
28. "FOGA Was Self-Appointed Tribunal, High Court Finds," *Women's Wear Daily*, March 4, 1941, 1.

Chapter 2

1. Alphonsus Haire, "Pirated Designs," *The New York Times*, January 20, 1913, 10.
2. Ralph S. Brown, "Design Protection: An Overview," *UCLA Law Review* 34 (1986–1987): 1337–404. The history of the apparel industry is often misunderstood or not completely taken into account in legal reviews. In Christine Magdo's *Harvard Law School* article, she stated, "American designers traditionally did not copy each other," and argued that it was contemporary technology that made copying fast, easy, and widespread. This is clearly not the case when the historical record is examined. Christine Magdo, "Protecting Works of Fashion from Design Piracy," *LEDA at Harvard Law School* (2000): 1–15.
3. *The Semiconductor Chip Protection Act of 1983: Hearings on S. 1201 Before the Subcomm. on Patents, Copyrights and Trademarks of the Senate Judiciary Comm.*, 98th Cong., 1st Sess., 66, 75–76 (1983).
4. Linda Marx, "Knockoff King Jack Mulqueen Is Stealing Designers Blind, and There's No Stopping Him," *People*, November 9, 1981, 119–22.
5. Jennifer Mencken, "A Design for the Copyright of Fashion," *Boston College Intellectual Property and Technology Forum*, December 12, 1997, 121–201; Anne Theodore Briggs, "Hung Out to Dry: Clothing Design Protection Pitfalls in United States Law," *Hastings Communications and Entertainment Law Journal* 24 (Winter 2001–2002): 169–213; Leslie J. Hagen, "A Comparative Analysis of Copyright Laws Applied to Fashion Works: Renewing the Proposal for Folding Fashion Works in the United States," *Texas International Law Journal* 26 (1991): 341–88.
6. Myrna B. Garner and Sandra J. Keiser, *Beyond Design: The Synergy of Apparel Product Development* (New York: Fairchild, 2012).

7. U.S. Const. art. I, § 8.
8. Erastus S. Allen, "Legal Protection for Artistic Designs," *The Bulletin of the American Ceramic Society* (1944): 423–27.
9. While fabric prints may be protected under copyright, there is concern that "copyright trolls" push the envelope of protection and in essence extort designers, manufacturers, and even retailers over potential copyright infringement. Noah Smith, "Are Copyright Trolls Taking Over the Fashion Industry?" *Fortune*, October 7, 2015, http://fortune.com/2015/10/07/patent-trolls-fashion/.
10. S. Priya Bharathi, "There Is More than One Way to Skin a Copycat: The Emergence of Trade Dress to Combat Design Piracy of Fashion Works," *Texas Tech Law Review* 27, no. 4 (1996): 1667–79.
11. Robert Hoke, "Brush Up on the Basics of Intellectual Property," *The Iowa Lawyer* (2003): 24.
12. Quoted in Sylvan Gotshal and Alfred Lief, *The Pirates Will Get You: A Story for the Fight for Design Protection* (New York: Columbia University Press, 1945).
13. Quoted in Robert A. Buckles, "Property Rights in Creative Works—A Comparison of Copyright Laws and Patent Laws," *Journal of the Patent Office Society* 32, no. 6 (June 1950): 414–38.
14. Briggs, "Hung Out to Dry," 169–213.
15. US Department of Commerce, *Design Patents* (Washington, DC: US Department of Commerce, 1983).
16. Arnold B. Silverman, "What Are Design Patents and When Are They Useful?" *JOM: The Journal of the Minerals, Metals & Materials Society* 45, no. 3 (1993): 63.
17. "Protection for the Artistic Aspects of Articles of Utility," *The Harvard Law Review* 72, no. 8 (June 1959): 1520–36; Kal Raustiala and Christopher Sprigman, "The Piracy Paradox: Innovation and Intellectual Property in Fashion Design," *Virginia Law Review* 92, no. 8 (2006): 1687–777; William D. Shoemaker, *Patents for Designs* (Washington, DC: H. D. Williams Company, 1929); Harry Aubrey Toulmin, *Handbook of Patents* (Cincinnati, OH: The W. H. Anderson Company, 1949).
18. Erin Geiger Smith, "Fashion Designers Look to Patents to Fight Knockoffs," Reuters, http://www.reuters.com/article/2013/09/12/us-usa-fashion-new york-patents-idUSBRE98B0H420130912.
19. Quoted in Briggs, "Hung Out to Dry," 169–213.
20. John P. Nikonow, "Patent Protection for New Designs of Dresses," *Journal of the Patent Office Society* 17 (1935): 253–54. President Obama signed the

America Invents Act in September 2011 to help reform and speed up the patent process. It offered startup and growing companies (but not established companies) an opportunity to have patents reviewed in twelve months, rather than the typical wait time of three years. The White House Office of the Press Secretary, "American Jobs Act," September 16, 2011, http://www.whitehouse.gov/the-press-office/2011/09/16/president-obama-signs-america-invents-act-overhauling-patent-system-stim.

21. Martin Morrison, "Registration of Designs," *Congressional House Reports*, 64th Cong., 1st sess., vol. 3 (1916): 2.
22. Allen, "Legal Protection for Artistic Designs," 423–27; Richard Stim, "Can't Prove a Copyright Copied?," *Crafts Law* (2001): 40–41; Toulmin, *Handbook of Patents*; Roger E. Meiners and Robert J. Staaf, "Patents, Copyrights, and Trademarks: Property or Monopoly?," *Harvard Journal of Law and Public Policy* 13 (Summer 1990): 911–34; Magdo, "Protecting Works of Fashion from Design Piracy"; Safia Nurhabhai, "Style Piracy Revisited," *New York State Builders Association* 10, no. 3 (Winter 2001): 1–11; Peter Shalestock, "Forms of Redress for Design Piracy: How Victims Can Use Existing Copyright Law," *Seattle University Law Review* 21 (Summer 1997): 113–26.
23. Although obtaining patents was a slow and expensive process, shoe, handbag, and jewelry designers achieved some success protecting their products' appearance through this form of protection. "Urges Protection for Dress Designs," *The New York Times*, July 9, 1941, 30.
24. Toulmin, *Handbook of Patents*.
25. Quoted in Robert A. Buckles, "Property Rights in Creative Works: A Comparison of Copyright Laws and Patent Laws," *Journal of the Patent Office Society* 32, no. 6 (June 1950): 431.
26. "Design Patent in Dispute," *Women's Wear Daily*, April 3, 1935, 2.
27. "Urges Protection for Dress Designs," *The New York Times*, July 9, 1941, 30.
28. Smith, "Fashion Designers Look to Patents."
29. Kristi Ellis, "Feds Bust Counterfeit Operation," *Women's Wear Daily*, December 14, 2012, 2. Fiber manufacturers have taken steps to prevent the counterfeiting of their fibers. Brand logos and other identifying information can be embedded within a manufactured fiber, and a DNA marker can be applied at the ginning stage of cotton. "The DNA Revolution," *Textiles*, no. 4 (2008): 8–10.
30. "Please Don't Fool with the Star," *The Haberdasher* 10, no. 6 (June 1899): 88.
31. The high cost of obtaining a trademark to protect an element of a brand must be noted. A 2006 *Women's Wear Daily* article estimated the costs of protecting elements of a fictitious handbag including the *WWD* trademark, fabric copy-

right, design patent on bag shape, utility patent on the clasp, and so on. The costs ranged from a conservative $10,200 to a high of $19,500 if the process was complicated by legal challenges. Regarding worldwide trademark registration, the price tag could reach $3 million. Liza Casabona, "Fighting Knockoffs by Protecting a Brand," *Women's Wear Daily*, February 1, 2006, 12–13.

32. Gotshal and Lief, *The Pirates Will Get You*.

33. Maurice A. Weikart, "Design Piracy," *Indiana Law Journal* 19 (1943–1944): 235–57; David Goldenberg, "The Long and Winding Road: A History of the Fight over Industrial Design Protection in the United States," *Journal of the Copyright Society of the U.S.A.* 45, no. 1 (1997): 21–62.

34. Goldenberg, "The Long and Winding Road," 25.

35. Gotshal and Lief, *The Pirates Will Get You*.

36. Weikart, "Design Piracy," 245.

37. Ibid., 27–38.

38. Oscar Geier, "What Has Been Accomplished Towards Protecting Textile Designers," *Journal of the Patent Office Society* 16 (1934): 221–27.

39. Sylvan Gotshal, *Today's Fight for Design Protection* (New York: Sylvan Gotshal, 1957); Irene Blunt, "Fighting the Design Pirate," *Journal of the Patent Office Society* 15 (1933): 29; Henry Williams, "Report of the Committee on Protection of Designs," *Journal of the Patent Office Society* 15 (1933), 807–13; Geier, "What Has Been Accomplished"; Joseph Rossman, "Proposed Registration of Designs," *Journal of the Patent Office Society* 17 (1935): 995–98; Walter Derenberg, "Commercial Prints and Labels: A Hybrid in Copyright Law," *Journal of the Patent Office Society* 22 (1940): 452–68; Thomas Hudson, "A Brief History of the Development of Design Patent Protection in the U.S.," *Journal of the Patent Office Society* 30 (1948): 380–400.

40. Alterman's bill required that petitioners file a statement of the styles of dresses, coats, and suits with the county clerk and the secretary of state. Unlawful use was punishable by fines and imprisonment. "Every Dress Manufacturer Is Faced with a New Style Control Menace," *Women's Wear Daily*, March 13, 1935, 8; "State Style Measure Explained by Assemblyman," *Women's Wear Daily*, March 5, 1935, 2.

41. "Campaign Against Design Piracy," *Journal of the Patent Office Society*, November 1946, 845.

42. "Fashion Designer Asks Piracy Ban," *The New York Times*, July 22, 1947, 20.

43. "Full Text of Design Protection Bill," *Women's Wear Daily*, April 3, 1947, 36; "NRDGA Against Design Bill, If Changed or Not," *Women's Wear Daily*, February 25, 1948, 1.

44. Leonard Sloane, "Design Pirating Sets Off Battle," *The New York Times*, January 4, 1964.

45. The term of registration was two years, later reduced to one year, later to six months or a season. Renewals were possible. There was a $4 fee for registering and a $1.50 fee for renewal. Gotshal, *Today's Fight for Design Protection*; "Silks: Textile Design Registration at Bureau Gains: More than 100 a Day Are Being Handled, It Is Reported—Greater Sales Promotion Possibilities Seen," *Women's Wear Daily*, August 19, 1931, 12. The Design Protection Association was formed in 1931 to combat piracy in the textile trade. Sylvan Gotshal was counsel to the group. "Forming Design Protection Association," *Women's Wear Daily*, May 15, 1931, S11, 1.
46. The National Association of Style Creators, incorporation papers, November 1934, New York Department of State, New York County Clerk, New York, NY.
47. "No Copycat in St. Louis," *Retailers Market News*, January 20, 1940, 29.
48. "Announcing the Formation of the Junior Fashion Creators' League of America, Inc.," *Women's Wear Daily*, October 3, 1933, 9.
49. "Campaign Against Design Piracy," *Journal of the Patent Office Society* 28 (November 1946): 845.
50. Bergdorf Goodman Oral History, Manuscript Collection x181, Fashion Institute of Technology Special Collections and College Archives, New York, NY.
51. Schmidt, "Designer Law," 861–80.
52. *Wm Filene's Sons Co v. FOGA*, 14 F. Supp. 353 (1936).

Chapter 3

1. Jean L. Parsons, "No Longer a 'Frowsy Drudge': Women's Wardrobe Management, 1880–1930," *Clothing and Textiles Research Journal* 20 (2002): 33–41. Portions of this chapter rely on the research in this article.
2. For discussion of the growth of ready-to-wear during this period see Bernard Smith, "A Study of Uneven Industrial Development: The American Clothing Industry in the Late 19th and Early 20th Centuries" (PhD diss., Yale University, 1989).
3. Louis Levine, *The Womens' Garment Workers: A History of the International Ladies' Garment Workers' Union* (New York: B. W. Huebsch, Inc., 1924).
4. US Department of Commerce, *Census of Manufacturers: Clothing, 1914* (Washington, DC: Government Printing Office, 1914); Paul H. Nystrom, *Economics of Fashion* (New York: The Ronald Press Co., 1928).
5. For garment industry labor history, see, for example, Levine, *The Women's Garment Workers*; Karen Pastorello, *A Power Among Them: Bessie Abramowitz Hillman and the Making of the Amalgamated Clothing Workers of America* (Urbana: University of Illinois Press, 2008); Nancy L. Green, *Ready-to-Wear and Ready-to-Work: A Century of Industry and Immigrants in Paris and New*

York (Durham, NC: Duke University Press, 1997); Carolyn Daniel McCreesh, *Women in the Campaign to Organize Garment Workers, 1880–1917* (New York: Garland Publishing, 1985).

6. "Women Here and There," *The New York Times*, June 16, 1901, 16.
7. "Smart Fashions for Limited Incomes," *Vogue*, June 11, 1896, vi.
8. R. H. Macy & Co. advertisement, *The Ladies' Home Journal* (July 1894): 24.
9. Rob Schorman, *Selling Style: Clothing and Social Change at the Turn of the Century* (Philadelphia: University of Pennsylvania Press, 2003).
10. Jean Parsons and Jennifer Schulle, "The Shirtwaist: Changing the Commerce of Fashion," Costume Society of America Regional Meeting, Cincinnati, Ohio, 2003.
11. Cohen, *Law and Order in Industry*, 88.
12. "The Woman's Waist Department," *The Haberdasher*, November 1895, 59; and *The Haberdasher*, July 1896, 62. *The Haberdasher* was a major trade publication for the men's furnishings industry.
13. Levine, *The Women's Garment Workers*, 145.
14. By the early 1900s, stores began to use elaborate window displays to entice customers. In 1902, the novelist Theodore Dreiser described the allure as "stirring up in onlookers a desire to secure but a part of what they see." Quoted in Leach, *Land of Desire*, 40.
15. Edna Woolman Chase and Ilka Chase, *Always in Vogue* (Garden City, NY: Doubleday, 1954), 40.
16. See, for example, "Arrival of Buyers," *The New York Times*, September 6, 1900, 2. For this date, buyers came from as far west as Topeka, Kansas, and arrivals also included buyers from Canadian stores.
17. Jessica Daves, *Ready-Made Miracle: The American Story of Fashion for the Millions* (New York: G. P. Putnam, 1967); Leonard Drake and Carrie Glaser, *Trends in the New York Clothing Industry* (New York: Institute of Public Administration, 1942), 25.
18. See *The New York Daily Tribune*, May 26, 1895, 2.
19. "Convict-Made Shirt," *The Haberdasher*, March 1895, 61; and "Waists for Women," *The Haberdasher*, December 1895, 61.
20. We use the term *style* here to indicate variations in details on a garment, such as the size and shape of sleeves or collar, or the shape of the yoke, or number of pleats in the front.
21. Leach, *Land of Desire*.
22. J. Lawrence Laughlin, "Economic Effects of Changes of Fashion," *The Chautauquan* 19 (April 1894): 12–13.
23. The men's furnishings industry included shirts, ties, and other accessories, essentially everything in a man's wardrobe except suits and coats.

24. Florence S. Richards, *The Ready-to-Wear Industry, 1900–1950* (New York: Fairchild Publications, 1951).
25. Smith, "A Study of Uneven Industrial Development"; Richards, *The Ready-to-Wear Industry*.
26. Gregory, "Fashion and Monopolistic Competition."
27. *The Haberdasher*, November 1896, 22–23.
28. *Women's Wear*, October 29, 1910, quoted in Bernard Smith, "A Study of Uneven Industrial Development."
29. Haire, "Pirated Designs," 10.
30. "A Woman's Department in a Man's Shop," *The Haberdasher*, May 1903, 59.
31. There are many examples of writers who criticized the extravagant appearance of working-class girls, especially those in stores and factories. See Rose H. Phelps Stokes, "The Condition of Working Women from the Working Woman's Viewpoint," *The Annals of the American Academy* 27 (January–June 1906): 634, and Cochran Wilson, "Women and Wage-Spending," *Outlook* 84 (October 1906): 375–77. Bosworth also described a conversation between two "shop girls" concerned about their reputation for extravagant dress. They justified their appearance by stating that the "plain clothes" were more expensive than the lowest-priced things, which were covered with cheap trims. See Louise Bosworth, *The Living Wage of Women Workers: A Study of Incomes and Expenditures of 450 Women in the City of Boston* (New York: Longmans, Green, and Co., 1911), 65.
32. Richardson, *The Woman Who Spends*, 77–78.
33. Kathy Peiss, *Cheap Amusements: Working Women and Leisure in Turn-of-the-Century New York* (Philadelphia: Temple University Press, 1986), 62–67.
34. Mrs. Le Roy-Huntington, "Children's Ready-to-Wear Clothing," *Good Housekeeping* 48 (May 1909): 620.
35. Drake and Glaser, *Trends in the New York Clothing Industry*; "Improving the Basement Store," *The New York Times*, May 17, 1914, XX12.
36. *Women's Wear Daily*, November 30, 1910, quoted in Bernard Smith, "A Study of Uneven Industrial Development," 192.
37. The idea of "one-of-a-kind" fashions was often assumed to be the prerogative of custom dressmakers, but even they were sometimes caught duplicating designs for different customers. Cranor warned readers that even the "best dressmaker" might duplicate designs. See Katherine Cranor, "Homemade Versus Ready-to-Wear Clothing," *The Journal of Home Economics* (May 1920): 230.
38. Schorman, *Selling Style*.
39. Mary Moss, "Machine-Made Human Beings," *Atlantic Monthly* 94 (1904): 265.

40. Ibid.
41. B. W. Parker. "The Commerce of Clothes," *Good Housekeeping* 48 (April 1909): 525.
42. See, for example, J. L. Ashlock, "The Cost of Women's Clothes," *The Journal of Home Economics* 9 (November 1917): 499–502; "Why Are We Women Not Happy?" *The Ladies' Home Journal*, December 1900, 22; C. Henry, "The Finances of a Single Woman," *Harper's Bazar*, January 1909, 68–69; and Helen Watterson Moody, "The American Woman and Dress," *The Ladies' Home Journal*, June 1902, 15, 18.
43. Pearl MacDonald, "Housekeeper's Department: Club Women Approve Sensible Styles in Dress," *The Journal of Home Economics* 7 (April 1915): 201–3.
44. Richardson, *The Woman Who Spends*, 69.
45. "Why Are We Women Not Happy?" *The Ladies' Home Journal*, December 1900, 22.
46. Quoted in Leach, *Land of Desire*, 92.
47. Abraham and Straus advertisement, *The New York Times*, June 9, 1910, 5.
48. Norris, *Advertising and the Transformation of American Society*, 104.
49. For examples of advertising language see Best & Co. advertisements, *The New York Times*, September 24, 1911, 9, and October 22, 1916, 7; and Gimbels advertisement, *The New York Times*, December 24, 1911, X10. For discussion of the changing approach to fashion and consumer demand, see Susan Porter Benson, *Counter Cultures: Saleswomen, Managers, and Customers in American Department Stores, 1890–1940* (Champaign, IL: University of Illinois Press, 1986). For advertisers' attempts to equate mass-produced clothing with style and modernity, see Schorman, *Selling Style*.
50. Mary Brooks Picken, *The Secrets of Distinctive Dress: Harmonious, Becoming, and Beautiful Dress; Its Value and How to Achieve It* (Scranton, PA: The Woman's Institute of Domestic Arts and Sciences, Inc., 1918), 191.
51. H. L. Johnson, "For the Homemaker: Women and Clothes; What the Clubs Are Doing in the Matter of Standardization," *The Journal of Home Economics* 9 (March 1917): 127–36.
52. Benjamin M. Selekman, *The Clothing and Textile Industries in New York and Its Environs* (New York: Regional Plan of New York and Its Environs, 1925).
53. Ibid., 75.
54. Mary Schenck Woolman, *Clothing: Choice, Care, Cost* (Philadelphia: J. B. Lippincott Co., 1920), 155. Others also compared ready-made and home-produced garments. For example, in Baker's (1916) study, ready-made were always more expensive, but if time was a factor, it was the clear choice. She estimated the time to make a fancy waist at seventeen hours, hardly worth the

small savings in cost except for those on the tightest budgets. Charlotte Gibbs Baker, "Clothing and the Income," *The Journal of Home Economics* 8 (July 1916).
55. Baker, "Clothing and the Income," 374.
56. Selekman, *The Clothing and Textile Industries in New York*; US Census of Manufactures, 1920: 30.
57. Allinson pointed out that the manufacturing branch of dressmaking was concentrated in New York and occurred on a sporadic scale in Boston. As early as 1884, the Bureau of Industrial Statistics and Information identified at least some dressmaking businesses in Baltimore as "factory labor." See Maryland Bureau of Industrial Statistics and Information, *First Biennial Report of the Bureau*, 1884–1885 (Baltimore: Maryland Bureau of Industrial Statistics and Information, 1886), 91–92.
58. US Census of Manufacturing, 1923.
59. For a discussion of the differences in development and culture of ready-to-wear in Paris and New York see Green, *Ready-to-Wear and Ready-to-Work*. Paris continued to have significant numbers of small dressmakers in addition to the haute couture designers.

Chapter 4

1. Sections of this chapter were originally published in Sara B. Marcketti and Jean L. Parsons, "American Fashions for American Women: Early Twentieth Century Efforts to Develop an American Fashion Identity," *Dress: The Journal of the Costume Society of America* 34 (2007): 79–95.
2. Thorstein Veblen, *The Theory of the Leisure Class* (New York: MacMillan, 1899); and George Simmel, "Fashion," Report in *American Journal of Sociology* 62 (May 1957): 541–58. Although the term *trickle down* is commonly used to describe class-based fashion, neither Veblen nor Simmel used this term. For description of the fashion process and critique of their approach, see Fred Davis, *Fashion, Culture, and Identity* (Chicago: The University of Chicago Press, 1992), 103–20.
3. "Mystery of the Fashions," *Women's Wear*, August 10, 1910, 5.
4. "Shall American Women Follow Paris Styles?" *The New York Times*, October 6, 1912, F8. This article presented the differing opinions of Edward Bok, the designers Joseph and Henri Bendel, and Maurice Renard.
5. Anna Burnham Westermann, "Can America Originate Its Own Fashion?," *Ladies' Home Journal* (1909): 11–12.
6. Edna Bryner, *The Garment Trades* (Cleveland, OH: The Survey Committee of the Cleveland Foundation, 1916).

7. Publications also used the anglicized version of the term—*commissioner*—but more often referred to them as commissionaires. They eventually were considered a significant problem by the Parisian fashion houses in their fight to stop design piracy. See "Plan Clearing House of Paris Fashions," *The New York Times*, February 5, 1916, 3.
8. "We Are Advertising Foreign Styles While They Are Copying Our Own Smart Women," *Women's Wear*, October 15, 1912, 11.
9. "Franco-American Board Reports on Exploitation of French Models," *Women's Wear*, May 19, 1919, 3.
10. For a more detailed explanation of copying practices of French haute couture, see Troy, *Couture Culture*, 239–40.
11. "Clearance of Exclusive French Models at Wanamaker Store," *Women's Wear*, January 1, 1921, 4.
12. The fashion press used a variety of terms for this movement, including "American styles for American women," "American fashions for American women," and other variants of the title.
13. Selected names of associations and start dates if available: American Dress Designers' Association; Associated Fur Manufacturers, 1911; National Association of Clothing Designers, 1910; International Association of Garment Manufacturers, 1908; Model Creators' Association; Model Makers' Association; United Cloak and Suit Designers' Mutual Aid Association of America; Retail Clothiers' and Furnishers' Association, 1923; Custom Tailors and Designers Association, 1880; National Garment Retailers' Association; The Greater New York Apparel Merchants; National Retail Dry Goods Association; American Cloak and Suit Manufacturers Association, 1919; The Cloak, Suit, and Skirt Manufacturers' Protective Association; Dress and Waist Manufacturers' Association; Merchants' Ladies' Garment Association Inc., 1917; National Association of House Dress Manufacturers, 1917; National Knitted Outerwear Association, 1918; New York Separate Skirt Manufacturers' Association; Associated Dress Manufacturers of New York; American Clothiers' Association; Pantsmakers' Union; Amalgamated Clothing Workers of America, 1915.
14. Other groups that promoted more uniformity of dress included the General Federation of Women's Clubs and certain home economists. Their concern, however, was the "tyranny of the ever-increasing changes of style" that meant throwing away clothing that was far from worn out. See H. L. Johnson, "For the Homemaker: Women and Clothes, What the Clubs Are Doing in the Matter of Standardization," *The Journal of Home Economics* 9 (March 1917): 127–36; and "Standardized Dress," *The Journal of Home Economics* 8 (June 1916): 326–27.

15. "Put 28-Inch Limit on Women's Coats," *The New York Times*, March 24, 1911, 20. The article described this as the first convention of the Cloak and Suit Designers.
16. "Informal Meeting of Waist and Dress Designers' Association Held Last Night," *Women's Wear*, September 20, 1911, 5; "Clothing Designers Meet," *The New York Times*, June 28, 1912, 11; "The Chicago Dressmakers' Club Convention," 1. Limited information is available regarding these associations and organizations.
17. "National Ladies' Tailors and Dressmakers' Association Plan Fashion Congress," *Women's Wear*, April 11, 1911, 5. James Blaine, Philip Friedman, and Walter Bartholomew were appointed officers. The object of the National Ladies' Tailors and Dressmakers' Association was "not to dictate styles to American women, but to offer the best efforts based upon all good ideas received . . . and if possible to create some uniformity in the showing of models throughout the country."
18. Ibid.
19. "American-Designed Dresses at Miss Hostetter's Wedding," *The New York Times*, October 5, 1914, X4.
20. "Without Waiting for Paris, American Designers Have Issued Certain Edicts for Autumn," *The New York Times*, August 10, 1913, X6.
21. Clara E. Simcox, "Why I Refused $25,000 a Year," *The Delineator* 79 (February 1912): 87. Simcox went on to describe how she had been instrumental in creating a focus on New York instead of Parisian fashions.
22. See Edward Bok, "A Woman's Questions," *Ladies' Home Journal* 18 (April 1901): 16.
23. May Allinson, *Industrial Experience of Trade School Girls in Massachusetts*, Studies in Economic Relations of Women, vol. 9 (Boston: The Department of Research: Women's Educational and Industrial Union, 1917), 217.
24. J. M. Gidding and Co. advertisement, *The New York Times*, March 9, 1913, 28.
25. "Home Fashions for America," *The New York Times*, December 8, 1912, 12.
26. As reported in *Women's Wear*, under the caption "American fashions for American women," the *New York World* commented editorially that the proposed revival of Robespierre styles demonstrated that "Paris was mentally and morally unbalanced. . . . It will be . . . a freak in New York. It is time for America to have American dress for American women." "American Fashions for American Women," *Women's Wear*, July 6, 1912, 15. In the article "Second Day of Style Congress," *Women's Wear*, June 28, 1912, 1, 11, the original president of the Boston branch of the National Ladies' Tailors and Dressmakers' Associ-

ation decried the very existence of Parisian fashion, which was reportedly met "with an outburst of applause."

27. "Home Fashions for America," 12.

28. Sara B. Marcketti and Jean L. Parsons, "Design Piracy and Self-Regulation: The Fashion Originators' Guild of America, 1932–1941," *Clothing and Textiles Research Journal* 24 (2006): 214–28.

29. The opera singer Madame Nordica complained of hastily and poorly sewn gowns, publicly doubting and even renouncing the renowned craftsmanship of Paris. "New York Says Paris Dressmakers Are No Longer Creators of Fashions, but Merely Adopters," *Women's Wear*, May 15, 1911, 5; "Parisians Adopt Uniform," *Women's Wear*, May 31, 1912, 1, 4; "Two More Prominent American Women Come Out for Open Recognition on Merit of American Styles and Merchandise and Announce Intention to Support Movement," *Women's Wear*, December 24, 1912, 7; "Paris Losing Its Vogue," *The New York Times*, December 1, 1912, 16; "Advisors on Modes Proposed in Paris," *The New York Times*, December 1, 1912, 3; "Nazimova for American Mode," *The New York Times*, December 14, 1912, 10; "How to Beat Paris at Her Own Game," *The New York Times*, December 19, 1912, 8.

30. "It Was America That Made Paris," *The New York Times*, December 22, 1912, 11.

31. See Troy, *Couture Culture*, 192, for a discussion of the "precarious balance that Poiret strove to maintain after 1909 between an allegedly disinterested commitment to high culture and the demands of an increasingly complex, sophisticated, and diversified commercial enterprise." Styles of both American and Parisian origination were copied at lower price points and flooded the market with cheap imitations of higher-end goods.

32. "Style vs. Quality," *Women's Wear*, December 13, 1912, 1; "That American Women Are the Peers of Those of Paris Evidenced by Comparing Original Drecoll Model with the American Made Copy," *Women's Wear*, October 28, 1912, 4. The perspective that France was an international style fount that the American originator consulted but altered to fit the "beautiful, willowy American figure" and her style of life continued to be an important argument even into the 1940s. Marshall Adams, "US Prepared to Accept Lead in Fashion," *The Washington Post*, July 19, 1940, 15.

33. R. H. Macy advertisement, *The New York Times*, September 24, 1913, 5.

34. A few years later, in 1918, the US company that produced dresses under the brand name Peggy Paige was denied a US trademark because it was "a mere proper name."

35. "Paris Labels," *Women's Wear*, October 18, 1912, 2.

36. Samuel Hopkins Adams, "The Dishonest Paris Label: How American Women Are Being Fooled by a Country-Wide Swindle," *Ladies' Home Journal*, March 1913.
37. "Two More Prominent American Women Come Out for Open Recognition on Merit of American Styles and Merchandise"; "Paris Labels" and "Costumes," *Women's Wear*, October 25, 1912, 12.
38. "Publicity," *Women's Wear*, December 24, 1912, 7.
39. "American Fashions for American Women," 12.
40. "Costumes," *Women's Wear*, February 18, 1913, 1.
41. Paquin advertisement, *The New York Times*, March 7, 1913, 6.
42. "To Stop Pirating of Dress Fashion," *The New York Times*, May 29, 1914, 4.
43. "Warning Against False Labels," Poiret advertisement, *Women's Wear*, October 14, 1913, 3.
44. "Threaten to Bar American Buyers," *The New York Times*, March 4, 1914, 4; "To Stop Pirating of Dress Fashion," 4; "Modistes Gain Thirty Percent," *The New York Times*, February 15, 1913, 4.
45. For an in-depth analysis of the complications and ambivalent nature of original designs and reproductions as they evolved between the French and American trades, see especially chapter 4 of Troy, *Couture Culture*.
46. "Paris Dressmakers in Protective Union," *The New York Times*, October 24, 1915, sec. 3, 9.
47. "Paul Poiret Assails American Buyers," *The New York Times*, December 19, 1915, 17.
48. Ibid.
49. See *Woman's Home Companion*, particularly during the year 1915.
50. Megan Richardson and David Tan, "Wood v. Duff-Gordon and the Modernist Cult of Personality," *Pace Law Review* 28 (Winter 2008): 379–93.
51. "Francis of Paris Has Radical Views on the Present French Situation," *Women's Wear*, April 23, 1913, 1, 12.
52. "Grean Lectures to the Women Students at the Teachers College of Columbia on American Fashions," *Women's Wear*, November 23, 1912, 8–9.
53. "Head Designer for Thurn Comments on How America's Publicity Has Boosted Paris," *Women's Wear*, December 23, 1912, 6.
54. "December a Month of Peace in Styles to Most Women," *The New York Times*, December 13, 1914, X2.
55. The number of American firms rose sharply in the early twentieth century to keep up with the demand for the newest novelties. US Census Bureau, *Census of Manufacturers, 1921* (Washington, DC: Government Printing Office, 1924).
56. Although 1940 to 1944, when Paris was occupied by the Nazis, is most often

identified as a beginning of a true support and attention to US designers, the 1910s and World War I were a period of development that was also essential to the evolution of US ready-to-wear designers. Sandra S. Buckland and Gwendolyn S. O'Neal, "'We Publish Fashions Because They Are News': *New York Times*, 1940–1945," *Dress* 25 (1998): 33–41.

57. "Style Congress of Ladies Tailors and Dressmakers Opens," *Women's Wear*, June 27, 1912, 1. *The New York Times* and subsequent issues of *Women's Wear*, among others, printed related essays and editorials.

58. Edward Bok, "Gowns and Hats Fresh from Paris," *The New York Times*, September 15, 1912, 14.

59. Babette A. Muelle, "New York Dressmakers," *Good Housekeeping* 36 (1903): 302–3; "Home Fashions for America," *The New York Times*, December 8, 1912, 12; Sarah Bernhardt, "Can the American Woman Design Her Own Clothes?" *Ladies' Home Journal* (April 1912), 9; "What America Needs," *Women's Wear*, August 6, 1912, 1; Edward Bok, "If America Had Her Own Fashions," *The New York Times*, September 25, 1912, 7; "American Styles for American Women," *Women's Wear*, October 9, 1912, 1; "Those Artistic French Fashions," *The New York Times*, December 12, 1912, 9; "The Instinct of Dress," *The New York Times*, December 13, 1912, 14; "Worth Declares America Is Right," *The New York Times*, December 20, 1912, 12; "As to American Fashions," *The New York Times*, December 26, 1912, 8; "Geraldine Tarrar on American Styles," *The New York Times*, December 29, 1912, 11; "American or French," *Women's Wear*, February 24, 1913, 3, 6–7; "Fashion Contest for Times Readers," *The New York Times*, December 5, 1912, 9.

60. Anna Burnham Westermann, "Can America Originate Its Own Fashion?," *Ladies' Home Journal* (September 1909): 11–12.

61. Marlis Schweitzer, "American Fashions for American Women," in *Producing Fashion: Commerce, Culture and Consumers*, ed. Regina Blaszczyk (Philadelphia: The University of Pennsylvania Press, 2007).

62. Edward Bok, "Paris Fashions and Ours," *The New York Times*, September 6, 1912, 8.

63. "We Are Advertising Foreign Styles," 1.

64. Elizabeth Miner King, "War, Women, and American Clothes," *Scribner's Magazine* 21 (1917): 592–98.

65. "Paris May See End of Style Control," *The New York Times*, August 6, 1914, 15.

66. Troy, *Couture Culture*, 274–75. Troy also details the controversy surrounding the Syndicat during the war years.

67. Daniel Delis Hill, *As Seen in Vogue: A Century of American Fashion in Advertising* (Lubbock: Texas Tech University Press, 2007), 28–29.

68. Quoted in Troy, *Couture Culture*, 276–77.
69. Eleanor L. Dulles, *The French Franc, 1914–1928* (New York: The Macmillan Company, 1929), appendix, 143.
70. "Paris Advises Americans to Shop at Home," *Women's Wear*, December 12, 1919, 1, 17.
71. See "New Conspiracy to Smuggle Gowns," *The New York Times*, December 12, 1912, 24. Attempts to smuggle French dresses had in fact been occurring for years, with frequent notices of arrests in *The New York Times*. See, for example: "Charge Smuggling on Liner St. Louis," *The New York Times*, March 29, 1909, 1; and "Woman Confesses Smuggling Plot," *The New York Times*, March 28, 1913, 24.
72. "Simcox Is Bankrupt," *The New York Times*, October 1, 1916, 17. Apparently in addition to both customs duties and taxes, Simcox had a number of prominent customers who had not paid her.
73. "Our Views Endorsed," *The Dry Goods Economist*, March 1913, 31.
74. Charles R. Richards, *Art in Industry* (New York: The MacMillan Co., 1922). According to Richards, designers by and large no longer worked in factories by 1920 (p. 19).
75. Quoted in Joanne Ollian, "From Division Street to Seventh Avenue: The Coming of Age of American Fashions," in *A Perfect Fit: The Garment Industry and American Jewry, 1860–1960*, ed. Gabriel M. Goldstein and Elizabeth E. Greenberg (New York: Yeshiva University, 2012).
76. Farnan-Leipzig describes a slightly different breakdown of the types of designers in the 1930s. Sheryl Farnan-Leipzig, Jean L. Parsons, and Jane Farrell-Beck, "It Is a Profession That Is New, Unlimited, and Rich," *Dress* 35 (2008–2009).
77. Harry Collins advertisements, *The New York Times*, October 1, 1922, 2, and September 25, 1921, 8.
78. "Designers Establish Employment Bureau," *Women's Wear*, September 12, 1919, 3; "Leading Tailors and Dressmakers Organize for Protection and Elevation of Their Industry," *Women's Wear*, October 9, 1919, 1; "Associated Dress Industries of America," *Women's Wear*, January 17, 1919, 32–33; M. D. C. Crawford, "You Must Raise America's Standards of Design," *Women's Wear*, November 5, 1919, 2; M. D. C. Crawford, "America Lacks Costume Inspirational Sources—More Museums and Libraries of Costume Ideas Essential in Apparel Centers," *Women's Wear*, January 8, 1920, 3; "Need Retailers' Aid to Elevate American Style," *Women's Wear*, January 19, 1920, 1, 54; M. D. C. Crawford, "Suggests Establishment of Special Stores to Carry Merchandise of American Craftsman," *Women's Wear*, July 1, 1919, 2; "How American

Retailers Promote Foreign Goods," *Women's Wear*, October 18, 1912, 2, 6–9; "Nadoolman Says American Newspapers Force American Designers to Deny Their Own Style Creations," *Women's Wear*, October 22, 1912, 1.

79. Richards, *Art in Industry*.

80. The tailoring trade has been generally considered the domain of men, both as cutters and patternmakers. The dressmaking trade was overwhelmingly women. Other jobs were also gender segregated. Cutters, for example, were exclusively men, while stitchers were 80–90 percent women, depending on the type. N. I. Stone, *Wages and Regularity of Employment in the Dress and Waist Industry of New York City* (1915; repr., New York: Columbia University Libraries, 2008).

81. Charles Worth was sometimes referred to as a "bearded milliner," or "man milliner," suggesting the oddness of a man who made dresses for women. See Abigail Joseph, "'A Wizard of Silks and Tulle': Charles Worth and the Queer Origins of Couture," *Victorian Studies* 56 (Winter 2014).

82. Mary Donahue, "Design and the Industrial Arts in America, 1894–1940: An Inquiry into Fashion Design and Art and Industry" (PhD diss., The City University of New York, 2001).

83. "Designers, Stop Guessing!" *Women's Wear*, March 20, 1912, 9. For an overview of the various curricula and the conflicts between art education and practical, trade education, see Donahue, "Design and the Industrial Arts." Although some apparel design and sewing education existed in the newly organized home economics programs, much of the teaching was oriented to training consumers of apparel.

84. There is no way to know for sure how many were women, but sewing and fashion advertised extensively in women's publications.

85. "The Dressmakers' Club Convention," *Women's Wear*, March 15, 1911, 1, 2; "What Makes a Good Designer?" *Women's Wear*, April 18, 1913, 4.

86. "Grean Lectures on American Fashions," *Women's Wear*, November 23, 1912, 8–9.

87. Ibid.

88. Richards, *Art in Industry*, 12, 15.

89. Donahue, "Design and the Industrial Arts"; Ethelwyn Miller, "Americanism: The Spirit of Costume Design," *The Journal of Home Economics* 10 (May 1918): 207–11; Ann Marguerite Tartsinis, *An American Style: Global Sources for New York Textile and Fashion Design, 1915–1928* (New York: Bard Graduate Center, 2013). The American Museum of Art hosted a series of lectures by industrial experts, such as James Chittick, a textile expert in woolens, worsteds, silks, ribbons, and velvets. At the Metropolitan Museum of Art, Professor Chas

Pellew lectured to designers, salespeople, and buyers about dyestuffs of the ancient world. Ruth Wilmott of Columbia University lectured on fashion design, specifically the various colors, lines, and values of the proportions of the human body. On December 3, 1917, a textile gallery opened at the Metropolitan Museum of Art especially for textile designers studying primitive art at schools and museums.

90. "The Mallinson Campaign to Popularize American-Made Styles," *The American Silk Journal* 34 (October 1915): 38.
91. "To Get Recognition: The Chance the War Affords to American Manufacturers," *The New York Times*, October 18, 1914, XX12.
92. Madelyn Shaw, "American Silk from a Marketing Magician," *Textile Society of America 8th Biennial Symposium Proceedings*, Northampton, Massachusetts, September 26–28, 2002. Proceedings are available at DigitalCommons@University of Nebraska, http://digitalcommons.unl.edu/tsaconf/.
93. Miller, "Americanism," 207–11; Elizabeth Miner King, "War, Women, and American Clothes," *Scribner's Magazine* 21 (1917): 592–98. Crawford was a research fellow at the American Museum of Natural History until 1921 when he moved to the Brooklyn Museum.
94. In 1945, for example, the Metropolitan Museum of Art presented an exhibit of design by US designers using Enka rayon fabrics with prints inspired by objects in their collections.
95. King, "War, Women, and American Clothes," 592–98.
96. Tartsinis, *An American Style*.
97. Donahue, "Design and the Industrial Arts."
98. M. D. C. Crawford, "Museum Documents and Modern Costume," *American Museum Journal* 18 (1918): 286–97.
99. M. D. C. Crawford, "Antiquities of the New World Inspire American Textile Design," *Good Furniture Magazine* 10 (March 1918): 166–69. This entire issue of the magazine was focused on "mobilizing" industrial design in the United States to break a dependence on "foreign" sources, a direct response to the war.
100. Lauren D. Whitley, "Morris De Camp Crawford and the Designed in America Campaign, 1916–1922," *Textile Society of America Symposium Proceedings*, New York, September 24–26, 1998. Fashion Institute of Technology, New York. Proceedings are available at DigitalCommons@University of Nebraska, http://digitalcommons.unl.edu/tsaconf/.
101. M. D. C. Crawford, "One of Best Things Written on Subject," *Women's Wear Daily*, April 29, 1941, 21.
102. Davis adopted the name Tobé when she founded her style service.

103. "Rising Prestige of Knitted Outerwear," *American Cloak and Suit Review*, March 1922, 137.
104. *Harper's Bazar* changed its name to *Harper's Bazaar* in November 1929.
105. "Thus New York Designers Visualize the Mode," *Vogue*, October 1, 1919, 51–52, 124.
106. Ibid.
107. "The Unseen Label: The Contribution of the American Wholesale Designers," *Vogue*, October 27, 1930, 66–69, 101–2. *Vogue* did not devote an entire issue to American designers until 1938, although they included advertisements for US dressmakers. See Madelyn Shaw, "American Fashion," in *From Paris to Providence*, ed. Susan Hay (Providence: Museum of Art, Rhode Island School of Design, 2000), 107.
108. "It Was America That Made Paris," 11.
109. See, for example, Bonwit Teller & Co. advertisement, *The New York Times*, November 8, 1914, 3.
110. "[Clara] Simcox [Importer] Says Exclusive American Fashions Are Not Working Against Public Opinion but With It," *Women's Wear*, October 24, 1913, 1, 9. *Harper's Bazar* noted Simcox's design had a Paris inspiration. "From Fifth Avenue Shops," *Harper's Bazar*, March 1915, 53.
111. Arnold, Constable & Co. advertisement, *The New York Times*, August 30, 1914, 8.
112. *Harper's Bazar* advertisement, *The New York Times*, January 20, 1916, 9. The advertisement listed the designers of all the new styles that were in the next issue. This included twenty Paris designers and seven New York designers. Lucile was included in the New York list, having opened a salon there.
113. "American Fashions for American Women," *Women's Wear*, September 7, 1912, 13.
114. Some retailers with exclusive custom shops did advertise the services of their in-store designers by name. Shaw, "American Fashion," 117.
115. Ibid.
116. "Girls Who Apply for Positions," *Women's Wear*, April 18, 1913, 4.
117. "Things of Interest to Women: Thorough Training Now Offered to the American Girl Who Wants to Create Fashions," *The New York Times*, February 23, 1913, 78.
118. Farnan-Leipzig, Parsons, and Farrell-Beck, "It Is a Profession."
119. Richards, *Art in Industry*; and "Sues Over Dress Designer," *The New York Times*, April 22, 1928, 29. Salaries quoted by Richards varied by industry garment category.
120. Originally named the Traphagen School of Cooperative Fashion, Traphagen became a strong voice for American design.

121. The Bush Tower was conceived to provide office space for importers and manufacturers as well as a library specializing in books on manufacturing. It was built 1916–1918, located at 130 West Forty-Second Street in New York City.
122. M. D. C. Crawford, "Suggests Establishment of Special Stores to Carry Merchandise of American Craftsmen," *Women's Wear*, July 1, 1919, 2; "To Create US Styles for Bush Terminal Building," *Women's Wear*, July 3, 1919, 5; "Design Department," *Women's Wear*, August 22, 1919, 2.
123. Advertisement, *The New York Times*, August 22, 1920, X10.
124. Penikees advertisement, *The New York Times*, February 27, 1921, RP25.
125. *The New York Times*, April 3, 1921, 67.
126. "United States Government Cartridge Cloth," *The New York Times*, February 9, 1920, 15. Cartridge silk was silk noil or waste silk, up to this point not used in apparel. See *The New York Times*, March 9, 1920, and February 9, 1920.
127. Harry Collins advertisements, *The New York Times*, October 2, 1921, 8, and May 23, 1922, 6.
128. Elizabeth Hawes, *Fashion Is Spinach* (New York: Random House, 1938), 108–9.
129. "To Establish a Fashion Library," *The New York Times*, January 17, 1915, 5.
130. "Value of Showing American Styles," *The New York Times*, January 18, 1920, X8.
131. The American Society of Style Creators, incorporation papers, 1930, New York Department of State, New York County Clerk, New York, NY.
132. Richards, *Art in Industry*, 455.
133. *Ben Gershel & Co., and Abraham E. Lefcourt v. Hickson, Inc., and Richard J. Hickson*, July 29, 1920, Supreme Court of New York, Appellate Division, First Department.
134. "Simcox Announcement of Copyrighted Styles," *Women's Wear*, November 4, 1912, 1.
135. Sara B. Marcketti and Jean L. Parsons, "The Use of Design Patents to Protect Dress, 1910–1950," *Proceedings of the 70th Annual Conference of the International Textile and Apparel Association*, New Orleans, November 2013.
136. The trademark filing date was March 6, 1917, although they had clearly begun to use and advertise it in 1916. *The Official Gazette of the United States Patent Office*, May 1, 1917, 299.
137. "What the Betty Wales Label in a Dress Means," *Harper's Bazar*, January 1918.
138. "Exclusive Agency Takes Firmer Hold," *American Cloak and Suit Review* (February 1922): 113–14; "Dresses Fashioned by Peggy Paige," advertisement,

Harper's Bazar (May 1920): 47. The Peggy Paige name was trademarked in March 1921, although the company had been using the name for at least five years.

139. "Exclusive Agency Takes Firmer Hold," 113–14.
140. *Montegut et al. v. Hickson, Inc.*, May 4, 1917, Supreme Court of New York, Appellate Division, First Department. Sylvie Montegut and Jeanne D'Etreillis were the owners of design house Boue Soeurs.
141. "To Protect Dress Designs," *The New York Times*, September 2, 1921, 18.
142. "Business World: A New Check on Style Piracy," *The New York Times*, November 12, 1925, 42.
143. "Against Style Piracy," *The New York Times*, December 20, 1925, E19.

Chapter 5

1. Parts of this chapter originally appeared in Sara B. Marcketti and Jean L. Parsons, "Design Piracy and Self-Regulation: The Fashion Originators' Guild of America, 1932–1941," *Clothing and Textiles Research Journal* 24 (2006): 214–28.
2. "Couturiers to Organize," *The New York Times*, December 20, 1931, N19.
3. Fashion Originators' Guild of America, incorporation papers, March 1932, New York Department of State, New York County Clerk, New York, NY.
4. Bernard Barber and Lyle Lobel, "Fashion in Women's Clothes and the American Social System," *Social Forces* 31 (1952): 124–31.
5. Florence S. Richards, *The Ready-to-Wear Industry, 1900–1950* (New York: Fairchild Publications, 1951), 51.
6. Leonard Drake and Carrie Glaser, *Trends in the New York Clothing Industry* (New York: Institute of Public Administration, 1942). Figures for the interim years were average cost of $5.11 in 1929, $3.74 in 1931, $2.60 in 1933, and $2.95 in 1935.
7. To meet the need for cheapness, some manufacturers juggled pattern pieces to use the least amount of fabric possible. Although this saved on the cost of the garment, quality issues such as rippling and sagging of the fabric occurred. "Dress Trade's Growth Brings Union Problem," *Women's Wear Daily*, May 2, 1932, 13.
8. William Leach, *Land of Desire: Merchants, Power, and the Rise of a New American Culture* (New York: Vintage Books, 1993).
9. "Dress Trade's Growth Brings Union Problem," *Women's Wear Daily*, May 2, 1932, 13.
10. Drake and Glaser, *Trends in the New York Clothing Industry*.
11. Lazare Tepere, *The Woman's Garment Industry, an Economic Analysis* (New York: Educational Department of the International Ladies 'Garment Workers' Union, 1937).

12. "Plan Organization of Dress Industry," *The New York Times*, June 20, 1933, 35.
13. According to Ben Hirsch, president and treasurer of Melba Dress Company, a firm dealing in garments wholesaling at the lower, popular price of $6.75: "During the years that the public had money to spend, these [dress] men were doing well and were not so persistent in their claims of being creators, but since the public generally went broke in 1929, and since have been compelled to buy Chevrolets and Fords instead of Cadillacs and Lincolns, and $5 dresses instead of $25 dresses, they have been making life pretty miserable for both you and me by their persistence for monopoly." "Hirsch Hits Policies of Fashion Guild," *Women's Wear Daily*, October 21, 1935, 7; "Fashion Guild Tells Plans to Retail Stores," *Women's Wear Daily*, March 28, 1932, sec. 2, 5.
14. Original directors of the FOGA were Maurice Rentner, Herbert Sondheim, Edward Gerrick, Samuel Kass, Herman Florsheimer, Morris E. Zipper, and William Fox. In 1936 the officers included Rentner, Sondheim, Charles Gumprecht, J. A. Livingston, Albert M. Post, and James M. Golby. Before serving as executive director, Albert Post was the chairman of the Merchandising Division of the National Retail Dry Goods Association. Fashion Originators' Guild of America, incorporation papers, March 1932, New York Department of State; "Maurice Rentner Started His Business Career at 17," *Women's Wear Daily*, November 12, 1933, 1, 15; Findings and Facts of Law, Federal Trade Commission, Docket No. 2769.
15. "Minneapolis Forms Local Style Guild," *Women's Wear Daily*, October 1, 1935, 13.
16. The Uptown Retail Annex Guild comprised thirty-three retail establishments, including Bergdorf Goodman, Hattie Carnegie, Bonwit Teller, Milgrim, and Tailored Woman. "Minneapolis Forms Local Style Guild," *Women's Wear Daily*, October 1, 1935, 13.
17. "Design Protection Gains in Many Lines," *The New York Times*, May 6, 1934, sec. 2, 19; "Guild Begins Non-Copying Program Today," *Women's Wear Daily*, July 5, 1933, 5.
18. "Fashion Guild War," *Business Week*, December 28, 1935, 12, 14.
19. The National Retail Dry Goods Association changed its name to the National Retail Merchants Association in 1958. Then in 1990, it merged with the American Retail Federation and adopted the name the National Retail Federation.
20. Fashion Originators' Guild of America, Inc., advertisement, *Women's Wear Daily*, January 10, 1936, 11.
21. "Fashion Week to Begin Today," *The New York Times*, September 6, 1932, 30.
22. "Firm Admitted to Guild," *The New York Herald Tribune*, January 16, 1935,

34.

23. Among the proposals announced by Rentner were the following: couture houses establishing a New York headquarters to collaborate with the guild, the establishment of a passport system of admissions to the Parisian openings, and postponement of advertisement by American retailers of the new models to prevent "new styles being killed before the appropriate seasons are under way." "Suggests Guild and Couture Draft Code," *Women's Wear Daily*, August 3, 1933, 3; "Guild Eager to Cooperate with Britain," *Women's Wear Daily*, January 24, 1933, 40.

24. The registration bureau was established in 1933. *Wm Filene's Sons Co v. Fashion Originators' Guild*, 90 F.2d 556 (1937); "To Bring Back the Demand for Good Clothes," *Women's Wear Daily*, March 29, 1932, 9.

25. "Designs Filed at Peak," *The New York Times*, September 13, 1936, sec. 2, 8.

26. "Queries Cover FOGA Price Range Scope," *Women's Wear Daily*, April 23, 1936, 31; "Guild's Work Good in Upper Brackets," *The New York Times*, February 23, 1936, 17; "Designers of Today and Tomorrow," *Women's Wear Daily*, July 10, 1935, 5, and July 24, 1935, 5.

27. "Order Dress Guild Style Labels," *The New York Times*, August 6, 1933, 7; "No Change in Guild Plan," *The New York Times*, January 2, 1936, 57.

28. "Complete Text of Master's Report That Upholds FOGA's Style Protection Is No Monopoly," *Women's Wear Daily*, November 10, 1936, 39.

29. "Guild to Ask Buyers to Approve Code," *Women's Wear Daily*, June 14, 1933, 9.

30. In October 1936 the guild handled 691 complaints of piracy and found 408 of them justified. Maurice A. Weikart, "Design Piracy," *Indiana Law Journal*, vol. 19, *1943–1944*, 234–57; "Fashion Guild War," *Business Week*, December 28, 1935, 12, 14.

31. In the later Federal Trade Commission hearings regarding the legality of the FOGA, lawyers for the FTC and witnesses opposed to the FOGA likened red-carding to boycotting. "Sign Pact or Get No Goods, Guild Rules," *Women's Wear Daily*, December 7, 1932, 1.

32. "Stores Will Test Fashion Guild Ban," *The New York Times*, February 20, 1936, 38; "Fashion Guild Determines to Meet All Attacks on Program," *Women's Wear Daily*, February 18, 1936, 1; "All Parts of Country on Red Card List," *Women's Wear Daily*, February 18, 1936, 2.

33. "FOGA Adds Four Stores to 'Red Card' List," *Women's Wear Daily*, February 14, 1936, 1, 18.

34. "Imported Models Shown," *The New York Times*, June 2, 1936, 49; "May Be Fireworks," *Business Week*, February 29, 1936, 339.

35. The National Industrial Recovery Act (NIRA) was passed by Congress and approved by President Franklin D. Roosevelt on June 16, 1933. It was the centerpiece of Roosevelt's first one hundred days in office and was a deliberate attempt to restore industrial prosperity by positive governmental intervention. Title I of the NIRA, titled "Industrial Recovery," led to creation of the National Recovery Administration (NRA), suspended antitrust laws, and called for industries to create codes of industrial production in order to guard against the dangers of competition. Title II of the NIRA called for the creation of a Federal Emergency Agency for Public Works that would benefit Americans through direct government expenditure on public works projects. Albert U. Romasco, *The Politics of Recovery* (New York: Oxford University Press, 1983).

Chapter 6

1. Information from this chapter is derived from the hearings and debates of the NRA, Code of Fair Practices and Competition. During the time of the NRA, the courts largely kept out of decisions regarding unfair competition, one of the key features in arguments both for and against design protection, leaving defendants to the mercies of the Federal Trade Commission or the Better Business Bureau. For more information about the NRA and the women's dress-manufacturing code, see Sara B. Marcketti, "Codes of Fair Competition: The National Recovery Act, 1933–1935, and the Women's Dress Manufacturing Industry," *Clothing and Textiles Research Journal* (2010): 189–204.
2. Still debated today, there are legal arguments on both sides of this issue. See for example: C. Scott Hemphill and Jeannie Suk, "The Fashion Originators' Guild of America: Self-Help at the Edge of IP and Antitrust," in *Intellectual Property at the Edge: The Contested Contours of IP*, ed. Rochelle C. Dreyfuss and Jane C. Ginsburg (Cambridge: Cambridge University Press, 2013); Kal Raustiala and Christopher Sprigman, *The Knockoff Economy: How Imitation Sparks Innovation* (Cary, NC: Oxford University Press, 2012).
3. Rentner, November 15, 1934, NRA Hearing, 114.
4. Selekman, *The Clothing and Textile Industries in New York and Its Environs*, 19.
5. Alphonsus Haire, "Pirated Designs," *The New York Times*, January 20, 1913, 10.
6. "Dresses," *Printers' Ink Monthly*, January 1939, 55.
7. A low-priced copy was frequently said to "kill" the higher-priced dress, in that no more sales of the higher-end dress occurred. Aaron Johnston and Florence Fitch, "Design Piracy: The Problem and Its Treatment under N.R.A. Codes," National Recovery Administration Materials, ser. 52 (Washington, DC: The Administration, 1936).
8. "Fight Is Indicated over Dress Designs," *The New York Times*, September 2, 1934, sec. 2, 6.

9. *Wm Filene's Sons Co v. Fashion Originators' Guild*, 90 F.2d 556 (1937).
10. It seems that only when the copy was marketed in the same price bracket as the original did the issue of property rights become more important than the issue of price.
11. "Complete Text of Master's Report," 10.
12. Ernest L. Magee, November 15, 1934, NRA Hearing, 19.
13. Irene Blunt, November 15, 1934, NRA Hearing, 37.
14. Eugene Ackerman, November 15, 1934, NRA Hearing, 337 and 339.
15. Ruth O'Brien, *Boston Conference on Distribution* (Boston, MA: Retail Trade Board, Boston Chamber of Commerce, 1934).
16. Keating, November 15, 1934, NRA Hearing, 27.
17. Johnston and Fitch, "Design Piracy," 8.
18. "Fashion Originators' to Confer Shortly with High Grade Stores," *Women's Wear Daily*, March 7, 1932, sec. 2, 3.
19. "Retailer Decries False Sense of Security in Protected Styles," *Women's Wear Daily*, October 22, 1935, 17. This statement from Ohrbach's founder may not be surprising. In a 1999 article, Ohrbach's is mentioned for their fashion shows in which the original would parade down the runway next to the copy. Eric Wilson, "The Culture of Copycats: Divine Inspiration or Original Sin?" *Women's Wear Daily*, November 2, 1999, 8–10.
20. "St. Louis Market Has Curbed Piracy Under Voluntary Pact; Cleveland Sees Less Copying," *Women's Wear Daily*, March 6, 1941, 23.
21. "Stanley Marcus Favors Legal Aid Against Facsimile Copying," *Women's Wear Daily*, March 21, 1941, 7.
22. Paul H. Nystrom, *Fashion Merchandising* (New York: The Ronald Press Co., 1932); Paul H. Nystrom, *Economics of Fashion* (New York: The Ronald Press Co., 1928).
23. As stated in Paul M. Gregory, "Fashion and Monopolistic Competition," *The Journal of Political Economy* (1948): 71.
24. Leach, *Land of Desire*; Kidwell and Christman, *Suiting Everyone*; Madelyn Shaw, "American Fashion," in *From Paris to Providence*, ed. Susan Hay (Providence: Museum of Art, Rhode Island School of Design, 2000).
25. This was the finding of the lower courts against the FOGA. "Style Piracy Is Socially Desirable," *Women's Wear Daily*, March 4, 1941, 9.
26. Helen E. Meiklejohn, *Dresses: Impact of Fashion on a Business* (New York: McGraw-Hill, 1938), 337.
27. Rose H. Phelps Stokes, "The Condition of Working Women, from the Working Woman's Viewpoint," *The Annals of the American Academy* 27 (January–June 1906): 172.

28. Ibid., 151–60; Samuel Hartman, November 15, 1934, NRA Hearing, 156–66.
29. William Silverman, November 15, 1934, NRA Hearing, 156–66.
30. Kenneth Hutchinson, "Design Piracy," *Harvard Business Review*, 1940, 197.
31. Hawes, *Fashion Is Spinach*, 108–9.
32. While we could not find statistics for the number of returns per season, it is interesting to note that many of the antipiracy guilds included return policies in their regulations.
33. Clay Meyers, November 15, 1934, NRA Hearing, 242.
34. Samuel Zahn, 1934, NRA Hearing, 36.
35. S. Hartman, "Protest Move to Bar Dress Style Copying," *The New York Times*, September 25, 1934, 32.
36. Simon Larson, "Union Impact on Price in the Dress Industry" (master's thesis, City College of New York, 1963).
37. Johnston and Fitch, "Design Piracy," 40.
38. "Style Piracy Suit Decision Is Reversed," *Women's Wear Daily*, December 20, 1933, 1, 13; Edwin Levisohn, "The Design-Piracy Problem," *Journal of Retailing*, April 1933, 1–4.
39. Zahn, NRA Hearing, 41.
40. Johnston and Fitch, "Design Piracy," 135.
41. According to guild executive director Albert Post, the costs of manufacturing original designs ranged from $7,000 to $15,000. This included the expense of the designer, who would cost $200 a week, the viewing of new models in Paris, and the production of numerous samples. "Design Patent Keystone of New FOGA Plan," *Women's Wear Daily*, June 3, 1941, 13; "FOGA Official Tells of Style Piracy Methods," *Women's Wear Daily*, April 24, 1936, 1.
42. "State Style Measure Explained by Assemblyman," *Women's Wear Daily*, March 5, 1935, 2.
43. "League Members Upset Popular Misconceptions," *Women's Wear Daily*, April 3, 1935, sec. 2, 4.
44. "Design Patent Keystone of New FOGA Plan," 13.
45. "Witnesses Attack Piracy of Styles," *The New York Times*, May 29, 1936, 37.
46. Hutchinson, "Design Piracy," 197.
47. Chas Call, "Pleasing Guilds and Pleasing Chains Two Different Games," *Women's Wear Daily*, November 26, 1935, 14.
48. "Fashion Guild Members Praise Leadership of Maurice Rentner," *Women's Wear Daily*, November 22, 1933, 1, 14.
49. *Wm Filene's Sons Co v. FOGA*, 90 F.2d 556, 558 (1st Cir, 1937).
50. "Pittsburgh Struggles to Fight Off Style Piracy," *Women's Wear Daily*, June 25, 1941, 17.

51. "To Tell NRDGA Parley Design Patent Plan," *Women's Wear Daily*, June 2, 1941, 1, 32.
52. "Style Patent Speedup in Proposed FOGA Plan," *Women's Wear Daily*, June 3, 1941, 1, 29.
53. Johnston and Fitch, "Design Piracy"; May Allinson, *Industrial Experience of Trade School Girls in Massachusetts*, Studies in Economic Relations of Women, vol. 9 (Boston: The Department of Research: Women's Educational and Industrial Union, 1917), 217.
54. "Style Piracy Suit Decision Is Reversed," *Women's Wear Daily*, December 20, 1933, 1, 13.
55. "Widespread Collaboration by Representative Retailers Assures Effectiveness of Anti-Piracy Movement of the Fashion Originators' Guild of America," *Women's Wear Daily*, July 7, 1935, T5.
56. Interestingly enough, according to Rentner's son-in-law Arthur Jablow, Rentner never retained many designers. Jablow could only remember a "heavy-set woman, who worked [with Rentner] for many years." An article from *Women's Wear Daily* named Vera Jacobs as Rentner's designer, but it is not certain whether she remained with Rentner throughout Rentner's business career. Jacobs had patented about twenty dress designs during the 1930s and 1940s but did not assign a company name to the patents. Paula Neiman was named stylist for Maurice Rentner in a 1940 *Washington Post* article. Arthur Jablow, "The Reminiscences of Maurice Rentner," 1982, The Oral History Collection of the Fashion Institute of Technology Special Collections and College Archives, New York, NY, 5; "Miss Jacobs Joins Maurice Rentner," *Women's Wear Daily*, March 31, 1932, 20; Marshall Adams, "US Prepared to Accept Lead in Fashion," *The Washington Post*, July 19, 1940, 15.
57. S. Priya Bharathi, "There Is More than One Way to Skin a Copycat," *Texas Tech Law Review* 27, no. 4 (1996): 1–24.
58. Meyers, NRA Hearing, 240.
59. Meiklejohn, *Dresses*.
60. Federated Council on Art Education, *Costume Design* (New York: Federated Council on Art Education and the Institute of Women's Professional Relations, 1936), 14.
61. Kal Raustiala and Christopher Sprigman, "The Piracy Paradox: Innovation and Intellectual Property in Fashion Design," *Virginia Law Review* 92 (December 2006): 1687–777.
62. Meiklejohn, *Dresses*.
63. Ralph S. Brown, "Design Protection: An Overview," *UCLA Law Review* 34 (1986–1987): 1388.

Chapter 7

1. "Guild Extends Shopping Staff," *The New York Times*, September 1, 1936, 38; Waldon Fawcett, "The Proprieties of Protection by Boycott," *American Dyestuff Reporter*, July 27, 1936, 398–99.
2. This number was not corroborated by any other source. "Says Piracy Perils Style Leadership," *The New York Times*, August 11, 1940, 49.
3. "Counterclaim Filed in Guild Suit for Dues," *Women's Wear Daily*, April 29, 1935, 1, 20.
4. "Fashion Guild Wins Suit for Unpaid Dues: Counterclaim of Nathanson & Beck, Inc., for $570 on Ground Guild Failed to Protect It from Style Piracy Is Dismissed," *Women's Wear Daily*, October 7, 1936, 1.
5. "Style Importance Viewed Significant," *Women's Wear Daily*, April 3, 1935, sec. 2, 4.
6. Call, "Pleasing Guilds and Pleasing Chains," 14; "San Francisco Retailers Favor Protection of Style Campaign," *Women's Wear Daily*, December 11, 1935, 7; "NRDGA Sharply Attacks Many Points in Guild Program," *Women's Wear Daily*, December 20, 1935, 1; "Guild's Work Good in Upper Brackets," *The New York Times*, February 23, 1936, 17.
7. "A Statement by the Popular Priced Dress Mfrs.' Group, Inc.," *Women's Wear Daily*, February 28, 1936, 7.
8. "Hirsch Hits Policies of Fashion Guild," *Women's Wear Daily*, October 21, 1935, 7.
9. "Popular Price Dress Group Makes Public Declaration," *Women's Wear Daily*, October 23, 1935, 13.
10. "Sentiment at NRDGA Forum Against Guild Below $10.75," *Women's Wear Daily*, January 24, 1936, 11, 19, 23; "FOGA Policy Discussed by Merchants," *Women's Wear Daily*, February 10, 1936, 1; "AMC Rejects Guild Program Below $10.75," *Women's Wear Daily*, February 14, 1936, 1; "FOGA Policies Target of More Retail Groups," *Women's Wear Daily*, February 17, 1936, 1; "Chicago Shops Favor Original FOGA Program," *Women's Wear Daily*, February 20, 1936, 1, 26.
11. M. D. C. Crawford, "End of Rash Individualism Started Era of Good Trade," *Women's Wear Daily*, January 22, 1936, 4.
12. As early as 1933, the FOGA attacked the selling of goods in private apartments, but rules and regulations regarding this practice were not put into the Declaration of Cooperation until a later date. The FOGA rallied against apartment shops because they operated with negligible costs and required smaller markups than department stores with large overhead expenses, personnel structures, and slower ability to turn over styles.

13. The guild urged manufacturers to give retailers no more than an 8 percent EOM (end of month) discount. "Ban on Fashion Shows," *The New York Times*, November 26, 1933, 15; "Guild Avers New Pledge Is No Policy Shift," *Women's Wear Daily*, December 5, 1935, 1; "Guild Not to Copy Models of Retailers," *Women's Wear Daily*, April 11, 1935, 2; "Guild Warns Against Sales to Consumers," *Women's Wear Daily*, April 9, 1935, 25; *FOGA v. FTC*, 312 U.S. 457-468 (1941); Ira Rentner, "The Reminiscences of Maurice Rentner from Varying Perspectives," August 1982, The Oral History Collection of the Fashion Institute of Technology; *FOGA v. FTC* Respondent's Brief, 312 U.S. 457 (1941).

14. "Fashion Guild Insists It Does Not Want to Aggravate Returns," *Women's Wear Daily*, October 17, 1935, 15.

15. "$4.75 Manufacturers Plan Fight on Fashion Guild Pledge," *Women's Wear Daily*, October 10, 1935, 15; "Original Dress Does Not Exist, Mfr. Testifies at Guild Hearing," *Women's Wear Daily*, July 21, 1936, 1, 43; "Move to Form Dress Trade Returns Bureau," *Women's Wear Daily*, October 30, 1936, 1, 23; "Fashion Guild Registrations Increase," *Women's Wear Daily*, December 11, 1935, 7; "Dress Firm Assails Fashion Guild Stamp," *Women's Wear Daily*, July 24, 1936, 35.

16. "Rentner Raps Tactics Used by Retailers," *Women's Wear Daily*, August 9, 1936, 5; C. F. Hughes, "The Merchant's Point of View," *The New York Times*, February 16, 1936, sec. 3, 9.

17. "National Retail D. G. Ass'n Holds Guild Illegal," *Rayon and Melliand Textile Monthly* 17 (1936): 28.

18. "Dress War," *Time*, March 23, 1936, 27, 29–30.

19. "Gotshal Calls for Ending of Red Card Plan," *Women's Wear Daily*, February 20, 1936, 1.

20. Rudolf Callman, "Style and Design Piracy," *Journal of the Patent Office Society* (August 1940): 557–86.

21. "Blacklist Term Disputed at Guild Hearing," *Women's Wear Daily*, April 22, 1936, 1, 31.

22. "Extent of Guild Control Aired at Filene Hearing," *Women's Wear Daily*, May 20, 1936, 1, 35.

23. *Wm Filene's Sons Co v. FOGA*, 14 F. Supp. 353 (1936).

24. *Wm Filene's Sons Co v. FOGA*, 90 F.2d 556 (1937).

25. "Fashion Guild's New Battle," *Business Week*, April 25, 1936, 347; "FTC Files Complaint Against FOGA, Charging Trade Restraint," *Women's Wear Daily*, April 20, 1936, 1; "Commission Holds Guild a Monopoly," *The New York Times*, April 21, 1936, 42.

26. "Fashion Guild Trial to Move to Boston," *The New York Times*, July 25, 1936, 18; "Effect of Red Carding on J. L. Hudson Co. Is Related," *Women's Wear Daily*, August 17, 1936, 6; "FTC Hearing on Guild Going to Minneapolis," *Women's Wear Daily*, August 28, 1936, 1; "Guild Hearing, Adjourned in Chicago, Opens in Minneapolis," *Women's Wear Daily*, August 31, 1936, 1; "FOGA Wins a Point at Baltimore Hearing," *Women's Wear Daily*, November 10, 1936, 1.

27. "Says Piracy Perils Style Leadership," *The New York Times*, August 11, 1940, 49.

28. *FOGA v. FTC*, 114 F.2d 80 (1940); Sylvan Gotshal, *Today's Fight for Design Protection* (New York: Sylvan Gotshal, 1957), 13.

29. "Says Piracy Perils Style Leadership," *The New York Times*, August 11, 1940, 49.

30. *FOGA v. FTC*, 312 U.S. 457 (1941).

31. Ibid.

32. "Text of Decision in FOGA Case," *Women's Wear Daily*, March 4, 1941, 14.

33. "FOGA Approves Modified Style Piracy Plan," *Women's Wear Daily*, October 24, 1941, 1, 24.

34. "FOGA, NRDGA Move to Protect Designs," *Women's Wear Daily*, April 4, 1941, 1, 40; "Style Patent Speedup in Proposed FOGA Plan," *Women's Wear Daily*, June 3, 1941, 1, 29.

35. "To Tell NRDGA Parley Design Patent Plan," *Women's Wear Daily*, June 2, 1941, 1, 32.

36. *White et al. v. Leanore Frocks*, Inc., No. 307, Circuit Court of Appeals, Second Circuit, June 4, 1941, https://casetext.com/case/white-v-leanore-frocks-inc.

37. "Court Asks Law to Curb Style Piracy," *Women's Wear Daily*, June 10, 1941, 19.

38. "Text of Decision in FOGA Case," *Women's Wear Daily*, March 4, 1941, 14.

39. Albert Post, FOGA testimony before the Federal Trade Commission, January 13, 1938, 4427.

40. *Wm Filene's Sons Co v. FOGA*, 90 F.2d 556 (1937).

41. *FOGA v. FTC*, 312 U.S. 457 (1941).

42. Albert M. Post before Charles F. Diggs, trial examiner, Federal Trade Commission proceedings, January 13, 1938, 4326. In author's possession.

43. Federated Council on Art Education, *Costume Design*, 28; Meiklejohn, *Dresses*, 337.

44. "Fashion Guild Opening Set," *The New York Times*, August 24, 1952, F2.

45. "Couture Tradition to Be Upheld Here," *The New York Times*, June 22, 1940, 28.

46. Virginia Pope, "Style Leadership Called City's Due," *The New York Times*, August 5, 1940, 15.
47. Marshall Adams, "U.S. Prepared to Accept Lead in Fashion," *The Washington Post*, July 19, 1940, 15.
48. Maurice Rentner's name as a designer and manufacturer was mentioned in *The New York Times* throughout the 1940s and 1950s both in articles and in advertisements. He was known as "the Dean," "the King," and "Napoleon." According to his obituary published in *The New York Times* in July 1958, 60 percent of the industry's top executives had at one time worked for Rentner. He was perhaps most famous for serving as one of the original thirty-two stockholders who, in 1919, conceived of the idea of the Garment Center, which was the beginning of the vast Seventh Avenue–Broadway garment district. Maurice Rentner, Inc. merged with Anna Miller & Company, owned by Rentner's sister, in 1958. Bill Blass served as the head designer. Blass became the vice president and then owner of the firm. He organized the company under his own name in 1970. Virginia Pope, "Many Operations Mark New Styles," *The New York Times*, April 8, 1954; Virginia Pope, "Designer's Career a Story Book One," *The New York Times*, September 1, 1945, 24; "Heads Promotion Unit of N.Y. Dress Institute," *The New York Times*, March 19, 1941, 30; "Maurice Rentner Is Dead at 69," *The New York Times*, July 8, 1958, 27; "Maurice Rentner Started His Business Career at 17," *Women's Wear Daily*, November 12, 1933, 1, 15.
49. Virginia Pope, "Glamorous Styles Forecast for Fall," *The New York Times*, May 22, 1944, 22.
50. Jablow, "The Reminiscences of Maurice Rentner," 13.
51. Ibid., 17.

Chapter 8

1. Edmonde Charles-Roux, *Chanel and Her World* (New York: Vendome Press, 2005), 377.
2. See, for example, Susan Scafidi, "Intellectual Property and Fashion Design," *Intellectual Property and Information Wealth* 1, no. 115 (2006); Testimony of David Wolfe, Creative Director, The Doneger Group before the US House Subcommittee on Courts, the Internet, and Intellectual Property, Legislative Hearing on H.R. 5055, Washington, DC, July 27, 2006; "Is the Fashion Commons at Risk?" *On the Commons: Commons Magazine*, August 19, 2005, http://onthecommons.org/fashion-commons-risk.
3. "Even Karl Lagerfeld Can't Spot a Real Chanel Jacket from a Fake! Designer Admits 'There Are So Many Copies' It's Too Hard to Tell," MailOnline, http://

www.dailymail.co.uk/femail/article-2293459/Even-Karl-Lagerfeld-spot-real-Chanel-jacket-fake-Designer-admits-copies-hard-tell.html.
4. See, for example, Ida M. Tarbell, *The Business of Being a Woman* (New York: The Macmillan Co., 1912).
5. Roshco, *The Rag Race*, 51.
6. The designers he copied were probably less enthusiastic. Linda Marx, "Knock-off King Jack Mulqueen Is Stealing Designers Blind, and There's No Stopping Him," *People*, November 9, 1981, 119–22.
7. Kim Peiffer, "Get Kate Middleton's Dress for Less," *People*, May 2, 2011; Alexandra Steigrad, "The Copycat Threat," *Women's Wear Daily*, September 9, 2010, 1, 18.
8. Eric Wilson, "The Culture of Copy-Cats," *Women's Wear Daily*, November 2, 1999, 8–10.
9. Richard Martin, "Fashion in the Age of Advertising," *The Journal of Popular Culture* 29 (1995): 235–54.
10. "Guild Extends Shopping Staff," *The New York Times*, September 1, 1936, 38; Waldon Fawcett, "The Proprieties of Protection by Boycott," *American Dyestuff Reporter*, July 27, 1936, 398–99.
11. *FOGA v. FTC*, 312 U.S. 457 (1941).
12. Jaclyn Fierman, "High-Fashion Names Knock Themselves Off," *Fortune*, June 10, 1985, 73.
13. Teri Agins, "Fashion Knockoffs Hit Stores Before Originals as Designers Seethe," *Wall Street Journal*, August 8, 1994, 1.
14. This is certainly not a new process, as the intricate cuts of Vionnet in the 1930s were particularly difficult to copy. Betty Kirke, *Madeleine Vionnet* (San Francisco: Chronicle Books, 2012).
15. Cheryl Lu-Lien Tan, "Copy Protection for Fall Fashion," *Wall Street Journal*, October 27–28, 2007, W1.
16. Meenal Mistry, "Style That Can't Be Copied," *Wall Street Journal*, January 31–February 1, 2015, D1–D3.
17. Mistry, "Style," D2.
18. Ben Winograd and Cheryl Lu-Lien Tan, "Can Fashion Be Copyrighted?," *Wall Street Journal*, September 11, 2006, 1.
19. In this case the courts held that the red sole did indeed constitute a legal trademark as long as it was in contrast to the shoe color.
20. Lauren Sherman, "Mansur Gavriel Responds to 'Proof' of Copying," *The Business of Fashion*, September 21, 2015, http://www.businessoffashion.com/articles/news-analysis/mansur-gavriel-responds-to-proof-of-copying.
21. Yoga-athletic maker Lululemon Athletica accused Calvin Klein Inc. of

infringing on design patents for its "Astro Pant." The case was settled in a confidential settlement out of court. Ashby Jones, "Downward Docket: The Yoga Pants War," *Wall Street Journal*, September 11, 2012, http://online.wsj.com/news/articles/SB10000872396390443696604577645891750143350; Erin Geiger Smith, "Fashion Designers Look to Patents to Fight Knockoffs," Reuters, http://www.reuters.com/article/2013/09/12/us-usa-fashion-newyork-patents-idUSBRE98B0H420130912.

22. Diane Von Furstenberg, board chairman of the CFDA, helped launch Fordham Law's Fashion Law Institute as well as the You Can't Fake Fashion campaign. Kristi Ellis, "No Law in Sight: Fashion World Forges New Path on Piracy," *Women's Wear Daily*, March 21, 2012, 1, 12.

23. Amy Spindler, "Company News: A Ruling by French Court Finds Copyright in a Design," *The New York Times*, May 19, 1994.

24. Cathy Horyn, "Is Copying Really a Part of the Creative Process?" *The New York Times*, April 9, 2002.

25. "Chanel Loses Lawsuit Over Crochet Design," AsiaOne, November 23, 2012, http://news.asiaone.com/print/News/Latest%2BNews/Diva/Story/A1Story20121123-385320.html.

26. Eric Wilson, "The Culture of Copy-Cats," *Women's Wear Daily*, November 2, 1999, 8.

27. Randy Cohen, "Acceptable Knockoffs," The Ethicist, *New York Times Magazine*, May 22, 2005.

28. Agins, "Fashion Knockoffs," 1; Horyn, "Is Copying Really a Part of the Creative Process?," 1.

29. "Fashion and the Democracy of Style," The Norman Lear Center, http://learcenter.org/event/fashion-the-democracy-of-style.

Sources

Books

Allinson, May. *Industrial Experience of Trade School Girls in Massachusetts.* Studies in Economic Relations of Women, vol. 9. Boston: The Department of Research: Women's Educational and Industrial Union, 1917.

Benson, Susan Porter. *Counter Cultures: Saleswomen, Managers, and Customers in American Department Stores, 1890–1940.* Champaign, IL: University of Illinois Press, 1986.

Bosworth, Louise. *The Living Wage of Women Workers: A Study of Incomes and Expenditures of 450 Women in the City of Boston.* New York: Longmans, Green, and Co., 1911.

Byrner, Edna. *The Garment Trades.* Cleveland, OH: The Survey Committee of the Cleveland Foundation, 1916.

Charles-Roux, Edmonde. *Chanel and Her World.* New York: Vendome Press, 2005.

Chase, Edna Woolman, and Ilka Chase. *Always in Vogue.* Garden City, NY: Doubleday, 1954.

Cohen, Julius Henry. *Law and Order in Industry: Five Years' Experience.* New York: The Macmillan Co., 1916.

Crawford, M. D. C. *The Ways of Fashion.* New York: Fairchild Publishing Co., 1941.

Daves, Jessica. *Ready-Made Miracle: The American Story of Fashion for the Millions.* New York: G. P. Putnam, 1967.

Davis, Fred. *Fashion, Culture, and Identity.* Chicago: The University of Chicago Press, 1992.

Donahue, Mary. "Design and the Industrial Arts in America, 1894–1940: An Inquiry into Fashion Design and Art and Industry." PhD diss., The City University of New York, 2001.

Doyle, Tracy. *Patterns from Finished Clothes: Re-Creating the Clothes You Love.* New York: Sterling Pub. Co. Inc., 1996.

Drake, Leonard, and Carrie Glaser. *Trends in the New York Clothing Industry.* New York: Institute of Public Administration, 1942.

Dulles, Eleanor L. *The French Franc, 1914–1928.* New York: The Macmillan Company, 1929.

Federated Council on Art Education. *Costume Design.* New York: Federated Council on Art Education and the Institute of Women's Professional Relations, 1936.

Funderburk, Jane A. U. "The Development of Women's Ready-to-Wear, 1865 to 1914: Based on *New York Times* Advertisements." PhD diss., The University of Maryland, 1994.

Garner, Myrna B., and Sandra J. Keiser. *Beyond Design: The Synergy of Apparel Product Development.* New York: Fairchild, 2012.

Glock, Ruth E., and Grace I. Kunz. *Apparel Manufacturing: Sewn Products Analysis.* Upper Saddle River, NJ: Prentice Hall, 2004.

Goldstein, Gabriel M., and Elizabeth E. Greenberg, eds. *A Perfect Fit: The Garment Industry and American Jewry, 1860–1960.* New York: Yeshiva University, 2012.

Gotshal, Sylvan. *Today's Fight for Design Protection.* New York: Sylvan Gotshal, 1957.

Gotshal, Sylvan, and Alfred Lief. *The Pirates Will Get You: A Story for the Fight for Design Protection.* New York: Columbia University Press, 1945.

Green, Nancy L. *Ready-to-Wear and Ready-to-Work: A Century of Industry and Immigrants in Paris and New York.* Durham, NC: Duke University Press, 1997.

Hawes, Elizabeth. *Fashion Is Spinach.* New York: Random House, 1938.

Hemphill, C. Scott, and Jeannie Suk. "The Fashion Originators' Guild of America: Self-Help at the Edge of IP and Antitrust." In *Intellectual Property at the Edge: The Contested Contours of IP,* edited by Rochelle C. Dreyfuss and Jane C. Ginsburg, 159–79. New York: Cambridge University Press, 2013.

Hill, Daniel Delis. *As Seen in Vogue: A Century of American Fashion in Advertising.* Lubbock: Texas Tech University Press, 2007.

Hollahan, Lee. *How to Use, Adapt, and Design Sewing Patterns: From Store-Bought Patterns to Drafting Your Own.* Hauppauge, NY: Barron's Educational Series, 2010.

Hollen, Norma R., and Carolyn M. Kundel. *Pattern Making by the Flat-Pattern Method.* Upper Saddle River, NJ: Prentice Hall, 1993.

Johnston, Aaron, and Florence Fitch. "Design Piracy: The Problem and Its Treatment Under N.R.A. Codes." National Recovery Administration Materials, ser. 52. Washington, DC: The Administration, 1936.

Kidwell, Claudia, and Margaret Christman. *Suiting Everyone: The Democrati-*

zation of Clothing in America. Washington, DC: The Smithsonian Institution Press, 1974.

Kirke, Betty. *Madeleine Vionnet*. San Francisco: Chronicle Books, 2012.

Larson, Simon. "Union Impact on Price in the Dress Industry." Master's thesis, City College of New York, 1963.

Leach, William. *Land of Desire: Merchants, Power, and the Rise of a New American Culture*. New York: Vintage Books, 1993.

Levine, Louis. *The Women's Garment Workers: A History of the International Ladies' Garment Worker's Union*. New York: B. W. Huebsch, Inc., 1924.

Marcketti, Sara B. "Design Piracy in the United States Women's Ready-to-Wear Apparel Industry: 1910–1941." PhD diss., Iowa State University, 2005.

Maryland Bureau of Industrial Statistics and Information. *First Biennial Report of the Bureau, 1884–1885*. Baltimore: Maryland Bureau of Industrial Statistics and Information, 1886.

McCreesh, Carolyn Daniel. *Women in the Campaign to Organize Garment Workers, 1880–1917*. New York: Garland Publishing, 1985.

Meiklejohn, Helen E. *Dresses: Impact of Fashion on a Business*. New York: McGraw-Hill, 1938.

Norris, James D. *Advertising and the Transformation of American Society, 1856–1920*. New York: Greenwood Press, 1990.

Nystrom, Paul H. *Fashion Merchandising*. New York: The Ronald Press Co., 1932.

———. *Economics of Fashion*. New York: The Ronald Press Co., 1928.

O'Brien, Ruth. *Boston Conference on Distribution*. Boston, MA: Retail Trade Board, Boston Chamber of Commerce, 1934.

Ollian, Joanne. "From Division Street to Seventh Avenue: The Coming of Age of American Fashions." In *A Perfect Fit: The Garment Industry and American Jewry, 1860–1960*, edited by Gabriel M. Goldstein and Elizabeth E. Greenberg, 114–28, Lubbock, TX: Texas Tech University Press, 2012.

Pastorello, Karen. *A Power among Them: Bessie Abramowitz Hillman and the Making of the Amalgamated Clothing Workers of America*. Urbana: University of Illinois Press, 2008.

Payne, Blanche, Geital Winakor, and Jane Farrell-Beck. *The History of Costume*. New York: Longman, 1992.

Peiss, Kathy. *Cheap Amusements: Working Women and Leisure in Turn-of-the-Century New York*. Philadelphia: Temple University Press, 1986.

Picken, Mary Brooks. *The Secrets of Distinctive Dress: Harmonious, Becoming, and Beautiful Dress; Its Value and How to Achieve It*. Scranton, PA: The Woman's Institute of Domestic Arts and Sciences, Inc., 1918.

Raustiala, Kal, and Christopher Sprigman. *The Knockoff Economy: How Imitation Sparks Innovation*. Cary, NC: Oxford University Press, 2012.

Richards, Florence S. *The Ready-to-Wear Industry, 1900–1950*. New York: Fairchild Publications, 1951.

Richards, Charles R. *Art in Industry*. New York: The MacMillan Co., 1922.

Richardson, Bertha June. *The Woman Who Spends: A Study of Her Economic Function*. Boston: Whitcomb & Barrows, 1904.

Romasco, Albert U. *The Politics of Recovery*. New York: Oxford University Press, 1983.

Roshco, Bernard. *The Rag Race*. New York: Funk & Wagnalls Company, 1963.

Schorman, Rob. *Selling Style: Clothing and Social Change at the Turn of the Century*. Philadelphia: University of Pennsylvania Press, 2003.

Schweitzer, Marlis. "American Fashions for American Women." In *Producing Fashion: Commerce, Culture and Consumers*, edited by Regina Blaszczyk. Philadelphia: The University of Pennsylvania Press, 2007.

Selekman, Benjamin M. *The Clothing and Textile Industries in New York and Its Environs*. New York: Regional Plan of New York and Its Environs, 1925.

Shaw, Madelyn. "American Fashion." In *From Paris to Providence*, edited by Susan Hay. Providence: Museum of Art, Rhode Island School of Design, 2000.

Shoemaker, William D. *Patents for Designs*. Washington, DC: H. D. Williams Company, 1929.

Smith, Bernard. "A Study of Uneven Industrial Development: The American Clothing Industry in the Late 19th and Early 20th Centuries." PhD diss., Yale University, 1989.

Stone, N. I. *Wages and Regularity of Employment in the Dress and Waist Industry of New York City*. 1915. Reprint, New York: Columbia University Libraries, 2008.

Stuart, Jessie. *The American Fashion Industry*. Boston, MA: Simmons College, 1951.

Tarbell, Ida. *The Business of Being a Woman*. New York: The Macmillan Company, 1912.

Tartsinis, Ann Marguerite. *An American Style: Global Sources for New York Textile and Fashion Design, 1915–1928*. New York: Bard Graduate Center, 2013.

Tepere, Lazare. *The Woman's Garment Industry, an Economic Analysis*. New York: Educational Department of the International Ladies' Garment Workers' Union, 1937.

Toulmin, Harry Aubrey. *Handbook of Patents*. Cincinnati, OH: The W. H. Anderson Company, 1949.

Troy, Nancy. *Couture Culture: A Study in Modern Art and Fashion*. Cambridge, MA: The MIT Press, 2003.

US Department of Commerce. *Design Patents*. Washington, DC: US Department of Commerce, 1983.

Veblen, Thorstein. *The Theory of the Leisure Class.* New York: MacMillan, 1899.

Woolman, Mary Schenck. *Clothing: Choice, Care, Cost.* Philadelphia: J. B. Lippincott Co., 1920.

Periodicals

Allen, Erastus S. "Legal Protection for Artistic Designs." *The Bulletin of the American Ceramic Society* (1944): 423–27.

Ashlock, J. L. "The Cost of Women's Clothes." *The Journal of Home Economics* 9 (November 1917): 499–502.

Baker, Charlotte Gibbs. "Clothing and the Income." *The Journal of Home Economics* 8 (July 1916): 373–78.

Barber, Bernard, and Lyle Lobel. "Fashion in Women's Clothes and the American Social System." *Social Forces* 31 (1952): 124–31.

Beltrametti, Silvia. "Evaluation of the Design Piracy Prohibition Act: Is the Cure Worse than the Disease? An Analogy with Counterfeiting and a Comparison with the Protection Available in the European Community." *Northwestern Journal of Technology and Intellectual Property* 8 (2010): 147–73.

Bharathi, S. Priya. "There Is More than One Way to Skin a Copycat." *Texas Tech Law Review* 27, no. 4 (1996): 1667–79.

Blunt, Irene. "Fighting the Design Pirate." *Journal of the Patent Office Society* 15 (1933): 29.

Briggs, Anne Theodore. "Hung Out to Dry: Clothing Design Protection Pitfalls in United States Law." *Hastings Communications and Entertainment Law Journal* 24 (Winter 2001–2002): 169–213.

Brown, Ralph S. "Design Protection: An Overview." *UCLA Law Review* 34 (1986–1987): 1337–404.

Buckland, Sandra S., and Gwendolyn S. O'Neal. "'We Publish Fashions Because They Are News': New York Times, 1940–1945." *Dress* 25 (1998): 33–41.

Buckles, Robert A. "Property Rights in Creative Works: A Comparison of Copyright Laws and Patent Laws." *Journal of the Patent Office Society* 32, no. 6 (June 1950): 414–38.

Callmann, Rudolf. "Style and Design Piracy." *Journal of the Patent Office Society* (August 1940): 557–86.

"Campaign Against Design Piracy." *Journal of the Patent Office Society* (November 1946): 845.

Cranor, Katherine. "Homemade Versus Ready-Made Clothing." *The Journal of Home Economics* (1920): 230–33.

Crawford, M. D. C. "Museum Documents and Modern Costume." *American Museum Journal* 18 (1918): 286–97.

Derenberg, Walter. "Commercial Prints and Labels: A Hybrid in Copyright Law." *Journal of the Patent Office Society* 22 (1940): 452–68.

Farnan-Leipzig, Sheryl, Jean L. Parsons, and Jane Farrell-Beck. "It Is a Profession That Is New, Unlimited, and Rich." *Dress* 35 (2008–2009): 29–47.

Fawcett, Waldon. "The Proprieties of Protection by Boycott." *American Dyestuff Reporter* (July 27, 1936): 398–99.

Geier, Oscar. "What Has Been Accomplished Towards Protecting Textile Designers." *Journal of the Patent Office Society* 16 (1934): 221–27.

Goldenberg, David. "The Long and Winding Road: A History of the Fight Over Industrial Design Protection in the United States." *Journal of the Copyright Society of the U.S.A.* 45, no. 1 (1997): 21–62.

Gregory, Paul M. "Fashion and Monopolistic Competition." *The Journal of Political Economy* (1948): 69–75.

Hagen, Leslie J. "A Comparative Analysis of Copyright Laws Applied to Fashion Works: Renewing the Proposal for Folding Fashion Works in the United States." *Texas International Law Journal* 26 (1991): 341–88.

Harchuck, Kimberly A. "Fashion Design Protection: The Eternal Plight of the 'Soft Sculpture.'" *Akron Intellectual Property Journal* 4, no. 1 (2010): 73–118.

Hoke, Robert. "Brush Up on the Basics of Intellectual Property." *The Iowa Lawyer* (2003): 24.

Hudson, Thomas. "A Brief History of the Development of Design Patent Protection in the U.S." *Journal of the Patent Office Society* 30 (1948): 380–400.

Hutchinson, Kenneth. "Design Piracy." *Harvard Business Review* (1940): 191–98.

"The IDPPPA—Is the Third Time a Charm?" *Columbia Business Law Review* 2015, no. 2. http://cblr.columbia.edu/archives/11357.

"Is the Fashion Commons at Risk?" *On the Commons: Commons Magazine*, July 1, 2014. http://onthecommons.org/fashion-commons-risk.

Johnson, H. L. "For the Homemaker: Women and Clothes; What the Clubs Are Doing in the Matter of Standardization." *The Journal of Home Economics* 9 (March 1917): 127–36.

Joseph, Abigail. "'A Wizard of Silks and Tulle': Charles Worth and the Queer Origins of Couture." *Victorian Studies* 56 (Winter 2014): 251–79.

King, Elizabeth Miner. "War, Women, and American Clothes." *Scribner's Magazine* (1917): 592–98.

Laughlin, J. Lawrence. "Economic Effects of Changes of Fashion." *The Chautauquan* 19 (April 1894): 12–13.

Leach, William. "Transformations in a Culture of Consumption: Women and Department Stores, 1890–1925." *The Journal of American History* 71 (September 1984): 319–42.

Levisohn, Edwin. "The Design-Piracy Problem." *Journal of Retailing* (April 1933): 1–4.

Loangkote, Linna T. "Fashioning a New Look in Intellectual Property: Sui Generis Protection for the Innovative Designer." *Hastings Law Journal* 63, no. 1 (2011–2012): 297–322.

MacDonald, Pearl. "Housekeeper's Department: Club Women Approve Sensible Styles in Dress." *The Journal of Home Economics* 7 (April 1915): 201–3.

Magdo, Christine. "Protecting Works of Fashion from Design Piracy." *LEDA at Harvard Law School* (2000): 1–15.

Marcketti, Sara B. "Codes of Fair Competition: The National Recovery Act, 1933–1935, and the Women's Dress Manufacturing Industry." *Clothing and Textiles Research Journal* (2010): 189–204.

Marcketti, Sara B., Kate Greder, and Heather Sinclair. "Is Anything Ever New? Fashion Design Students' Perceptions of Piracy." *International Journal of Costume and Fashion* (2014): 17–28.

Marcketti, Sara B., and Jean L. Parsons. "The Use of Design Patents to Protect Dress, 1910–1950." *Proceedings of the 70th Annual Conference of the International Textile and Apparel Association*, New Orleans, November 2013.

———. "Design Piracy and Self-Regulation: The Fashion Originators' Guild of America: 1932–1941." *Clothing and Textiles Research Journal* 24 (2006): 214–28.

———. "American Fashions for American Women: Early Twentieth Century Efforts to Develop an American Fashion Identity." *Dress: The Journal of the Costume Society of America* 34 (2007): 79–95.

Martin, Richard. "Fashion in the Age of Advertising." *The Journal of Popular Culture* 29 (1995): 235–54.

Meiners, Roger E., and Robert J. Staaf. "Patents, Copyrights, and Trademarks: Property or Monopoly?" *Harvard Journal of Law and Public Policy* 13 (Summer 1990): 911–34.

Mencken, Jennifer. "A Design for the Copyright of Fashion." *Boston College Intellectual Property and Technology Forum* (December 12, 1997): 121–201.

Miller, Ethelwyn. "Americanism: The Spirit of Costume Design." *The Journal of Home Economics* 10 (May 1918): 207–11.

Moody, Helen Watterson. "The American Woman and Dress." *The Ladies' Home Journal* (June 1902): 15, 18.

Nikonow, John P. "Patent Protection for New Designs of Dresses." *Journal of the Patent Office Society* 17 (1935): 253–54.

Nurhabhai, Safia. "Style Piracy Revisited." *New York State Builders Association* 10, no. 3 (Winter 2001): 1–11.

Parsons, Jean L. "No Longer a 'Frowsy Drudge': Women's Wardrobe Management, 1880–1930." *Clothing and Textiles Research Journal* 20 (2002): 33–41.

Parsons, Jean, and Jennifer Schulle. "The Shirtwaist: Changing the Commerce of Fashion." Presented at the Costume Society of America Regional Meeting, Cincinnati, Ohio, 2003.

Phelps Stokes, Rose H. "The Condition of Working Women from the Working Woman's Viewpoint." *The Annals of the American Academy* 27 (January–June 1906): 634.

"Protection for the Artistic Aspects of Articles of Utility." *The Harvard Law Review* 72, no. 8 (June 1959): 1520–36.

Raustiala, Kal, and Christopher Sprigman. "The Piracy Paradox: Innovation and Intellectual Property in Fashion Design." *Virginia Law Review* 92, no. 8 (2006): 1687–777.

Richardson, Megan, and David Tan. "Wood v. Duff-Gordon and the Modernist Cult of Personality." *Pace Law Review* 28 (Winter 2008): 379–93.

Rossman, Joseph. "Proposed Registration of Designs." *Journal of the Patent Office Society* 17 (1935): 995–98.

Scafidi, Susan. "Intellectual Property and Fashion Design." *Intellectual Property and Information Wealth* 1, no. 115 (2006): 115–31.

Shalestock, Peter. "Forms of Redress for Design Piracy: How Victims Can Use Existing Copyright Law." *Seattle University Law Review* 21 (Summer 1997): 113–26.

Shaw, Madelyn. "American Silk from a Marketing Magician." *Textile Society of America 8th Biennial Symposium Proceedings*, Northampton, MA, September 26–28, 2002.

Silverman, Arnold B. "What Are Design Patents and When Are They Useful?" *JOM: The Journal of the Minerals, Metals & Materials Society* 45, no. 3 (1993): 63.

Simmel, George. "Fashion." Report in *American Journal of Sociology* 62 (May 1957): 541–58.

"Standardized Dress." *The Journal of Home Economics* 8 (June 1916): 326–27.

Stim, Richard. "Can't Prove a Copyright Copied?" *Crafts Law* (2001): 40–41.

Walsh, Margaret. "The Democratization of Fashion: The Emergence of the Women's Dress Pattern Industry." *The Journal of American History* 66 (1979): 299–313.

Weikart, Maurice A. "Design Piracy." *Indiana Law Journal* 19 (1943–1944): 234–57.

Whitley, Lauren D. "Morris De Camp Crawford and the Designed in America Campaign, 1916–1922." *Textile Society of America Symposium Proceedings*, New York, September 24–26, 1998.

Williams, Henry. "Report of the Committee on Protection of Designs." *Journal of the Patent Office Society* 15 (1933): 807–13.

Wilson, Cochran. "Women and Wage-Spending." *Outlook* 84 (October 1906): 375–77.

Primary Sources

The American Society of Style Creators. Incorporation papers, 1930. New York Department of State, New York County Clerk, New York, NY.

Bergdorf Goodman Oral History. Manuscript Collection x181. Fashion Institute of Technology Special Collections and College Archives, New York, NY.

Fashion Originators' Guild of America. Incorporation papers, March 1932. New York Department of State, New York County Clerk, New York, NY.

Morrison, Martin. "Registration of Designs." Congressional House Reports, 64th Cong., 1st sess., vol. 3 (1916).

The National Association of Style Creators. Incorporation papers, November 1934. New York Department of State, New York County Clerk, New York, NY.

National Recovery Administration. *Hearing on the Code of Fair Competition for the Dress Manufacturing Industry*. Washington, DC: Government Printing Office, 1934.

"The Reminiscences of Maurice Rentner from Varying Perspectives." August 1982. The Oral History Collection of the Fashion Institute of Technology Special Collections and College Archives, New York, NY.

The Semiconductor Chip Protection Act of 1983: Hearings on S. 1201 Before the Subcomm. on Patents, Copyrights and Trademarks of the Senate Judiciary Comm. 98th Cong., 1st sess, 66, 75–76 (1983).

US Census Bureau. *Census of Manufacturers, 1921*. Washington, DC: Government Printing Office, 1924.

US Department of Commerce. *Census of Manufacturers: Clothing*. Washington, DC: Government Printing Office, 1914.

Index

Page numbers in *italic* refer to illustrations.

Abercrombie & Fitch, 103
Abraham & Straus, 51, 111
A.B.S. by Allen Schwartz, xii, 152
Ackerman, F. Eugene, 116
Adelman, Jack, *34*
advertising, 14, 44, 49, 51–52, 57, 84, 87, *113*; Bonwit Teller, *12*; brand name dresses, *94*, 95; designers named in, *62*, 82; FOGA, *8*, 101, *103*, 105–6; John Wanamaker, *9*; Gimbels, *50*; Martin's, *13*; Rosen Bros., *20*; Saks, *62*; shirtwaist dresses, *17*; Stein & Blaine, *89*; Weingarten & Pearl, *67*. *See also* American Styles for American Women campaign
Albert Blum, 87
Alice Maynard, *17*
Alterman, Meyer, 31, *32*, 124, 164n40
Amelia Earhart designs, 103, *104*, 105
America Invents Act, 162–63n20
American Apparel & Footwear Association, xvi
American Cloak and Suit Manufacturers Association, 59, 170n13
American Cloak and Suit Review, 63, 82
American Council of Style and Design, 31–32, 35
American Dress Designers' Association, 58, 170n13
American Dress Manufacturers' Association, 58
American Indian motifs, 79
American Museum of Art, 176n89
American Museum of Natural History (AMNH), 79, 80, *80*, 81, 176n89, 177n93
American Style Protective Association, 33, *34*
American Styles for American Women campaign, 58, 71
Anna Miller & Company, 190n48
Anne Klein II, 148
antitrust laws, 135, 137, 142
Arens, E., 118–19
Arnold Constable and Co., *xiv*, 84
Art in Industry (Richards), 76, 78–79, 85, 90
art schools, 77–78
Associated Garment Manufacturers, 87
Associated Merchandising Corporation (AMC), 25, 105, 111, 132
Association of Dress Manufacturers, 96
"authorized copies," 10, 18, 35, 57, 63–64, 67–68, 92, 145

Baker, Charlotte, 168–69n54
Balenciaga, 151

Baltimore, 102, 111, 169n57
bankruptcy, 75, 100, 114, 117
bargain basements, 49, 124
Beer. *See* Maison Beer
Bendel, Henri, 83
Ben Gershel & Co., *91*
Bercovici, Joseph, 96
Bergdorf Goodman, 32, 88, 90, 103, 181n16
Bessette, Carolyn, xi
Better Business Bureau, 183n1
Betty Wales dresses, 93, *94*, 95
Bharathi, S. Priya, 19
big-box stores, 149
Black, Graeme, 149
Black, Hugo, 14, 137, 142
blacklisting. *See* red-carding
Blaine, James, 62–63, 69–70, 83
Blakely, Joanna, 152
Blass, Bill, 149, 190n48
Bloomingdale's, 103, 111, 146
blouses, 33, 75, 76. *See also* shirtwaists
Blum, Albert, 87
Blunt, Irene, 111, 116
Bok, Edward, 71–72, *86*, 87
Bonwit Teller, xii, *xiii*, *12*, 82, 181n16
Boston, 111, 125, 130, 169n57, 171–72n26
Bosworth, Louise, 167
Boue Soeurs, 95
Bramley trademark, 23, 92
branding, 5, 10, 92–95 passim, *94*, 149
Brewster, Elisha, 35, 136
bridal gowns. *See* wedding dresses
Britain. *See* United Kingdom
Brooklyn Museum, 79, 81–82, 177n93
Brown, Ralph, 16, 129
Bryner, Edna, 56–57
B. Siegel Co., 117, 140
Bureau of Home Economics, 116
Bush Terminal Sales Building (Bush Tower), New York City, 87, 179n121

business failure, 126–27, 129. *See also* bankruptcy
buyers, 45, 49, 57, 59, 67, 82, 90, 117, 126; FOGA and, 110, 135; French views, 68, 69, 72–73; syndicates, 132

Call, Chas, 125
Callot Soeurs, 65, 66, *66*
Calvin Klein, 150, 192n21
Cashin, Bonnie, 25
catalog sales, 46, *47*
celebrities, xi–xii, 61, 79, 88, 146
chain stores, 87, 149
Chanel, Coco, 145, 151
Chanel logo, 26
Charles A. Stevens & Bros., 46
Charles Lang & Parnes, 85
Cheney Brothers v. Doris Silk Corp., 29–30
Chéruit, Louise, 66, 70, 82
Chicago, 40, 46, 60, 78, 101, 132
Chittick, James, 176n89
Christian Dior Couture, 150
Christian Lacroix, 146
Christian Louboutin, 149
Christman, Margaret, 119
class, 7, 47–48, 54, 55, 77, 119. *See also* middle-class women; working-class women
Cleveland, 40, 132
Cloak and Suit Designers' Mutual Aid Association, 77, 170n13
Cloak and Suit Manufacturers. *See* American Cloak and Suit Manufacturers Association
cloaks, 36, 77
coats, 33, 54, 59, 77, *115*
Cohen, Julius Henry, 27, 39
Cohen, Randy, 152
Collins, Harry, 76, 82, 83, 84, 87, 88, *88*, 92
Columbia University, 78, 177n89

Index

communications technology, 41, 146, 147, 149
computer chip industry. *See* semiconductor industry
Congress, US. *See* US Congress
consumers, 46–50, 69–70, 147–48; Depression-era, 98–99, 112, 117; entitlement to fashion, xii, 117–23
contests. *See* design contests
contracting system. *See* subcontractors and subcontracting
Copeland, Jo, 82. *See also* Jo Copeland (store)
copies, authorized. *See* "authorized copies"
copyright, xv, 10, 18–21 passim, *20*, 29–35 passim, 136, 148–52 passim, 162n9; Clara Simcox and, 92; fabric, 163–64n31; France, 150, 157n1
Copyright Act of 1790, 19
Copyright Office. *See* US Copyright Office
corsets, *21*, 36, 87
Costa, Victor, 150
Council of Fashion Designers of America (CFDA), xv, *xv*, 150
counterfeit designer labels. *See* false designer labels
counterfeiting, xi, xiii, 26, 152
court cases, 29–30, *91*, 92, 95, 140–42 passim; FOGA, xvii, 14, 35, 114, 130, 136–38, 142; France, 150, 158n10; patent infringement, 23, 24–25, 150, 158n10
Cranor, Katherine, 167n37
Crawford, M. D. C., 11–12, 14, 79–82, 160–61n21, 177n93
customs duties, 75

Davis, Tobé Coller ("Taubé"), xi, 82, 93
Dayton Co., 111
De la Renta, Oscar, 150

department stores, 4, 13–14, 46–55 passim, 83, 93, 117, 119, 125–26; FOGA relations, 103–5, 111, 117; labels, 84
Depression, 97, 98–101, 111, 113, 126, 129
design contests, 85, *86*, 87
Design Copyright Service Bureau, 33
Design Creators' League, 128
designer labels, false. *See* false designer labels
design patents, 21–25, *22*, 92, 138–41 passim, *139*, 150, 164n31
Design Piracy Prohibition Act, xv
Design Registration League, 29
design schools. *See* schools of design and fashion
Dior, Christian, 144. *See also* Christian Dior Couture; House of Dior
display windows. *See* window display
disposability, 51, 52. *See also* obsolescence, planned and rapid
division of labor, gendered. *See* gendered division of labor
Dix, Dorothy, 69
DKNY, 148–49
DNA markers, 163n29
Donnelly Act (New York State), 135
Doris Silk Corporation, 29–30
Doucet, Jacques, *62*, 66, 82
drawing, 78. *See also* sketches and sketching
Drecoll gowns, 63
Dreiser, Theodore, 166n14
Dress Control Returns Bureau, 134
Dress Creators' League of America, 107, 111, 121, 122, 124, 130
dresses, 59–60, 77, 120–21, 149; ads, *34*, 89; brand names, 93, *94*, 95; design contests, *86*, 87; design patents, *139*; industry value, 142; in litigation exhibits, *91*; "Mondrian," *xiv*; prices, 63, 75, 99, 100,

107, 114, 116, 121, 130–34 passim, 181n13; quality, 117; Sears, Roebuck, 68; trade associations, 58. *See also* shirtwaist dresses; wedding dresses
dressmakers, 53, 60, 63, 71, 75–77, 176n80
Dry Goods Economist, 45, 75
duties and tariffs. *See* customs duties; tariffs

Earhart, Amelia, 103, *104*, 105
Ed. Schuster Company, 111
education, xiii, 77–79, 85, 128, 176n83. *See also* home economics
Edward, Duke of Windsor, xii
Egyptian motifs, 11, *12*
Elizabeth II, Queen of Great Britain, 146
Emanuel, 148
employment. *See* labor
Ernst Kern Co., 117
espionage. *See* spies and spying
Esterel, Jacques, 158n10
Europe, 54, 76, 157n1. *See also* France; United Kingdom
Ewing, Thomas 29
exhibitions and style shows, *59*, *64*, *67*, 67, 84, 87, 90, *103*, 184n19; expense of, 152
exhibitions, museum, 81

fabrics and textiles, xvi, 117, 149; cheapness and quality, 116; "Lastex," *104*; legal aspects, 19, 20, 163–64n31; museums, 176–77n89, 177n94; naming, 83; print design, 33, 79, 162n9, 177n94; retail sales, 52; trade associations, 107, 111
false designer labels, 64–70, 84
Fashion Art League, 60
fashion illustration, 78, 79. *See also* sketches and sketching

Fashion Is Spinach (Hawes), 120
Fashion Originators' Guild of American (FOGA), xvi, 14, 33, 98–114 passim, *99*, 127–48 passim; ads, *8*, 101, *103*, 105–6; attack on "apartment shops," 187–88n12; inaugural announcement, *102*; labels, *106*, 109–10, *109*, *138*; member list (1936), 153–56; PPDMG and, 132–34, *133*; registration bureau, 101, 107, 136, 148; in *Women's Wear Daily*, *15*, 105–7, *105*. *See also FOGA v. Federal Trade Commission (FTC)*
fashion schools. *See* schools of design and fashion
fashion shows. *See* exhibitions and style shows
Federal Trade Commission (FTC), xvii, 136–37, 139, 183n1
Fenning, Karl, 31
Ferragamo, 149
fibers, *104*, 163n29. *See also* rayon; silk
Filene's. *See* Wm Filene's Sons Co.
Filene's v. FOGA. See *Wm Filene's Sons Co. v. FOGA*
Fisk, Clark and Flagg, 7
Fitch, Florence, 123
Flora Dress Company, 140–41
FOGA. *See* Fashion Originators' Guild of American (FOGA)
FOGA v. Federal Trade Commission (FTC), xvii, 14, 136–37, 142, 145
Forever 21, xv
Forsch, Benjamin Co. v. Morris W. Haft & Bros., *24*, 25
Forstmann Woolen Company, 116
Fox, Irving, 127
France, 4, 5, 54–92 passim, 96, 146, 172n32; FOGA and, 107, 109; lawsuits and court cases, 150, 151, 158n10; "Mondrian" dress, *xiv*; protective system, xi. *See also* Paris

Index

Francis (French designer), 68–69
Franklin Simon & Co., *23*, 25, 63, 82, 92, *93*
FTC. *See* Federal Trade Commission (FTC)
functional nature of clothing. *See* utilitarian nature of clothing

Gavriel, Floriana, 150
gendered division of labor, 77, 176n80
General Federation of Women's Clubs, 52
Gershel & Co. *See* Ben Gershel & Co.
Ghesquière, Nicolas, 149, 151
Gibbs, Charlotte Baker, 53
Gimbel, Adam, 35
Gimbels, *50*
Goldman Costume Co., 93, *94*, 95
Good Housekeeping, *38*, 48, 95
Goodman, Andrew, 35
Gotshal, Sylvan, 134–35
Gray, Florence, 85
Grean, Alexandre, 78, 85
Great Britain. *See* United Kingdom
Great Depression. *See* Depression
guarantees, 93, 116
guilds, retail. *See* retail guilds

The Haberdasher, 45
Haft & Bros. *See* Morris W. Haft & Bros.
Hagen, Leslie, 18
Haire, Alphonsus, 16, 45–46
H&M, xv, 149
Hand, Learned, 30, 136
handbags, *27*, 151, *151*, 163n23, 163–64n31
Harding, Florence, 88
Harper's Bazaar, 83
Hartley, Fred A., Jr., 32
Hartman, Samuel, 121–22
hats, 14, 65, *86*, 87
Hattie Carnegie, 88, 103, 181n16

Hawes, Elizabeth, 88, 90, 109, 120
Henri Bendel, 32, 45, 90
Henry Rothschild and Co. *See* V. Henry Rothschild & Co.
Herrera, Carolina, 149
Hickson, Inc., 88, 91, 92, 95
Hirsch, Ben, 12–13, 132
home economics, 51, 52. *See also* Bureau of Home Economics
homemade clothing, 52, 120, 168–69n54
Hoover, Herbert, 30
House of Dior, 151
Howie, Frances, 150
H. R. Mallinson & Co., 79
Hudson's. *See* J. L. Hudson Company
Huntington, Mrs. Le Roy. *See* Le Roy-Huntington, Mrs.
Hutchinson, Kenneth, 13, 120, 125
Hutchinson, Pierce & Co., 27

illustration. *See* fashion illustration
immigrant labor, 39, 44, 77
imports, 74–75
Inch, Robert A., 24–25, 140, *141*
Industrial Design Registration Bureau, 107–8
industry groups. *See* trade associations
injunctions, 30, 130, 135
Innovative Design Protection and Piracy Prevention Act (ID3PA), 158n12
intellectual property laws, xi, 16–19 passim, 28
International Ladies' Garment Workers' Union (ILGWU), 99–100
International News Service v. Associated Press, 29–30
inventors and inventions, 16–25 passim, 29, 79, 128, 140, *141*

Jablow, Arthur, 144, 186n56
Jack Adelman, Inc., *34*

jackets, 59, 149, 150, 158n10
Jacobs, Vera, 186n56
Jay Thorpe, 32, 103
Jenny, Madame, *62*, 68, *69*
J. L. Hudson Company, 111
Jo Copeland (store), 103
Johnston, A. C., 123
John Wanamaker, *9*, *80*, 103
Junior Fashion Creator's League of America, 33
junior wear, 107

Kahn Act, 28–29
Kaner, Joan, 152
Karan, Donna, 148–49
Katrantzou, Mary, 149
Keating, John, 116
Kennedy, John F., Jr., xi
Kern Co. *See* Ernst Kern Co.
Kidwell, Claudia, 119
King, Elizabeth Miner, 81
Klein, Anne, 148
Klein's, *xiii*

labels, false. *See* false designer labels
labels, FOGA. *See* Fashion Originators' Guild of American (FOGA): labels
labor, 127–29, 142, 159–60n7. *See also* gendered division of labor; immigrant labor; pay; unions
Ladies' Home Journal, 51, 71, 95
Lagerfeld, Karl, 145
law journals. *See* legal press
lawsuits, 24–25, *24*, 29–30, 85, 92, 132, 136–40 passim, 150; copyright infringement, 151
Leach, William, 119
Leanore Frocks, 140–41
Lefcourt, Abraham E., *91*
legal press, xvi, xvii, 10, 16, 145
legislation, xi, xv, 10, 16–21 passim, 25–35 passim, 96, 148, 158n12; copyright, 19, 21, 152; New York State, 31, *32*, 96, 124, 135, 164n40; NIRA, 111, 183n35; patents, 10, 18–21 passim. *See also* antitrust laws
Le Roy-Huntington, Mrs., *38*, 48
Levine, Louis, 37, 39
licensing, 66, 67, 109
logos, xi, 26, 93, 95, 107, 163n29
Lombardy Dresses, Inc., 24, 140
London, 54, 107
Long, Dorothy, *22*, 25
Lord & Taylor, xii, 92, 103
Los Angeles, 132, 144
Louboutin, Christian, 149
Louise and Co., 45
Louis Vuitton, 26, 149
Lucile, 68, 178n112
Lululemon Athletica, 150, 192n21

Macy's. *See* R. H. Macy & Co.
Madame Jenny. *See* Jenny, Madame
Madame Nordica. *See* Nordica, Madame
Magdo, Christine, 161n2
mail order. *See* catalog sales
Mainbocher, 9
Maison Beer, *62*, 68
Mallinson & Co. *See* H. R. Mallinson & Co.
M&H Rentner, 95
Mansur Gavriel, 150
manufacturers' trade associations, 31, 58, 59, 96, 121, 132
Marcus, H. Stanley, 117
Marie Claire, xi
Martin's (Brooklyn), *13*
Mayer Chic, 87
Mayer, Edward L., 81
Maynard's. *See* Alice Maynard
McDonald, Pearl, 51
Meiklejohn, Helen Everett, 128
menswear, 26–27, 38, 43, 46
Metropolitan Museum of Art, 79, 176–77n89, 177n94

Meyers, Clay, 120–21, 128
middle-class women, 4, 38, 48, 50, 88, 90
Middleton, Kate, 146, *147*
Milgrim, Sally, 25, 82
Milgrim (store), 76, 82, 181n16
Minneapolis, 101, 111
Mizrahi, Isaac, 149
Morrison, Martin A., 24, 29
Morris W. Haft & Bros., *24*, 25
Moss, Mary, 50
Mulqueen, Jack, 18, 146
museums, 75, 79, 80, 176–77n89, 177n94
musical recordings, 18, 152

Nathanson & Beck, 130
Nathanson Dress Co., 34
National Association of Clothing Designers, 60, 170n13
National Association of Style Creators, 33
National Committee for Effective Design Legislation, 32
National Consumer League, 51
National Federation of Textiles, 107, 111, 137
National Garment Retailers' Association, 58, 90, 170n13
National Industrial Recovery Act (NIRA), 111, 183n35
National Ladies' Tailors and Dressmakers' Association, 60, 71, 171n17, 171–72n26
National Recovery Administration (NRA), xvii, 111, 112, 121, 183n35–1
National Retail Dry Goods Association, 58, 105, 127, 132, 134, 138, 170n13, 181n14; name change, 181n19
Native American motifs. *See* American Indian motifs
Neiman-Marcus, 117

Neiman, Paula, 143, 186n56
Nettie Rosenstein, 103
New York City, 39–40, 60–61, 159–60n7; counterfeit French labels in, 65; design contests, 85, *86*, 87; "Fashion Fete" (1914), *73*, 74; garment district, 44, 190n48; manufacturers, 44, 53–54; retailers, 9, *13*, *17*, 20, 39, 40, 46, 90, 111; retail guilds, 101; schools of design and fashion, 77–78; World War II, 143
New York School of Design, 77
New York School of Fine and Applied Arts, 77
New York State, 31, *32*, 96, 124, 164n40; Donnelly Act, 135; Supreme Court, 136
New York Times, 65, 84, 85
Nordica, Madame, 61, 172n29
Novak, Syd, 140
NRA. *See* National Recovery Administration (NRA)

O'Brien, Ruth, 116
obsolescence, planned and rapid, 6, 128
O'Connell, P. A., 125
Ohrbach, Nathan, 117
Ohrbach's, 117, 184n19
Oldfield, William A., 29
Oppenheim, Collins and Co., 10, *11*

Panama-Pacific International Exposition, San Francisco, 1915, 28–29
pants, yoga. *See* yoga pants
paper pattern companies, 46
Paquin, Jeanne, *62*, 65, 66, 82
Paris, 25, 46, 54–91 passim, 96, 119, 129, 144; FOGA and, 107, 109; Hoover view, 30; Madame Nordica view, 172n29; Rentner view, 182; *Women's Wear Daily* on, 171–72n26

Parker, B. W., 51
Parsons School of Design, 77
patents, 10, 19–25, 92, 138–41 passim, 150, 162–63n20, 163n23
pattern companies. *See* paper pattern companies
patternmakers and patternmaking, 38, 77, 78, 176n80
Patterson, Bina, 117
Pattullo Modes, 82
pay, 53, 85
Peggy Paige dresses, 95, 172n34
Peiss, Kathy, 48
Pellew, Chas, 177n89
Penikees Silk, 87
photography, 67, 147
Picart, Jean-Jacques, 146–47
Picken, Mary Brooks, 52
Pittsburgh, 126, 128
planned obsolescence. *See* obsolescence, planned and rapid
Poiret, Paul, 62–63, 65–66, 68, 73, 77, 82, 83, 172n31
Polo/Ralph Lauren, 158n10
Popular Priced Dress Manufacturers Group (PPDMG), 31, 121, 132, *133*, 134
Post, Albert, 105, 107, 109, 138, 139, 181n14
Pratt Institute, 77, 78
prices: dresses, 63, 75, 99, 100, 107, 114, 116, 121, 130–34 passim, 181n13; retail, 99, 112, 116–29; wholesale, 74, 107, 130, 131
Price-Schlesinger, *34*
print design, 33
Prohibition, 90, 114
purses. *See* handbags

quality, 110, 120; decline of, 52, 99–100, 116–17, 180n7
Queen Elizabeth. *See* Elizabeth II, Queen of Great Britain

Ralph Lauren, 150, 158n10
rayon, 107, 117, 177n94
"red-carding," 110–11, 133, 135, 138
Redfern Corset Company, 87
registration bureaus, 33, 96, 101, 107–8, 116, 136, 148
Rentner, Ira, 33
Rentner, Maurice, 32, 33, *99*, 107–12 passim, 128, 130, 182n23, 190n48; designers and stylists, 186n56; FOGA founding, 14, 98, 101; on *FOGA v. FTC*, 136–37; Jablow on, 144; speech in honor of, 125; World War II, 143–44. *See also* M&H Rentner
retailers' trade associations, 30, 33, 58, 90, 105
retail guilds, 101–2, 132, 181n16
returns of merchandise, 133, 134, 185n32
R. H. Macy & Co., 37, 40, 46, 63, 103
R. H. White and Co., 111
Richards, Charles: *Art in Industry*, 76, 78–79, 85, 90
Richards, Florence, 99
Richardson, Bertha June, 7, 48, 51
Ringer, Barbara, 18
Robbins, C., 101
Rodriguez, Narciso, xi–xii
Roosevelt, Franklin Delano, 20
Rosemary dresses, 95
Rosen Bros., *20*
Rosenstein, Nettie, 25, *26*
Roshco, Bernard, xii
Rothschild & Co. *See* V. Henry Rothschild & Co.
Rubin, Louis, 96
Russeks, 13–14

Saint Laurent, Yves, *xiv*, 150, 158
St. Louis, 33, 40, 132
Saks and Co., *62*
sales representatives, 45

Index

sales showrooms. *See* showrooms
San Francisco World's Fair. *See* Panama-Pacific International Exposition, San Francisco, 1915
schools of design and fashion, 77–79, 90, 128
Schorman, Rob, 49
Schuster's. *See* Ed. Schuster Company
Schwartz, Allen B., xii, 152
seamstresses, 3, 36, 53, 76
Sears, Roebuck, 68
semiconductor industry, 18
Sheldon, Roy, 118–19
Shelton Looms, 87
Sherman Act, 135, 137, 142
shirtwaist dresses, *17*, 41, *43*, 50, 54
shirtwaists, 7, 37–41, *38*, *43*, 50, 54, 59; ads, *28*, *42*
shoddiness. *See* quality: decline of
shoes, 149–50, 163n23, 191n19
showrooms, 5, 8, 40, 44, 45
Siegel, Ernest, 117, 140
silhouette, 3, 41, 42, 49, 56, 78
silk, 66, 79, 87, 117, 179n126
Silk Association of America, 33, 116
Simcox, Clara, 60, 75, 84, 92, 171n21
Simmel, Georg, 55
Simons, Raf, 150
Simpson Crawford Co., 63
Simpson, Wallis, xii
sketches and sketching, 5, 8–9, 57, 96, 107–8, 111
skirts, 41, 56, 77
sleeve styles, *42*, 52
smuggling, 75
social class. *See* class
Sondheim, Herbert, *108*, 124–25, 139–40, 181n14
spies and spying, 5, 8–9, 110, 138
Star brand, 28, *42*
Stehli, Henry E., 31–32, 35
Stein and Blaine, *73*, 82, *89*, 90
Steinmetz, E. M. A., 82, 84, *89*
Stella McCartney Limited, 150

Stevens Department Store (Chicago). *See* Charles A. Stevens & Bros.
Stewart & Co., 63
stitchers, 53, 77, 176n80
store buyers. *See* buyers
Strawbridge and Clothier, 111
Style Piracy Bureau, 33
style registration bureaus. *See* registration bureaus
style shows. *See* exhibitions and style shows
subcontractors and subcontracting, 44, 45, 100
suits, 33, *34*, 50, *50*, 54, *56*, 77; Chanel's, 145; prices, 126
Supreme Court, US. *See* US Supreme Court
Syndicat de Défense de la Grande Couture Française, 66–68, 75

tailors, 3, 36, 60, 78, 176n80
Tappe, Herman Patrick, 81–82, 84
Tarbell, Ida, 5–6, *118*
tariffs, 74
technical training, 78, 85, 90, 128, 176n83
Textile Design Registration Bureau, 33, 116
textiles and fabrics. *See* fabrics and textiles
theft, 9, 68
Thurn, 62, 88
Tracy, Ellen, 149
trade associations, xvi, 30–33 passim, 58–60 passim, 71, 90, 121, 148, 170n13; male nature of, 77; silk industry, 33, 116. *See also* Fashion Originators' Guild of American (FOGA); manufacturers' trade associations; retailers' trade associations
trademarks, 10, *23*, 25–28, 65, 92–93, 95, 163–64n31, 172n34; shoes, 191n19

training, technical. *See* technical training
Traphagen, Ethel, 87
Traphagen School of Fashion, 78, 87, 178n120
Troy, Nancy, 4–5
Turner, Jessie Franklin, 81, 82

undergarments, *21*, 36, 41, 87
Ungaro, Emanuel, 148
unions, 33, 58, 99–100, 170n13
United Kingdom, 54, 107, 157n1; designers, 68, 149
United Women's Wear League, 96
Uptown Retail Annex Guild (New York), 101, 181n16
Uptown Retail Guild (New York), 35
US Commerce Department, 25
US Congress, xv, 10, 18, 21, 28–33, 35, 96, 141; NIRA, 111, 183n35
US Copyright Office, 19, 30, 31, 32, 136, 158n12
US Department of Agriculture, Bureau of Home Economics. *See* Bureau of Home Economics
US Patent and Trademark Office, 20, 21, 30, 32, 140, 150
US Supreme Court, xvii, 14, 25, 111, 136–37, 142
utilitarian nature of clothing, 16, 19, 35

Valvo, Carmen Marc, 149
Veblen, Thorstein, 55
Vestal, Albert H., 30–31
vests, 71, 151
V. Henry Rothschild & Co., 7, 39, 45
Viktor & Rolf, 149
Vionnet, Madeleine, *115*
vocational training. *See* technical training
Vogue, 37, 40, 74, 83, 84, 95, 178n107

waistcoats. *See* vests
Walker, Joset, 25
Wanamaker's. *See* John Wanamaker
Wang, Vera, 149
wedding dresses, xi–xii, *xiii*, 60, 106, 146, *147*
Weingarten & Pearl, 67
White's (Boston). *See* R. H. White and Co.
White v. Lombardy Dresses, Inc., 140
Wholesale Fashion Trades Association of London, 107
wholesale showrooms. *See* showrooms
Wm Filene's Sons Co., 35, 103, 111
Wm Filene's Sons Co. v. FOGA, 114, 126, 135, 142
Wilmott, Ruth, 177n890
window display, 48, 166n14
Wolfenstein, 135
Woman's Home Companion, 68, 69
women, middle-class. *See* middle-class women
women, working-class. *See* working-class women
Women's Wear Daily, xii, 5, 6, *8*, 11, 15, 55, 80; competitions, 87; FOGA in, 105–7, *105*
Wong, Kaisik, 151
Woolman, May Schenck, 52–53
working-class women, 3–4, 7, 47–48, 50, 77, 167
World War, I, 68–84 passim, 90, 96–97
World War II, 143
Worth, Charles Frederick, 4, 61, 73, 77

yoga pants, 150, 192n21
YSL, 150

Zadeh, Maryam Nassir, 149–50
Zahn, Samuel, 111, 121, 138, *139*
Zara, xv, 149

About the Authors

Sara B. Marcketti is an associate professor in the Apparel, Events, and Hospitality Management Department at Iowa State University and the Associate Director of Scholarship of Teaching and Learning at the Center for Excellence in Learning and Teaching. She is coauthor of *Survey of Historic Costume*, sixth edition.

Jean L. Parsons is an Associate Professor at the University of Missouri in the Textile and Apparel Management Department and coauthor of *20th-Century Dress in the United States*.